Writers at Home

Writers at Home

NATIONAL TRUST STUDIES

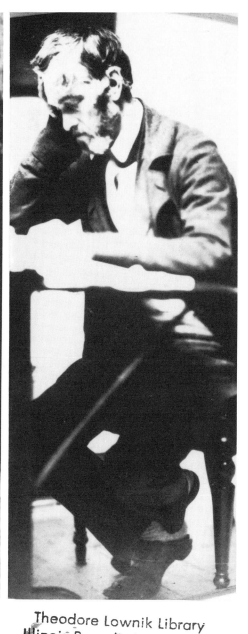

Facts On File Publications
New York, New York ● Oxford, England

To Robin Wright

First published in the United States by
Facts On File, Inc.
460 Park Avenue South
New York, New York 10016

Library of Congress Cataloging in Publication Data
Main entry under title:

Writers at home.

"Published in association with the National Trust."
1. Literary landmarks—Great Britain.   2. Authors,
English—Homes and haunts.   3. Dwellings—Great Britain.
4. Great Britain—Description and travel—1971-
5. Authors, English—Biography.   I. Jackson-Stops,
Gervase.   II. National Trust (Great Britain)
PR109.W75 1986   941.1'04858   85-12900
ISBN 0-8160-1318-7

Printed in England by BAS Printers, Over Wallop.

Jacket front: *A Chelsea Interior* by Robert Tait;
jacket back: view from Virginia Woolf's 'hut'.

Coleridge Cottage, No. 35 Lime Street, Nether Stowey,
Bridgwater, Somerset. At the western end of the village, on the
south side of the A39. *Station:* Bridgwater (8 miles).

Carlyle's House, No. 24 Cheyne Row, Chelsea, London SW3.
Off Cheyne Walk, between Battersea and Albert Bridges on
Chelsea Embankment, or off Oakley Street.

Shaw's Corner, Ayot St. Lawrence, near Welwyn, Hertfordshire.
At the south-western end of the village, one mile north-east of
Wheathampstead. *Bus:* London Country route 304 from
St Albans or Hitchin, alight Gustardwood, 1¼ miles. *Station:*
Welwyn Garden City (6 miles).

Lamb House, West Street, Rye, East Sussex. Facing west end of
the church in West Street.

Clouds Hill, Wareham, Dorset. 9 miles east of Dorchester, 1½
miles east of Wadlock Crossroads, one mile north of Bovington
Camp. *Bus:* Wilts & Dorset routes 186-9 to Tolpuddle. *Station:*
Wool or Moreton (3½ miles).

Hardy's Cottage, Higher Bockhampton, near Dorchester,
Dorset. 3 miles north east of Dorchester, ½ mile south of the A35.
Bus: Wilts & Dorset routes 184-7 from Weymouth, Dorchester,
Salisbury and Bournemouth (½ mile). *Station:* Dorchester South
(4 miles).

Monk's House, Rodmell, Lewes, East Sussex. 2½ miles south
east of Lewes, off the former A275 (now C7) in Rodmell village,
near Church. *Bus:* Southdowns route 123, 823 from Lewes and
Newham, 2 hourly, not Sunday. *Station:* Southease (1 mile).

Bateman's, Burwash, Etchingham, East Sussex. ½ mile south of
Burwash (A265). Approached by road leading south from west
end of village or north from Woods Corner (B2096). *Station:*
Etchingham (3 miles).

Wordsworth's House, Main Street, Cockermouth, Cumbria.
Bus: Cumberland routes 34/5, 58, 60 from Whitchaven, Maryport,
Wigton & Keswick stop within 200 yards. *Station:* Maryport
(6½ miles).

Charleston Farm House, Firle, East Sussex, is in the process of
restoration. An appeal has been launched to enable the National
Trust to open the property to visitors. Contributions should be
addressed to the Charleston Trust, 85 Elgin Crescent, London,
W11.

Contents

Foreword

Gervase Jackson-Stops

The National Trust is generally associated in the public imagination either with open spaces – coastal paths in Devon and Cornwall, nature reserves on the Norfolk marshes, ancient forests saved from the encroaching tentacles of the industrial Midlands – or with great country houses set in spreading parkland, filled with the accumulated treasures of many generations. But one type of property owned by the Trust tends to be overlooked: the smaller, more everyday houses and cottages that have acquired special significance because of their literary associations.

These may be modest architecturally; they may have few contents (for writers are not often avid collectors); yet they can speak to us as many better known 'sights' cannot. In a simple view from a window across a cornfield, in a rickety bookshelf crammed with dog-eared volumes, a wind-up gramophone, or an abandoned eighteenth-century wig-stand, one can arrive at a fuller understanding of a mind already revealed to us with such intensity in another medium.

The founding fathers of the Trust themselves acted from instincts that were essentially literary. Their early attempts to preserve the Lake District were a response not only to the poetry of Wordsworth and his contemporaries, but to the writings of Ruskin. Like him, they saw that 'historic interest' and 'natural beauty', the two sides of preservation, met in the written word, the only truly immutable element in our lives. So it is that these often humble, sometimes hideous places (for who would otherwise consider preserving Shaw's Corner or Max Gate?) have an effect on us that can be as powerful as Proust's *madeleine*, summoning up our own past as well as the writer's. To find Mr. McGregor's cabbage patch still thriving at Hill Top, to walk down Porpoise Lane at Rye half-expecting to see Miss Mapp twitching back the net-curtains, to see Disraeli's banks of primroses at Hughenden or the housekeeper's room at Uppark where H.G. Wells' mother sat in state, may be to experience what we have already lived in thought.

We are deeply grateful to the authors of these essays for bringing their people and places, poetry and prose, so vividly to life, to James Lees-Milne and to Simon Blow for helping to conceive the whole shape of the book and to Jonathan Marsden who has borne the brunt of the editing and picture research.

Introduction

James Lees-Milne

Recently there have been plenty of books about the influence of literature on landscape and architecture; fewer about the influence of landscape and architecture on literature. In a sense this book redresses the balance.

One of the many odd notions about themselves which the British people cherish is that their poets and writers have been inspired by nature to a far greater extent than foreign ones. In this assumption they are probably mistaken, but on the other hand they have taken the lead among western countries in the conservation of nature and wild life. There are several reasons for it. The British Isles are restricted in size; most of the land is gentle, well tended, loveable pasture and (with the exception of parts of Scotland and Wales) the opposite of savage and rebarbative. Because this country is on a small scale and easily accessible to town-dwellers it is very vulnerable. During the past half century it has sustained serious damage through a multitude of causes, principally over-population and the spread of cities. The more the English landscape is eroded the more precious it becomes to its inhabitants, while in the large European countries like France, Germany and Spain nature is more expendable and therefore held less dear.

Throughout the changing fashions of landscape design the British have always contrived to make their parks look like tamed reproductions of the natural environment. Our nearest neighbour France, with hundreds of thousands of acres of uncultivable land to spare, has on the contrary been under no such necessity. She has moulded, trimmed and dragooned her parks. The regimented formalism of Le Nôtre reflected, so our Georgian ancestors liked to claim, the absolutism of the French monarchy, whereas the picturesque disorder of William Kent, Capability Brown and their followers illustrated the United Kingdom's much vaunted love of freedom and independence of authority.

It may well be argued that the inconstancy of our climate has had a profound effect upon our poets and descriptive writers. True, they have been no more able to ignore it than the rest of us. The extremes of heat and cold, rain and sun, tempest and calm in the British Isles are relieved only by brief interludes of temperate weather. But short though our summers may be, what, when they are vouchsafed at all, could be more beautiful? From the extremes of our climate have evolved the extremes of our national temperament, causing us to veer from gaiety to melancholy, from exultation to the deepest despair, all within 24 hours. In fact, our weather renders the British the most mercurial people on the earth's surface. It has made poets of us. It has made us the masters of the lyric and the ode, which can be composed within a matter of days, whereas in painting, an art which requires a longer time and more sustained mood for composition, we have not pre-eminently excelled. Now just as extremes of temperament affect men's sensibilities, extremes of weather cause rapid changes in the aspect of landscape. We have merely to think of the Sussex Downs basking under a blue sky and fleecy white clouds in the morning and swept by horizontal prongs of icy hail on the afternoon of the same day. The verdant and elusive English landscape cannot be taken for granted like the parched and stable scenery of the Mediterranean. Its beauty is transient from storm purple to pigeon grey, and from pigeon grey to fiery gold. Too often, alas, it is pigeon grey. It is no coincidence therefore that the first two poems in the English language begin with references to the weather. William Langland's opening lines of 'The Vision Concerning Piers Plowman' run as follows:-

> In the summer season when soft was the sun
> In rough cloth I robed me...

continuing,

> ...on a May morning on Malvern Hills,
> A marvel befel me – sure from Faery it came...

In other words it was a fine day, and the hero of the story was actually able to lie down on a broad bank and fall asleep 'by a merry-sounding burn'. Chaucer's opening lines of the Prologue to *The Canterbury Tales* are equally weather-conscious.

> When April with its showers of gentle rain
> The soil which March had dried hath pierced again,
> And bathed each vein in dew.

Whereafter neither of these long, late-fourteenth century masterpieces makes further reference to nature, her habits or her works.

For the next two hundred years and more writers continued to ignore nature. Indeed why should they not? They were surrounded by it, immersed in it, overwhelmed by it. It was at worst something to be feared and disliked, at best taken for granted; in short, something not to be loved. Then came Shakespeare. This giant of literature was the first English poet to refer to nature with more than a touch of contemptuous familiarity, more than a passing nod of patronising approval. His immediate predecessors of the Italian Renaissance, even Michelangelo and Tasso, both observant men, had been content to acknowledge the presence of 'bei fiori' and 'l'erba fresca' as conventional decorative backcloths to scenes of passion or courtly dalliance. Not so Shakespeare. He used his senses as well as his eyes. He looked at the natural world around him with keen scrutiny, and absorbed it. Flowers meant more to him than pretty, if chancy, decoration, grass more than jolly green stuff, just as winter was more than simply cold. Not for nothing was he brought up in a small market town in the heart of England which gave instant access to the open country. The landscape he evoked in *A Midsummer Night's Dream, As You Like It* and even the sonnets, arcadian though it was, is a recognizable portrayal of the richly wooded Forest of Arden and the dappled meadows bordering the river Avon. His evocations of the seasons may be fractional, mere word sketches dropped into the text without warning like beech husks into pale streams. Phrases like 'proud-pied April, dressed in all his trim', 'the darling buds of May', 'a bank where the wild thyme blows, where oxlips and the nodding violet grows', 'the barky fingers of the elm', 'old December's bareness', 'where icicles hang by the wall, and Dick the shepherd blows his nail', and a hundred others are no literary conceits, but direct, close observations of natural phenomena, transmuted of course into immortal art. Shakespeare's recognition of and respect for nature had a profound influence upon his successors' development of the literature of the English landscape. His love of his native Warwickshire is proved by his purchase in 1597 of New Place, the second largest house in Stratford-upon-Avon for his retirement 14 years later. There 'our life, exempt from public haunt' (to quote the good Duke exiled in the Forest of Arden) found 'tongues in trees,

Shakespeare's Birthplace, Stratford-upon-Avon.

books in the running brooks, sermons in stones, and good in everything'. Alas, New Place was demolished by a later owner who could not endure the number of trippers it attracted, but Shakespeare's father's house, which is his birthplace, and the little town itself, are his enduring shrine.

In very many respects Shakespeare was far in advance of his time. He even saw beauty in the savagery of nature. Romance in the blasted heath (*Macbeth*) and rugged coastline (*King Lear*) aroused no sympathetic response in subsequent poetic bosoms for quite another two hundred years. Nor was scenery of a benign kind to be more than cursorily explored in the seventeenth century. Descriptions of it are scrappy. Herrick's 'Hesperides' makes a half-hearted attempt. Herrick pays grudging tribute to the scenery of Devon, where, until the outbreak of the Civil War, he, a confirmed Londoner, was exiled to a remote parsonage. Nevertheless Herrick, addressing his honoured friend Endymion Porter in a poem entitled 'The Country Life', is aware of the exacting calls upon the good landowner as well as the moral responsibilities.

> No, thy ambition's masterpiece
> Flies no thought higher than a fleece;
> Or how to pay thy hinds, and clear
> All scores, and so to end the year:
> But walk'st about thine own dear bounds,
> Nor envying others larger grounds,
> For well thou know'st 'tis not th' extent
> Of land makes life, but sweet content.
> When now the cock, the ploughman's horn,
> Calls forth the lily-wristed morn,
> Then to thy corn-fields thou dost go,
> Which, though well soiled, yet thou dost know
> That the best compost for the lands
> Is the wise master's feet and hands...
> Thou go'st; and as thy foot there treads,
> Thou see'st a present Godlike power

> Imprinted in each herb and flower,
> And smell'st the breath of great-eyed kine,
> Sweet as the blossoms of the vine.

In these lovely lines we have got far away from the courtier's vison of nature through the closed windows of a palace. We can positively inhale the reek of cow stalls and the stench of manure heaps. Herrick's fellow metaphysical poets, like Donne and Cowley, are more abstract and less realistic than Herrick. Of the next generation Milton, whom Horace Walpole was to call the poetic inspiration of English landscape gardening of the eighteenth century, is one of the first English poets to make abbreviated, we might almost say accidental, reference to certain places. This he does by deft nostalgic sketches in the staccato lines of *L'Allegro* and *Il Penseroso*. From his father's house at Horton in Buckinghamshire Milton's eye roamed across the flat landscape ('Russet lawns and fallows grey, Where the nibbling flocks do stray') to Windsor Castle on its eminence. ('Towers and battlements it sees Bosomed high in tufted trees.') And doubtless it was to St George's Chapel that he directed his 'due feet... To walk the studious cloysters pale, And love the high embowed roof, With antick pillars massy proof.' Even so these phrases are hardly topographical descriptions of the Home Counties. Rather they were meant to be idyllic vignettes of an environment deemed suitable for the archaic shepherds, Corydon and Thyrsis. We can call them artificial, the adjective which that indefatigable horsewoman Celia Fiennes at the turn of the century was to choose as the highest expression of praise for the gardens of the country houses she visited. John Evelyn, who was just as enthusiastic an admirer of landscape as Celia, was no less prosaic in his descriptions. The eminent sylviculturist would call the most famous gardens of his time 'pretty' or even 'convenient'.

With the Georgians came a dramatic change in the enlightened man's attitude to nature. It came with the cult of the Picturesque, a powerful movement in literature as well as painting and landscape gardening. Indeed, the change cannot be overlooked because the wild English shires were turned almost overnight into one enormous tamed landscaped park. Christopher Hussey in his perceptive book *The Picturesque* (1927) maintained that the English really derived no visual pleasure from their surroundings until they became familiar with the paintings of Claude, Salvator Rosa, Ruysdael and Hobbema; that the hundred years (1730-1830) of the idealised Picturesque was an interregnum between the Classical and Romantic periods:

> It occurred at a point when an art shifted its appeal from the reason to the imagination. An art that addresses the reason, even though it does so through the eye does not stress visual qualities. The reason wants to *know,* not to experience sensations. The romantic movement was an awakening of sensations, and, among the other sensations, that of sight required exercising.

Art may have addressed Milton's reason through his eyes but rarely did it awake sensations that were not cerebral. His descriptions of the Garden of Eden in *Paradise Lost* are not imaginative but patently interpretative of landscape paintings. Alexander Pope was the first important poet to attempt to translate what he saw in the works of the landscape painters, notably Claude and Rosa, into verse as well as garden design, but even his discernment was limited. His poetry failed to do more than generalise about nature, which he kept within a classical allegorical straight-jacket. As Hussey has pointed out, his 'Windsor Forest' contains no trees worthy of the name – they are in fact given no names –

> Here waving groves a chequered scene display...
> There, interspersed in lawns and opening glades,
> The trees arise that show each other's shades.

Alfred's Hall, Cirencester Park, built in the 1720s by Lord Bathurst and *(right)* Alexander Pope *(National Portrait Gallery)*.

What were they? Full grown willows, elms, sycamores, or merely saplings? We are not told.

Christopher Hussey found it remarkable that western civilization remained indifferent to nature until the eighteenth century. The Chinese, he pointed out, had loved nature centuries before Christ was born. He believed that European indifference, which he preferred to call positive hostility, to nature was deliberately fostered by Christianity. Whereas Holy Men in China sought the mountains and forests to commune more closely with the divine through nature, Christians saw in nature things fearful, sinister and sinful. The Saints withdrew to the wilderness as a penance, in order to combat evil spirits and unmentionable temptations begotten of isolation. Not till the slackening of blind acceptance of the Church's dogmas and the daring cult of paganism in Renaissance times did nature become a source of scientific study and a purveyor of beauty and joy. With the opening up of roads and travel, the Grand Tour made available to educated Englishmen as they rode or drove from one private gallery to another not only the landscape paintings of Europe but the very scenery depicted in the paintings. So intoxicated did the English landowners in Georgian times become with the infinite constituents they found in the Picturesque that protagonists of the beautiful, the fearful and the sublime arose among them. In a succession of obstreperous and sometimes silly treatises they gave voice to conflicting precepts that were usually academic and always in deadly earnest. There is no need to investigate here the divergent theories of what constituted correct landscape layout, from the 3rd Earl of Shaftesbury's *Characteristics* of 1711 to Uvedale Price's *Essay on the Picturesque* of 1794.

The literary shrines of the early eighteenth century are largely those country houses whose owners were either busily rebuilding their ancestral seats or replanning the parks in which they stood, and often both at once. These owners were cultivated patrons delighting in the entertainment of men of letters who might share their interest in architecture and landscape design. They would receive the poets, writers and painters as social equals, allowing them to stay, often for weeks on end, particularly if they were engaged in composition. In 1718 Gay and Pope spent the summer at Oakley Grove which was being rebuilt as Cirencester House in the absence of their host, the 1st Earl Bathurst. Pope wrote that Oakley Wood was inspiring Gay 'like the cave of Montesinos'. To his confidante Martha Blount he wrote that 'we draw plans for houses and gardens, open avenues, cut glades, plant firs, contrive water-works all very fine and beautiful in our imagination.' In 1726 Pope, this time accompanied by Swift, was at Cirencester again. The two friends lodged with a tenant farmer and had to walk a couple of miles each day to dine with the Earl. Mrs Delany on a subsequent visit to Cirencester wrote Swift a long letter. She told him that the farmer's cottage was having to be enlarged because it had 'burst with pride... after entertaining so illustrious a person' as him. It was renamed Alfred's Hall, and so venerable did it look in the new guise of a Gothic castle that an eminent antiquarian seriously mistook it for one of King Arthur's. Until his death in 1744 Pope continued to take a lively interest and pride in his part in creating the 'as yet visionary beauties that are to rise in these scenes' and he looked upon himself 'as the magician appropriated to the place, without whom no mortal can penetrate the recesses of those sacred shades'. The good-natured Lord Bathurst smiled indulgently at his distinguished guest's little vanities.

At Rousham in Oxfordshire, Pope, Gay and Horace Walpole were frequent guests of General Dormer, then employing William Kent to design gardens, terraces, and temples on the banks of the Cherwell which runs through the grounds. At Stowe in Buckinghamshire, the seat of Lord Cobham, Pope addressed to his host the first of his *Moral Essays* (1733); and to Stowe he referred in the lines of the 'Epistle to Lord Burlington' which begin:

> Consult the genius of the place in all;
> That tells the waters or to rise, or fall,
> Or helps th'ambitious hill the heavens to scale,
> Or scoops in circling theatres the vale.

and end:

> Nature shall join you; Time shall make it grow
> A work to wonder at – perhaps a STOW.

Pope, in spite of his lamentable health was a tireless frequenter of country houses whose owners were men of culture. To all of them he proffered his advice on the improvement of their architecture and landscape. Wimpole Hall, Sherborne Castle and Prior Park near Bath were among his other favourite retreats. At the first Matthew Prior and at the last Fielding, Richardson and Smollett were welcome visitors. Nuneham Courtenay in Oxfordshire was likewise a hospice for intellectuals. There the 1st Earl Harcourt (who ultimately met his death by drowning in a well in the park) entertained Oliver Goldsmith, author of 'The Deserted Village'. The poem was meant to be a sharp reproof to his host for having destroyed the village of Nuneham Courtenay because it obscured a distant view of Harcourt's magnificent new 'nest of pleasure.'

> Ill fares the land, to hastening ills a prey,
> Where wealth accumulates, and men decay.

The poet laureate, William Whitehead, however, rebutted Goldsmith's charge. On the contrary he extolled the compassion shown to one of his ancient tenants by the 'indulgent' Earl in allowing her to end her days in her 'clay-built cot'. The 2nd Earl was an admirer of Rousseau, who stayed at Nuneham and planted in the park the seeds of wild flowers, including periwinkle, clematis and bryony, mentioned in *La Nouvelle Héloise*. Lord Harcourt also entertained the Rev. William Mason, who was encouraged to lay out the flower garden, Horace Walpole, William Gilpin and Fanny Burney, who lost her way in the rambling old house.

The eighteenth century marked the veritable heyday of the English country house. In no other century were writers, artists and musicians so lavishly entertained, so prudently encouraged to create, and so liberally treated. Of all the rural centres of the arts, Hagley in Worcestershire under the reign of George Lord Lyttelton probably attracted more distinguished men of letters than any other. Here James Thomson, Horace Walpole, Addison, Pope again, Shenstone, Dr Johnson and Mrs Thrale (who, in their own judgement, were received coldly and made to feel unwanted) were at different times guests. In addition to men of letters a galaxy of architects and landscape designers visited and left their mark upon both house and park. Here Thomson in 1743 added lines to the section 'Spring' in *The Seasons,* inspired by the abrupt contours of the newly created park besprinkled with classical temples and baronial towers. The popularity of *The Seasons* was immense. The blank verse displayed the picturesque ideal with looser, broader, more colourful brushstrokes than the constrained alexandrines of Pope. Every page of this otherwise pedestrian poem described natural scenery as though it were paintings by Claude of mountain, cliff and coast. Nature henceforth was something to be enjoyed in the same way as a landscape scene composed on canvas.

Tamed nature was at last a friend to man. Savage nature was still beyond the pale. It is true that Charles Cotton a hundred years before had invoked the wilder scenery of Derbyshire:

> Oh, my beloved rocks that rise
> To awe the earth and brave the skies,
> From some aspiring mountain's crown,
> How dearly do I love,
> Giddy with pleasure, to look down,
> And from the vales, to view the noble heights above!

Cotton's verses beseeched his old piscatorial friend Isaac Walton, then dwelling in London, to visit him in Dovedale. Even so one may surmise that Cotton felt happier viewing the noble heights above than looking, giddy, down upon the flattened plain below. And the Peaks were not anything like as wild and blasted as either the Highlands of Scotland, or the English Lake District whose turn was to come with the poets and writers Walter Scott and Wordsworth, Coleridge, Southey and de Quincey, helped by painters like Wilson, Girtin and Turner. With them dawned the Romantic Movement in literature. The imagination of British writers expanded by means of vesting the violent and awful aspects of nature with attributes of heroic myth and ancient legend.

Young Walter Scott's interest in the history of the Scotch Lowlands was first awakened in the 1720s by the old Border tales and ballads, particularly Percy's *Reliques* and immersion in the pre-Renaissance poetry of France, Italy and Germany. While a practising barrister, he devoted his spare time to exploring the Border country. In 1799 he published a translation of Goethe's *Goetz von Berlichingen.* Three years later he published his *Minstrêlsey of the Scottish Border.* It was followed by 'The Lay of the Last Minstrel', 'Marmion' and 'The Lady of the Lake'. His first novel *Waverley* (1814) revived the dormant but by no means abeyant romance of the Stuart tragedy in Scotland. The spell of Jacobite loyalties and intrigues, the daring of Prince Charles Edward's adventures, the romance of the plaid and philibeg and the melancholy beauty of Highland scenery captivated his readers' imagination. Walter Scott's novels were a revelation to several generations, not only in the British Isles, but overseas. In the 1830s and 40s, the German Mendelssohn was inspired to compose *Fingal's Cave* after a voyage to Staffa in the Hebrides, the Frenchman Berlioz composed the overture *Waverley* and the Italian Donizetti the opera *Lucia di Lammermoor.*

What Walter Scott did for Scotland, Wordsworth and his group of friends did for the Lake Country, that is to say open the eyes and arouse the senses of their readers to the beauties of mountains, dales and lakes in language simple and unaffected, fervent and from the heart. The Lake poets were also known as the Nature poets because their view of the world around them was strictly interpretative, free from classical allegory, courtly concepts and all the didactic conceits about beauty, sublimity, morality and sentiment which the landed-gentry theorists like Payne Knight, Uvedale Price and William Mason had worked to death. Wordsworth expressed contempt for theoretical expositions of nature, asserting that picturesque analysis of scenery 'was never much my habit'. It was a remarkable thing in English literary history, he said, that, save for a passage or two in Pope's 'Windsor Forest', English poetry from *Paradise Lost* to Thomson's *The Seasons* contained not a single original image of external nature. Southey went even further. 'For the beauties of nature', he averred 'the English poets from Dryden to Pope seem to have had neither ear, nor eye, nor heart.' These organs were, thanks to the precedent of the Lake poets, still further attuned to nature by a slightly younger generation of poets and artists in different parts of the country – Blake and Samuel Palmer at Shoreham, Keats and Constable at Hampstead, Crabbe at Aldeburgh and Hawker the Vicar of Morwenstow in distant Cornwall.

Another pioneer of natural scenery was the Rev. William Gilpin, who was gardener, painter and writer combined. His illustrated tours of the river Wye ('relative chiefly to Picturesque beauty'), the mountains and lakes of Cumberland and Westmorland, and furthermore the Highlands of Scotland, published between 1782 and 1800, were so widely read and studied that in the words of *The Gentleman's Magazine*, they virtually 'opened a new class of travels'.

With the newly awakened appreciation of the variety of natural scenery which the British Isles afforded, communications by road to hitherto inaccessible parts of the country improved. Travellers became curious to visit the haunts of the famous writers who had revealed to them the mysteries and beauties of their environments. The cult of the literary shrine took root. In 1769, ten years after the demolition of New Place had caused righteous indignation among the townsfolk, David Garrick organised a commemorative Shakespeare jubilee at Stratford-upon-Avon. In pouring rain it was attended by that celebrity-hunter of the living and dead James Boswell, the Shakespearean actor Arthur Murphy and other notables. The poet's birthplace in Henley Street (not bought by the Birthplace Trust till 1847) became the goal of pilgrims. Distinguished visitors, including Scott, Carlyle and Isaac Watts flocked to scratch their names on the window panes of the birth chamber. Later pilgrims were the American Washington Irving and Nathaniel Parker Willis, and the English Mrs Gaskell and Marie Corelli. The latter, coming in 1901, bought a house in the town, drove along the streets in a miniature carriage drawn by Shetland ponies, skimmed down the Avon in a gondola, and inhabited Stratford until her death. Other writers, like Crabb Robinson, Emerson and Hawthorne, were attracted to the Lakes in order to gaze upon the ageing Wordsworth who further heightened the curiosity of tourists by himself writing a *Guide through the district of the Lakes*. Among young literary aspirants paying homage, Clough, whom the testy Carlyle condescendingly described as 'a diamond sifted out of the general rubbish heap', and Ruskin, whose *Modern Painters* found a place in the library at Rydal Mount, were presumably not unwelcome. Swinburne, aged eleven, taken to see him in 1848, was reduced to tears by the patriarch's parting words, 'I do not think, Algernon, that you will forget me.'

Matthew Arnold visited the Brontë parsonage in the West Riding a matter of months after Charlotte Brontë's death in 1855 and wrote a memorial poem, 'Haworth Churchyard':

Brontë Parsonage, Haworth, West Yorkshire, in the 1860s and *(right)* Charlotte Brontë by George Richmond, 1850 *(National Portrait Gallery)*.

Where behind Keighley the road
Up to the heart of the moors
Between heath-clad showery hills
Runs, and the colliers' carts
Poach the deep ways coming down,
And a rough, grimed race have their homes
There on its slope is built
The moorland town.

Twelve years later William Johnson Cory followed suit. He found the parsonage 'a miserable homestead, choked with big gravestones, with no garden but the merest strip, no bigger than a bedroom passage,' and marvelled that 'out of that prison the little Charlotte put forth a hand to feel for the world of human emotion'. But Arnold also slogged all the way to Newstead Abbey in the middle of the coal pits of Nottinghamshire where his interest was, strangely, distracted from Byron's 'cry, stormily sweet, his Titan-agony', by the portrait of a Byron ancestor who in a momentary rage had struck his little son a death blow.

What exactly constitutes a literary shrine? Often a mere birthplace may seem accidental to the career of a famous person, having little reference to his or her future mode of life, and little bearing upon his or her style of writing. Few people associate Isaac Newton with the tiny manor-house of Woolsthorpe in Lincolnshire where he was born, where he watched the famous apple fall outside his window, and where, in retreat from London during the Great Plague, he formulated three prodigious discoveries: the differential calculus, the composition of light, and the law of gravity. That Elizabeth Barrett Browning, the delicate, valetudinarian mid-Victorian poet who escaped to live and die in Florence, should have been born in a remote Herefordshire country house built by her father in the Turkish style 'crowded with minarets and domes, and crowned with metal spires and crescents' (as she described the place to her future husband) seems totally incongruous. Yet in *Aurora Leigh* she referred to her childhood home, Hope End, with affection. Field Place, a pretty, tranquil, Wren-style house near Horsham, is an unlikely source for the turbulent spirit which animated Percy Bysshe Shelley. In later life he always referred to it with aversion. That Ouida, flamboyant author of 45 novels about fashionable life and languishing Guards officers, miracles of male strength, valour and beauty, should have been born in Hospital Road, Bury St Edmunds, seems as anomalous as Mrs Radcliffe writing *The Mysteries of Udolpho* in snug Stafford Row a few yards from the present Victoria railway station, London SW1. Even a writer's own choice of their life's setting sometimes bears no recognizable relation to their output. Who would suppose that the Pole Conrad, wedded to the sea, and the Hungarian Baroness Orczy, creator of *The Scarlet Pimpernel* and *Beau Brocade,* chose to live in cosy Kent villages among the hop orchards?

On the other hand there are writers whose native roots were deep enough to have coloured a whole lifetime of expression. There is Wordsworth of course who was born in Cumberland and after a flirtation with Somerset returned to the Lakes for the remaining 51 years of his life. There is Robert Burns who was born, bred and lived and died in an Ayrshire but-and-ben where his poems were composed in the Lowlands dialect. There is poor John Clare whose fragile muse knew only the flat pastoral meadows and woods of Northamptonshire. Crabbe's Suffolk centred on Aldeburgh: 'Thou awful sea! Upon this shingly beach of Aldeburgh I pace: my gazing eye Thy world of waters lost in the dim sky Admiring.' The poetry of Anna Seward, 'the Swan of Lichfield' who could quote the whole of *L'Allegro* before she was three and of whom a sister author, Mary Russell Mitford wrote bitchily, 'She is all tinkling and tinsel – a sort of Dr. Darwin [her co-citizen] in petticoats', was as provincial as her home town. When she ventured to describe the ocean around the North Pole in a poem about Captain Cook she got sadly out of her depth. The verse and novels of James Hogg, the 'Etrick Shepherd', are as dim as his native Selkirkshire which he never left and in which they are steeped. The total identification of Hardy with Wessex needs no emphasis; nor does the aloof, morose, almost alien strain of Tennyson's poetry escape the influence of his native Lincolnshire wolds. The Brontës are inextricably associated with the weird, wild moors round Haworth where the sisters were all born, and where they wrote and died. Jane Austen was born in Steventon in Berkshire and although she occasionally travelled to Bath and sometimes stayed with relations in her own county of Hampshire she spent the greater part of her life at Chawton, in a house as compact, neat and trim as those she made the homes of her heroines in fiction. Of more recent date we have Flora Thompson whose minor classic, *Lark Rise to Candleford*, calls upon her experiences as a girl assistant in Fringford Post Office, Oxfordshire.

Let us also not forget in this context of native roots the hunting stories of Somerville and Ross, all written in Castletownshend village, County Cork, and the humorous sporting novels by the creator of Jorrocks, R.S. Surtees at his home, Hamsterley Hall, Co. Durham; or those chronicles of everyday life which have passed into the realms of art, Gilbert White's *Natural History and Antiquities of Selborne*, recorded in the Hampshire village where he was born and where he died; and Parson Woodforde's diary ('I breakfasted, dined, supped and slept again at home') in Weston Longville village, Norfolk.

Identification of a writer with a certain place or region does not necessarily signify that he was born or even brought up there. Carlyle was not born in Chelsea, Kipling at Batemans, nor Bernard Shaw at Ayot St Lawrence, although the latter always referred to his horrid little house, Shaw's Corner, in postcards to me as 'the birthplace'. For instead of helping to form the author's character and influence their writings, they were themselves formed and fashioned by their incumbents. The same argument can apply to regions. A.E. Housman, forever connected with Shropshire, did not live in that county. He was born outside Bromsgrove in Worcestershire and when composing 'A Shropshire Lad' was living in Highgate and Pinner. Similarly,

I The 6th Earl of Dorset (1637-
1706), 'courtier, poet, and patron
of poets', by Sir Godfrey Kneller
(*Knole*). See page 18.

II Charles Dickens (1812-1870)
by William Powell Frith *(Victoria &
Albert Museum)*. See page 21.

III Sir Walter Scott (1771-1832), an unfinished study by Sir Edwin Landseer *(National Portrait Gallery)*. See page 25.

IV Vita Sackville-West's study in
the Tower at Sissinghurst Castle,
Kent. See page 26.

V *Cockermouth Castle* by J.M.W. Turner, exhibited 1810 and purchased by the 3rd Earl of Egremont *(Petworth House)*. The ruined castle was one of the Wordsworth children's favourite playgrounds. See pages 35-40.

VI Allan Bank, Grasmere where
Wordsworth lived from 1808-11.
See pages 41-47.

VII Hardy's Cottage, Higher Bockhampton, Dorchester. See pages 77-91.

VIII Kipling's house Batemans from the east. See pages 111-117.

IX Kipling's study at Batemans.

X & XI One of Helen Allingham's watercolours of Carlyle. On the wall behind him is a portrait of one of his 'heroes', Oliver Cromwell, and *(opposite)* the same room at Carlyle's House today. The walls are covered in a modern paper which closely follows the original. Carlyle's reading chair and several of the pictures remain in place. See pages 61-75.

XII Lawrence's cottage Clouds Hill. See pages 141-157.

XIII Shaw in the garden on the occasion of his ninetieth birthday and at the time of his donation of Shaw's Corner to the National Trust. See pages 119-139.

XIV The dining table and chairs made for Virginia Woolf by Duncan Grant and Vanessa Bell in around 1929 *(Monk's House)*. See pages 159-167.

XV Leonard Woolf by Vanessa Bell, 1940 *(National Portrait Gallery)*. See pages 159-167.

XVI The Garden Room at Charleston.

L.P. Hartley, whose novels take place along the Norfolk coast, was born amongst the brickfields of Bedfordshire and spent most of his adult life in London. As a boy however Housman was frequently taken in the holidays to Shropshire and the Bredon Hills, while Hartley's parents rented a beautiful red brick Georgian house, Bradenham Hall in Norfolk to which their son became deeply attached and which he made the scene of his best known novel, *The Go Between*. All of which help to prove that boy and girlhood memories are among the most vivid of an artist's life. Further evidence of this is found in Rupert Brooke's strong attachment to Grantchester where he took rooms as an undergraduate at Cambridge. His poem 'The Old Vicarage, Grantchester', was written in Berlin in nostalgia for the radiant days of his youth and beauty when, so he confided to a friend, he was 'as happy as the day's long'.

A belated infatuation for a region as distinct from a dwelling, may influence a writer's work just as strongly as a childhood love affair. While training to become a Jesuit at St Beuno's College, Asaph, Gerard Manley Hopkins fell head over heels in love with North Wales, its scenery and inhabitants. 'I have got a yearning for the Welsh people,' he informed his mother, and when he saw the mountains of Clwyd with the clouds lifting, 'it gives me a rise in the heart.' To Coventry Patmore he wrote towards the end of his life that North Wales was 'the true Arcadia of wild beauty.'

> Lovely woods, waters, meadows, combes, vales,
> All the air things wear that build this world of Wales.

The district was made sacred to this tormented convert to Catholicism by the proximity of St Winefred's holy well which inspired one of his longest religious poems. Hopkins's contemporary, also a priest but of the Anglican persuasion, R.F. Kilvert, was likewise smitten while in his thirties by the inhabitants and scenery of the South Wales borders. Kilvert's surviving diaries were mostly written while he was curate to his father at Clyro. He was of a very different caste to the reclusive Jesuit Hopkins, no less sensitive to suffering and distress, no less receptive to the sublimity of mountains and valleys, but an unashamed enjoyer of the social diversions of the neighbourhood. Others whose adopted regions came to permeate their writings were the Edinburgh-born Kenneth Grahame and the London-born Edward Thomas. On retiring from the secretaryship of the Bank of England Grahame chose to live in the Thames Valley where as a child he had stayed with his grandmother. At Pangbourne his best known novel, *The Wind in the Willows,* was conceived. Thomas moved in 1906 to the village of Steep near Petersfield which remained his home till his death in action in 1917. The pastoral scenery of this southern corner of Hampshire turned him in later life to poetry and infused his verse with 'an impassioned, almost trance-like delight in things natural, simple, "short-lived and happy-seeming"', to quote the tribute of his friend, Walter de la Mare.

Quite another kind of literary shrine is the *ménage,* or circle of writers, either assembled round the figurehead of an important patron, or a group without a leader or guiding star. In the first category Penshurst Place in Kent and Wilton in Wiltshire are among the earliest shrines presided over by owners of outstanding qualities and gifts. A fifteenth-century owner of Penshurst, 'the good Duke Humphrey' of Gloucester, patronised Lydgate and Capgrave. The Duke was learned in Latin and Italian, and formed a great collection of books which he bequeathed to Oxford University for the foundation of the Bodleian Library. In the following century Penshurst was acquired by Sir Philip Sidney's grandfather and young Philip and his brother Robert were born in the house. Philip inherited shortly before his legendary death on the field of battle ('Thy necessity is greater than mine'). Robert, later to be knighted and created Earl of Leicester, succeeded his brother in 1586. It was during

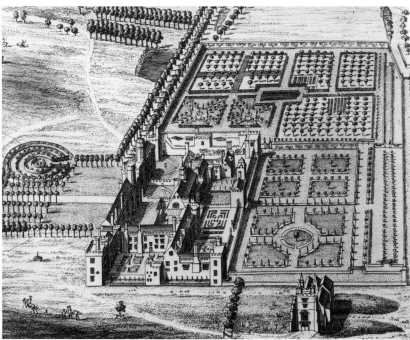

(*Left*) Sir Philip Sidney, and (*right*) Johannes Kip's aerial view of Penshurst.

his time that so many of his brother's fellow poets and writers, like Spenser, Fulke Greville, Hervey, Dyer and Ben Jonson, congregated within the venerable walls. Penshurst was one of the first country houses to be celebrated in verse in Jonson's famous poem addressed 'To Penshurst': 'Thou art not, Penshurst, built to envious show of touch or marble', and containing the lines:

> And though thy wals be of the countrey stone,
> They're rear'd with no man's ruine, no man's groan;
> There's none that dwell about them wish them downe;
> But all come in, the farmer and the clowne....

is probably the first generous acknowledgement of the democratic spirit within a great country house. Wilton, under Philip Sidney's sister, Mary, Countess of Pembroke, 'the subject of all verse', whose sons were to become Shakespeare's 'incomparable paire of brethren', must vie with Penshurst as the most famous meeting place of early seventeenth-century writers. Here they gathered around a woman of rare enlightenment. In 1603 *As You Like It* was performed at Wilton in the presence of King James I.

Knole is another great country house where successive owners have been patrons of artists and literary men. In Virgina Woolf's *Orlando*, based on Knole, the poet Nick Green enjoys Orlando's patronage and comes to stay. The 3rd Earl of Dorset was the friend of Jonson, Fletcher, Drayton and Donne. The last preached in the chapel so eloquently that he reduced the susceptible Countess Anne Clifford to tears. The 6th Earl of Dorset, himself author of the lyric, 'To all you ladies now on land,' was boon companion of Charles Sedley and Rochester, and friend and patron of Dryden who dedicated two essays to him, and of Prior who owed him his education at Cambridge. Prior wrote that 'A freedom reigned at his table which made every one of the guests think himself at home.' The dining-room, of which the walls are lined with portraits of the Earl's literary coterie, is known as the Poets' Parlour. The 6th Earl's generosity was inexhaustible. If he suspected that one of his literary friends was in need of cash he would slip a £100 note under his plate.

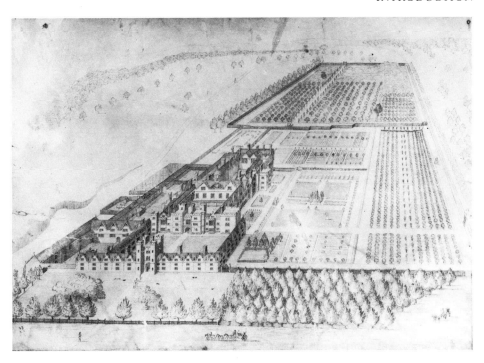

An aerial view of Knole in the late seventeenth century attributed to Thomas Badeslade.

We have already referred to those men of letters who in the eighteenth century assembled round the table of the estimable Ralph Allen (Fielding's Squire Allworthy) at Prior Park, of Lord Lyttelton at Hagley, Lord Harcourt at Nuneham and Lord Cobham at Stowe. In the nineteenth century Clevedon Court, Somerset, was presided over by Sir Charles Elton, 6th Baronet. Sir Charles was an accomplished poet and first-class classical scholar who translated Hesiod. He was a regular contributor to the *London Magazine*. He befriended John Clare, Charles Lamb, Robert Southey and S.T. Coleridge to whom he leased a cottage on the estate for his honeymoon. The baronet's sister married Henry Hallam the historian, and he thus became the uncle of Arthur, the lamented subject of Tennyson's threnody, *In Memoriam*. When Arthur Hallam died in Vienna in 1833 his body was brought back to Clevedon and buried in the Elton vault of the church.

> The Danube to the Severn gave
> The darken'd heart that beat no more;
> They laid him by the pleasant shore,
> And in the hearing of the wave.

Tennyson stayed at Clevedon Court in order to visit Hallam's tomb in 1850, the year *In Memoriam* was published. 'It seemed', the bereaved poet wrote, 'a kind of consecration to go there.' Thackeray often stayed at Clevedon Court where *Henry Esmond* was partly drafted, and Lady Castlewood was modelled on Sir Charles's youngest daughter, Jane Octavia, with whom the novelist fell in love. Drawings by Thackeray still hang in the house. Sir Charles was also patron of a local school of artists, Rippingille, Bird and Barker of Bath, the last of whom he commissioned to paint his wife and ten of his children.

Lady Gregory lived at Coole Park, County Galway, from the date of her marriage in 1880 until her death in 1932. In her book *Coole* she described the house in detail, particularly the drawing-room where she wrote plays and kept her secret journals. She told how Bernard Shaw would play the piano and sing folk songs, how Masefield composed ballads of the sea. But it is W.B. Yeats who is chiefly associated with Coole.

He first went there in 1898, was nursed to health after serious illness, and made it his home for many years occupying a room overlooking the lake. In 'The Wild Swans at Coole' the poet foretold the house's sad fate.

> Here, traveller, scholar, poet, take your stand
> When all those rooms and passages are gone,
> When nettles wave upon a shapeless mound
> And saplings root among the broken stone...

Coole was pulled down in 1941.

With the twentieth century we have Garsington Manor in Oxfordshire. Here the fabulous Lady Ottoline and Philip Morrell lived from 1913 to 1927 and entertained members of the group denominated 'Bloomsbury' as well as countless writers outside it. Lady Ottoline, who looked like a witch in *Macbeth* made up to resemble Helen of Troy, gave unflagging hospitality to those young writers who were professed pacifists during the First World War. Some of them repaid her kindness with vitriolic criticism. Aldous Huxley, then an undergraduate at Oxford, described his first visit to Garsington in December 1915:

> Lady Ottoline... is a quite incredible creature – arty beyond the dreams of avarice and a patroness of literature and the modernities.

Soon he was writing that the household was the most delightful he knew, 'always interesting people there and v. good talk.' That Christmas Middleton Murry and Katherine Mansfield, Lytton Strachey, Carrington and Clive Bell made up the party. Siegfried Sassoon found it 'enchanting' while on leave from the trenches in 1916. D.H. Lawrence, T.S. Eliot and Rupert Brooke were inmates at different times and when the conscientious objectors became too many for the manor the bailiff's house

(Left) Lady Ottoline Morell by Henry Lamb *(National Portrait Gallery)* and *(right)* Garsington Manor, Oxfordshire.

across the road was made available for them.

Unfortunately Garsington Manor no longer retains any of the Morrell's belongings then thought so extravagant. Even Lady Ottoline's red sealing-wax paint has been stripped from the wall panelling by a subsequent owner.

Two villages where writers congregated in a colony without a specific host are Limpsfield in Surrey and Dymock in Gloucestershire. In the former, Edward Garnett and his wife Constance, translator of Russian novels, lived at The Cearne, a house they built in 1896 overlooking the valley. Hudson, Cunningham Graham, Belloc, Edward Thomas, W.H. Davies and Galsworthy were sometime visitors. Ford Madox Hueffer (Ford) and his wife living nearby introduced D.H. Lawrence to the Garnetts who gave him lodging and Lawrence wrote many a poem seated at the open fireplace at The Cearne. Rupert Brooke, Bernard Shaw and E.V. Lucas used to meet at Champions, the home of their friends the Olivers. Lascelles Abercrombie settled at a house called Gallows in Dymock, in 1911. Two years later Rupert Brooke and John Drinkwater joined him; and Wilfred Gibson came to live at the Old Nail Shop, a red brick cottage with exposed beams and a thatched roof. From here the four poets contributed to *New Numbers.* In 1914 Robert Frost, the American poet, rented a black-and-white labourer's cottage in order to be near them.

Literary shrines may also take the form of places commemorated after brief visits. Stoke Poges is perhaps one of the most famous. The London-born Thomas Gray did not live there, and Cambridge became his final home; on the other hand he had as a boy stayed with relations at nearby Burnham Beeches where he walked and managed to discover 'mountains and precipices'. His mother was buried in Stoke Poges churchyard and the poet was eventually laid beside her. James Wyatt's handsome sarcophagus on a plinth commemorates the author of the *Elegy.* Church and monument are today an oasis overshadowed by abominations of wire and concrete. No longer are there fields through which the ploughman plods his weary way. No hoary-headed swains are to be met far from the madding crowd. Nor indeed are the distant spires and antique towers of Eton any longer visible through the electricity cables, factory blocks and the multi-storey car-parks of Slough.

Seaside resorts have many literary claims of a transitory nature. In No. 12 High Street, Broadstairs (since replaced by Woolworth's stores) Dickens wrote much of *Pickwick Papers;* at the Royal Albion Hotel *Nicholas Nickleby,* and at the Lawn House *The*

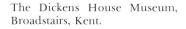

The Dickens House Museum, Broadstairs, Kent.

Old Curiosity Shop and *Barnaby Rudge.* In Bleak House where *David Copperfield* was finished, the novelist's study, bedroom and dining-room are furnished with some of his possessions. Dickens declared that Broadstairs beat 'all watering places into what the Americans call "sky blue fits".' *David Copperfield* was actually begun at Yarmouth on the Norfolk sands. In January 1849 Dickens arrived by coach from London with two companions and the next day walked 23 miles along the shore to Lowestoft and back. Dickens promptly made the wide dull waste of shingly beach at Yarmouth the site of the Peggotty's upturned boat-house and the home of Mrs Gummidge and Little Em'ly. Some coastal resorts have the most unlikely literary associations. Having temporarily escaped from his evil genüis Rimbaud in 1877, Verlaine took a job for nearly twelve months as French teacher in a Catholic boys' school in Bournemouth, 'on the top of the high cliffs covered with furze. I have seen leagues and leagues of sea in every direction, even as far as the first rocks of the shores of the Norman Islands,' he wrote to his mother nostalgically. Here he behaved impeccably, kept off the bottle and composed part of the masterpiece, *Amour.* But Bournemouth depressed him.

> Solitude de coeur dans le vide de l'âme,
> Le combat de la mer et les vents de l'hiver.

The boys ragged him unmercifully and when one winter day he was hit by a stone disguised as a snowball he had had enough, and returned to Arras.

The identification of definite places in fiction is never easy; nor should it be, any more than persons, who are seldom lifted wholly from life. Trollope's Barchester is a conflation of Salisbury and Winchester, Hugh Walpole's Polchester is a parody of Truro, and Hardy's Casterbridge only more or less a likeness of Dorchester. Rockingham Castle, Northamptonshire, was the model for Dickens's Chesney Wold in *Bleak House*, part of which was written there while he was staying with his friends the Watsons. The opening scene with Lady Dedlock, bored to death in her 'place' in Lincolnshire, where the waters are out, the park is 'punctured all over, all day long, with falling rain... and the heavy rain drops fall, drip, drip, drip, upon the broad flagged pavement, called, from old time, the Ghost's Walk, all night', is hauntingly descriptive. Haunting too are the dismal apartments with their portraits of lugubrious ancestors. But Dickens is not a good delineator of the upper classes and their ways of life. He is incapable of preventing his innate Radical prejudices from intervening between his pen and the land-owning gentry. Evelyn Waugh is more sympathetic towards the aristocracy, albeit of the 1920s and 30s, because he longed to be accepted as one of them. The physical Brideshead is probably Castle Howard in the North Riding, but inhabited by the Lygon family of Madresfield in Worcester-shire. The white and gold ballroom in Henry Green's *Loving* where Raunce the butler comes upon the two housemaids waltzing to the gramophone ('The little bitches, I'll show 'em') was partly taken from Birr Castle, King's County, Ireland where the novelist frequently stayed with his friends Lord and Lady Rosse, and partly from Petworth House, Sussex, his mother's old home. Of all the great houses celebrated by twentieth-century authors Knole in Kent is probably the best known, for not only did Vita Sackville-West describe the building in accurate detail as Chevron and the household and the house parties there before the first war in *The Edwardians*, but Virginia Woolf immortalized it as the setting for *Orlando* whose eponymous and epicene hero was modelled on Vita Sackville-West herself. As comedy Nancy Mitford's *Pursuit of Love* satirises her parents and sisters at Swinbrook, Oxfordshire, and Osbert Sitwell's autobiographical *Left Hand, Right Hand* chronicles his, his sister Edith and brother Sacheverell's Gothic youth at Renishaw under their father, the eccentric Sir George.

Individual houses have likewise given rise to some chronicles which are now minor classics. Vita Sackville-West's *Knole and the Sackvilles* (1923) portrayed its successive owners since the great house was given by Queen Elizabeth to her ancestor Thomas Sackville, a contributor to *Gorboduc,* one of the most boring tragedies in any language. *Earlham* (1922) is Percy Lubbock's story of his childhood among Quaker Gurney relations towards the end of the nineteenth century in the house of that name on the outskirts of Norwich. *Felbrigg, The Story of a House* (1962) by R.W. Ketton-Cremer, *Charlecote and the Lucys* (1958) by Alice Fairfax-Lucy, *Bowen's Court* (1942) by Elizabeth Bowen, the last and most distinguished representative of a line of Anglo-Irish owners since Cromwellian days, and *The Cecils of Hatfield House* (1973) by David Cecil are beautifully and lovingly written by members of the families who have owned the respective houses.

Of all categories of literary shrine the most illuminating are perhaps those actually built from the foundations by authors to express their ideologies and fantasies. They convey a far more vivid expression of a writer's personality and vision than the house he may have bought, beautified, cherished and lived in for decades, but which was built by a previous owner. Batemans at Burwash tells us what Kipling held dear, namely a pretty Jacobean manor house of Sussex stone set amid lawns and surrounded by streams, but it could just as well have been bought, lived in and loved by an appreciative stockbroker. Of the sort of 'created' shrine I have in mind the most ambitious, most lavish and in a sense most idiosyncratic, must have been Fonthill Abbey. It eclipsed in size and fancifulness Horace Walpole's Strawberry Hill – but William Beckford had the advantage over Walpole of being a millionaire. He was a spoilt and capricious elf, yet he was one of the greatest bibliophiles and collectors of works of art this country has produced. He was besides a competent musician and a landscape gardener on a vast scale. Above all he was a writer and it is as such he should primarily be remembered. His travel journals are among the best in the English language. His descriptions of the visits he paid to the Portuguese monasteries of Alcobaça and Batalha are both romantic and hilariously comical. His early fame was established by the well-known but underestimated oriental tale *Vathek*, composed in French reputedly within three days and nights. The eponymous hero of the tale was half the author's father, Alderman Beckford, and half young William

The south end of St Michael's Gallery, Fonthill, and *(right)* William Beckford by John Hoppner *(Salford Museum and Art Gallery).*

himself. Caliph Vathek was sensualist, tyrant and the personification of overweening ambition, ruthlessness and determination to get his own way. Although, alas, Fonthill Abbey has gone (it fell down conveniently a year or two after Beckford sold it for a colossal sum) there are so many records of it in prose and print, coloured lithographs and paintings by the numerous artists whom Beckford patronised, that we know precisely how every gallery and apartment looked, down to the placing of every single object of vertu. The stupendous size of the gimcrack abbey, the colourful Gothic windows, richly composed with armoreal escutcheons of the mediaeval families from whom William was descended through his mother (for his father was a parvenu), the wealth of marble, ormolu, gold and silver treasures encrusted with gems, not to mention the paintings by Bellini, Claude, Raphael, Elsheimer and other great masters, testified to the boundless potentialities of this frustrated genius who was his own worst enemy in more senses than one. Had Fonthill Abbey survived, it would undoubtedly be the most ambitious specimen in bulk and self-glorification of an English writer's illusion. Fonthill was indeed a reconstruction in stone and mortar (and, to its detriment, plaster) of those Portuguese monasteries, half sybaritic and half ascetic, which had haunted Beckford since his prodigal youth.

Clearly the Gothic style afforded greater scope than the classical to the literary imagination in the Augustan age. What eminent writer of those times raised for himself a habitation in the Palladian style? True, Matthew Prior commissioned James Gibbs to build him what might have been a partly Baroque country seat in Essex, but poor Prior's lack of means and early death prevented Down Hall getting further than a noble design on paper.

A shrine of the ambitious sort we are describing which has survived is Abbotsford in Roxburghshire. Here Sir Walter Scott at the height of his fame and fortune and the popularity of the Waverley novels commissioned William Atkinson to raise on the banks of the Tweed between 1812 and 1818 the heavy, gloomy pile out of a pre-existing farmstead. Abbotsford virtually set the fashion for nineteenth century Scotch baronial. Sir Walter was in his element. He nearly drove the architect mad by last minute alterations of design and detail, which he was determined to get 'right'. He need not have bothered for the result is an asymmetrical hash of little architectural merit. Scott was emphatic that his castle should be deliberately irregular and whimsical. He told Joanna Baillie in 1823, 'You cannot imagine how

Matthew Prior by Thomas Hudson *(National Portrait Gallery)*.

Scott's study at Abbotsford, where he wrote many of his later novels.

smart Abbotsford looks with its turrets and queer old-fashioned architecture.' But then Scott, whose literary output was immense, whose knowledge of Scotch history was unrivalled, whose industry was prodigious, was not the man of taste that Beckford could claim to be. Nevertheless, as a reflection of his personality and romantic notions Abbotsford, with its library, family portraits, museum, weapons and armour, its cumbersome, stuffy furniture and shoddy bric-à-brac which the novelist delighted to receive as gifts from admirers and friends, is one of the most rewarding literary shrines in the British Isles. It too is a fabric of illusion, for Scott was ambitious above all to be recognised and respected as a laird. He proceeded to ruin himself by buying up his neighbours' lands and increasing the acreage of his estate. He did not wish to be honoured as the author of the most widely read literature in Europe. He even denied to George IV, when taxed on the subject, that he was the author of the Waverley novels. The genial, kindly, child-like, gifted Sir Walter was a snob. He regarded the source of his fortune as slightly shameful and unbecoming a gentleman – it was as regrettable as trade. He was over-conscious of his friend and fellow poet the noble Lord Byron's professed contempt for scribbling. Byron also happened to own a country house and estate. The only difference was that Newstead Abbey was ancestral, having been in his family since the Reformation. So it was not Byron's creation. On the contrary it went far to create him. His romantic tales, like *The Giaour* and *The Corsair* and his doom-laden dramas like *Manfred* and *Cain*, derived from the melancholy influence Gothic Newstead had upon his formative imagination. Unhappily Byron was obliged to sell Newstead. Abbotsford is still the home of Sir Walter's descendants.

Another house created by a literary man or, to be strictly correct, a mansion transformed, is Knebworth in Hertfordshire. Actually the Lyttons had owned Knebworth House since Henry VII's reign; but the novelist Edward Bulwer-Lytton (1st Baron Lytton) destroyed two-thirds of the old house and re-edified the

Sir Edward Bulwer Lytton in his study at Knebworth by E.M. Ward *(Knebworth House)*.

remainder onto which he built extensions. The author of *The Last Days of Pompeii* and *Rienzi* was a deep-dyed egoist, valetudinarian, spiritualist and romantic, to whom nothing was so Romantic as himself. He ruthlessly imposed his own version of Tudor architecture upon the real thing in towers, turrets and a galaxy of crockets and gargoyles whose flavour remains irredeemably early Victorian. Bulwer-Lytton and Dickens acted in the great hall at Knebworth in Ben Jonson's *Every Man in His Humour* in 1850 and also the following year in Lytton's play, *Not so Bad as we Seem*, which Dickens disloyally pronounced to be rather worse than it seemed.

A twentieth-century creation is Sissinghurst Castle in Kent, the home of Harold Nicolson and his wife Vita Sackville-West from 1930 until their deaths there. Again Sissinghurst, another essentially Romantic composition, is in essence Gothic in that the castle remains, which the Nicolsons found in a state of utter dereliction, date from early Tudor times. The original builder happened to be a distant ancestor of Vita, a fact which in her eyes added lustre to the neglected site. If it could not take the place of Knole in her affections, it became the substitute on which she lavished her love and care. The Nicolsons made of the remains a habitation uniquely theirs. Few civilised couples would have been content, as they were, to sleep in one converted ruin, eat in another, and work and live separately in a third and fourth. Luxury meant nothing to them; seclusion and tranquility much; gardening everything. The detached fragments of tower, gate-house, priest's house and cottage became through their hands punctuations in a garden which they laid out, planted and made famous the world over. Only secondarily did they serve as parts of a dwelling. No literary shrine of recent date is more expressive of the joint labours and individual writings of a remarkable pair.

We should not forget those writers who grew up, so to speak, behind the green baize door of great country houses. George Eliot's father was not, to be accurate, a domestic servant, but he was born the son of a poor carpenter. An exceptionally intelligent lad, he rose to be agent to the Newdegate family of Arbury in Warwickshire. Mary Ann Evans, his youngest child, in order to avoid the lingering prejudice against female authors, adopted the pen-name, George Eliot. Her father was partly the model for Adam Bede; and Arbury Mill inspired *The Mill on the Floss*. In *Mr. Gilfil's Love Story* the crenellated Arbury Hall, with its astonishing mid-Georgian Gothic apartments of elaborate fan-vaulting and 'Perpendicular' wall panels, which the child Mary Ann must often have visited with her father when the family were from home, was translated accurately and photographically into Cheverel Manor.

> And a charming picture Cheverel Manor would have made that evening, if some English Watteau had been there to paint it; the castellated house of grey-tinted stone, with the flickering sunbeams sending dashes of golden light across the many draped panes in the mullioned windows, and a great beech leaning athwart one of the flanking towers, and breaking, with its dark flattened bough, the too formal symmetry of the front.

and elsewhere she describes the interior:

> anyone entering the dining-room for the first time, would perhaps have had his attention even more strongly arrested by the room itself, which was so bare of furniture that it impressed one with its architectural beauty like a cathedral. A piece of matting stretched from door to door, a bit of worn carpet under the dining-table and a sideboard in a deep recess, did not detain the eye for a moment from the lofty groined ceiling, with its richly carved pendants, all of creamy white, relieved here and there by touches of gold... The room looked less like a place to dine in than a piece of space enclosed simply for the sake of beautiful outline.

The housekeeper's room at Uppark, Sussex, and *(right)* H.G. Wells. Photograph by G.C. Beresford *(National Portrait Gallery)*.

H.G. Wells on the other hand was literally brought up behind baize doors at Uppark in Sussex where his mother was housekeeper. The contrast between upstairs and downstairs at Uppark was not quite as distinct as it seemed to the housekeeper's boy in view of the fact that Lady Fetherstonhaugh, the chatelaine of this large William and Mary house had been the dairy maid before her marriage. In her long widowhood she continued to live at Uppark with a younger sister. Wells in later life remembered the place with some affection. 'During my mother's thirteen years' sway at Uppark, and thanks largely to the reliefs and opportunity that came to me through that brief interval of good fortune in her life, I had been able to do all sorts of things.' He produced there a daily newspaper for the entertainment of the staff which he called *The Uppark Alarmist,* and contrived a miniature theatre in his mother's room where he staged simple plays. 'The place had a great effect on me' he wrote in his autobiography, 'it retained a vitality that altogether over-shadowed the insignificant ebbing trickle of upstairs life, the two elderly ladies in the parlour following their shrunken routines.' Furthermore Uppark features as Bladesover in Wells's novel, *Tono-Bungay,* a picture of English society in dissolution towards the end of the nineteenth century.

Not all writers were at home in the country. Far from it. William Cobbett's 'great wen' had and has – strange as it may seem – irresistible appeal. My friend Dormer Creston, author of *The Regent and His Daughter* and other excellent and under-rated biographies, assured me that without the roar of London's traffic she could neither think nor sleep. The two greatest literary Londoners are probably Samuel Johnson and Charles Dickens. The sights, sounds and smells of the metropolis are reflected and reproduced in the writings of both. 'When a man is tired of London', declaimed the Doctor, 'he is tired of life; for there is in London all that life can afford'. All! As though nature, the seasons, woods, pastures, downs, hills, lakes, wild life and flowers, tranquility and peace count for nothing. Johnson's verse lacks poetry, but his sonorous prose is like the notes of the organ heard in St Clement Danes against the clatter of cart wheels and pattens in the Strand. Johnson arrived in London in 1737 to embark upon the profession of literature. Boswell gives a list of sixteen houses in which he dwelt. Only one has survived, namely No. 17 Gough Square off Fleet Street, known as Dr Johnson's House. It is open to the public and in the garret

one can still picture him wrestling with the great Dictionary. Here too he wrote *Rasselas*, and here his wife, the florid, voluminous, portentous Tetty, 21 years his senior, died in 1752. He was grief-stricken by the loss of his 'pretty dear creature'. Eighteenth-century London, not the London of Lord Chesterfield's Mayfair but of Grub Street, the Strand, Fleet Street, the Temple, the dusky alleys leading off the main thoroughfares, and the murky taverns, the Mitre, the Devil and the Cheshire Cheese with its pew-like benches and sandy wooden floor, or what is left of them, is Johnson's memorial. Dickens's London of a century later was less picturesque but more smoke- and fog-laden, more squalid, more poverty-stricken and sinister. The Industrial Revolution had come and left a contagious blight upon alleys and river. The corpses of suicides were daily fished from the polluted waters of the Thames by the mudlarks who stripped them of rings and clothing. Dickens's London was the underworld of the nefarious dwarf Quilp, of Fagin and Bill Sykes as well as the shabby genteel Mrs Jellyby with her sprawling children and the Micawbers perpetually hovering on the brink of penury and shame. Dickens's London homes were, like Johnson's, numerous. No. 48 Doughty Street is the only survivor. While living in this house his reputation was established. Here he entertained to lively dinner parties Harrison Ainworth, Leigh Hunt and John Forster, his future biographer. Here he completed *Pickwick* and *Nicholas Nickleby* and wrote *Oliver Twist*. Here may be seen many personal relics, his portable desk, manuscripts and letters.

Whereas Johnson and Dickens may be considered 'natural' Londoners, although the first was born in Lichfield and the second in Portsmouth, Thomas Carlyle who moved to Chelsea at the age of 39 to spend the remainder of his days and to die there, never became a full-blooded Londoner. He always remained the aloof, exclusive

(Left) Dr Johnson by Sir Godfrey Kneller *(Knole)* and *(right)* Johnson's house in Gough Square, off the Strand, in London.

Scot, slightly contemptuous of the capital of his adopted country. Yet his house in Cheyne Row is the most evocative literary shrine in London. No. 24, brimful of his furniture and possessions, still preserves the flavour of his quirky, petulant spirit, still echoes the growls of his deep Lowlands voice, and in the rather foetid rooms the tensions which his wife Jane, that incomparable letter-writer, imparted to it, still reverberate.

If Johnson and Dickens had no understanding of the country, Carlyle had precious little. On the other hand two English poets whose pre-eminent descriptions of scenery and nature have been referred to, namely Herrick and Wordsworth, both appreciated and even loved London. That Herrick loved it is an understatement. He adored it. When this Devon parson was turned out of his remote incumbency during the Civil War his rejoicing was uncontained.

> From the dull confines of the drooping west,
> To see the day spring from the pregnant east.
> Ravisht in spirit, I come, nay more, I flie
> To thee, blest place of my nativitie!

Even Dr Johnson did not express his affection for the 'wen' in such strong terms as these:

> O place! O people! manners! fram'd to please
> All nations, customes, kindreds, languages!

Another Lowland Scot who adapted himself more readily to London than Carlyle, because he was socially more acceptable to the hostesses of his day, even to being enlisted among the Souls, was James Barrie. There is no particular house associated with his name unless it be No. 100 Bayswater Road where he lived for seven years. His memorial is the Peter Pan statue near the Westbourne Gate entrance to Hyde Park, designed by Sir George Frampton in 1912 at the author's expense. It marks the spot where Barrie – he never underestimated his importance – walked with his Newfoundland dog, Luath, the prototype of Nana in *Peter Pan, or the Boy who wouldn't grow up*. A true Londoner born and bred was George Grossmith the comedian and author, with his brother Weedon, of the immortal *Diary of a Nobody* (1874), the fictitious life of Charles Pooter of the Laurels, Holloway, an assistant in a mercantile business, whose beneficent intentions invariably went amiss and whose domestic and social gaucheries are catalogued with poignant irony. A plaque commemorates Grossmith on the house, No. 3 Spanish Place, W2, where he lived.

The two major university cities have claimed the exclusive allegiance of many a man and woman of letters since Grosseteste, first rector of the Franciscan Order in Oxford, became first Chancellor of the University in the thirteenth century. Roger Bacon lived in the Franciscan house (the site is now occupied by a car park) after his return from Paris in 1250. Mrs Humphrey Ward went to live in North Oxford immediately after her marriage and was peremptorily summoned to meet Mr Gladstone then staying at Keble College. The Grand Old Man strongly criticised her first novel *Elsmere* for being an attack on Christianity. William Cobbett was not the first low-brow to have a dig at the seat of pedantic intellectuals. 'Upon beholding the masses of buildings at Oxford,' he wrote 'devoted to what they call *learning*, I could not help reflecting on the drones that they contain and the wasps they send forth.' On the other hand Matthew Arnold and Gerard Manley Hopkins, both Balliol men, were unqualified admirers of Oxford, Arnold in the *Scholar-Gipsy* traced the rural haunts of the poor student wandering in North Hinksey, along Bagley Wood and on Cumnor Hill, whom the blithe riders, 'Returning home on summer-nights, have met Crossing the stripling Thames at Bab-Lock-hithe.' Of all the poets who have sung the city's praises – Spenser, Thomas Wharton, William Lisle Bowles, Southey, Wordsworth, J.B. Norton, Henry Glassford Bell, Walter Thornbury – none has described Oxford seen from a distance so tenderly and apprehensively as Hopkins in *Duns Scotus's Oxford* (1866):

> Towery city and branchy between towers;
> Cuckoo-echoing, bell swarmèd, lark-charmèd, rook-racked, river-rounded;
> The dapple-eared lily below; that country and town did
> Once encounter in, here coped and poisèd powers;

He reviled the brash new buildings then popping up in North Oxford between the old grey city and the open meadows.

> Thou hast a base and brickish skirt there, sours,
> That neighbour-nature thy grey beauty is grounded
> Best in; graceless growth, thou hast confounded
> Rural rural keeping – folk, flocks, and flowers.

And he deplored the brutal destruction of the poplars at nearby Binsey in the moving lines:

> My aspens dear, whose aery cages quelled,
> Quelled or quenched in leaves the leaping sun,
> All felled, felled, are all felled;
> Of a fresh and following folded rank
> Not spared, not one...

Cambridge of course has had as many devotees, Michael Drayton called it 'my most beloved town' in *Polyolbion* (1622) and Rose Macaulay, who as a young woman lived with her father, a lecturer in English at the University, lovingly recalled it in *Orphan Island*. Frances Cornford, who in childhood often visited her Darwin cousins, went to live off Madingley Road after her marriage in 1908 until her death in 1960. One of her frequent undergraduate visitors was Rupert Brooke whom she described as 'A young Apollo golden haired'. The Cornfords' home became the meeting place of artists and writers such as Will Rothenstein, Eric Gill, Lowes Dickinson, Bertrand Russell, Rabindranath Tagore and Frances's cousin, Gwen Raverat. Among her first collection of poems published in 1910 she celebrated in 'In the Backs' the poets who had frequented Cambridge over the centuries.

Bath, if not exactly a cosmopolitan city, was in the eighteenth century England's principal resort for pleasure, health and culture seekers. The number of eminent artists and writers who visited it season after season (indeed a selection of their names would occupy a page of this book) is almost legion, and the houses in which they lodged, as far as the exteriors are concerned, mostly remain. There are plaques in practically every street and square recording that such-and-such a great man and woman stayed in such-and-such a house. One of the most renowned, although in itself a modest little dwelling, is No. 33 St James's Square, in which Walter Savage Landor passed several stormy years. Dickens, accompanied by Forster and the painter Maclise, stayed with him there, to be inspired with the image of Little Nell and that of Laurence Boythorn, modelled on his boisterous host. Jane Austen was, over the years, a visitor to Bath and nearly all the houses in which she lodged with her parents and sister survive. In *Persuasion* and *Northanger Abbey* she wickedly satirised Bath society, minuting the absurd dumb show which was so strictly observed by the fashionable in the Assembly Rooms and Pump Room. Seldom was the conventional ritual of drinking the water and dancing stately minuets disregarded even by the unorthodox. But the widowed Mrs Thrale, having first shocked the staid by being

The Assembly Rooms, Bath, whose elaborate rituals are immortalised in the works of Jane Austen *(right, National Portrait Gallery)*.

married in St James's Church to Gabriele Piozzi a low bred Italian music master, and Roman Catholic to boot, scandalised all and sundry by dancing on her eightieth birthday a sprightly fandango with a young man a quarter of her own age. Many writers disparaged Bath, ('If I had not a mind to continue "to keep well" I would not remain here a day longer, for I am tired to death of the place.' – Walpole; 'Bath does not please me... incredibly dingy and wretched; and the infamous old men and youths carried in mechanical carriages round the smoking baths horrify me, a horror not softened by the tender glances of certain old women clad in flounces...' – Beckford; and 'The place looks to me like a cemetery, which the dead have succeeded in rising and taking... A dead failure!' – Dickens). Surprisingly, these denigrators returned to it year after year and some even chose to eke out the remainder of their days on its precipitous hills.

Other writers have captured provincial life in the smaller market towns of England. Mrs Gaskell was from the age of one brought up by an aunt in Knutsford, Cheshire. Here she was married and here buried. In *Cranford* she has portrayed small town life as a microcosm of society in the early decades of the nineteenth century. The ladies of Cranford were hedged about and their conduct dictated by infinite barriers of snobbery. The anecdotes about the choice of caps and headgear, the quality of porcelain tea services and the subservience to rank would be nauseating were they not told with such deft touches of humour. Two things particularly strike the reader of *Cranford* today. Firstly the quantity of middle-class townspeople who had absolutely nothing whatever to do, and secondly the close proximity of the country to the town. The author mentions casually what was then taken for granted, namely the fragrant smell on summer evenings wafted through the open windows from the neighbouring hayfields. Today it is the stink of diesel fumes from thundering lorries or the sulphurous stench from chemical factories that greet the nostrils of town dwellers. Mrs Sherwood, apart from the few years spent with her husband's regiment in India, never left Worcester, and in Britannia Square finished the last volume of her improving saga, *The Fairchild Family* (1847).

Olney in Buckinghamshire will always be associated with William Cowper. At the suggestion of a fanatical Evangelist, the Rev. John Newton, the poet and his saintly companion, Mrs Unwin, retired there in 1767 to occupy the western half of a house called Orchard Side in the marketplace. In Olney the poet's friends arranged for him to lead an ordered life in a vain attempt to keep his recurrent madness at bay. In

Orchard Side, now the Cowper and Newton Museum, he wrote some of his finest poems and lengthy letters to his friends, and played with his tame hares. The garden at the back still contains the 'nutshell of a summerhouse which is my verse manufactory.' His friend Lady Austen suggested that he try his hand at blank verse. When he replied that he could not think of a subject she said, without forethought, 'Write upon this sofa'. Soon after he began *The Task,* an epic in six books, the first of which he called 'The Sofa'. It includes the homely lines that synthesise the trouble-free routine which for a time enabled him to retain his tremulous sanity.

> Now stir the fire, and close the shutters fast,
> Let fall the curtains, wheel the sofa round,
> And, while the bubbling and loud-hissing urn
> Throws up a steamy column, and the cups,
> That cheer but not inebriate, wait on each,
> So let us welcome peaceful Ev'ning in.

The Task was an instant success and pilgrims thronged to gaze through the windows of Orchard Side at the sofa, and through the garden fence at the summerhouse.

From the dainty lace caps of the ladies of Cranford and the sofa and hissing tea-urn of Olney it is a far cry to the Midlands and the Potteries. Writers like Arnold Bennett and D.H. Lawrence sprang from very different backgrounds; essentially proletarian, murky, industrial and inelegant. Their novels were a stark reminder of the drab and often sordid surroundings of their working-class youth. They reflected the basic life as led by the struggling, unsentimental, tough miners and potters of Staffordshire and Nottinghamshire. Bennett and Lawrence belong to a no-nonsense school, nostalgic maybe, but realistic, political and positively anti-Picturesque. Bennett was born in 1867 above a small shop in Hanley, one of 'The Five Towns' of his novels and short stories. At the age of 22 he found work in a lawyer's office uncongenial, and left for London. Although he never returned to the Five Towns they provided the

(Left) William Cowper by Lemuel Francis Abbott *(National Portrait Gallery)* and *(right)* the poet's house, 'Orchard Side', at Olney, now the Cowper and Newton Museum.

substance and dun-coloured settings for all his stories. Lawrence, nearly a generation younger than Bennett, was born in the hill-top mining town of Eastwood, eight miles from Nottingham. He transposed many of the scenes he had witnessed in his youth into his books, calling his home town 'Bestwood', 'Woodhouse' and 'Beldover' in *Sons and Lovers*, *The Lost Girl* and *Women in Love*. When he was two his miner father and his mother moved to 28 Garden Road which he named 'The Bottoms' in *Sons and Lovers*. When he was six the family established itself at 12 Walker Street, from which the views of smoky cornfields were described by him as 'the country of my heart'. The small colliery where Walter Morel worked in *Sons and Lovers*, Lambclose House and the Reservoir were all taken from identical places in the close vicinity of his childhood homes.

Although James Joyce's Dublin background was not impecunious like Bennett's and Lawrence's it was uncouth; his father's boozy manner and broad language left an indelible impression upon the young James. Much of the verbal audacity of *Ulysses* derived from this parent. 'Hundreds of pages and scores of characters in my books', Joyce wrote in a letter, 'come from him.' At the age of twenty he left Dublin which he revisited only for brief spells. Just as he never lost, after years of living abroad, his strong Irish brogue, so he never forgot or ceased to recall in his writings the snatches of conversation and highly allusive scenes of lower middle-class life which were the inescapable legacy of his Dublin youth.

As the English countryside dwindles year by year, the tentacles of Metroland stretch further from the hub of the metropolis, and the provincial city centres become eviscerated by the developers, the little shops and dwellings bulldozed, to be replaced by supermarkets and stacked car-parks, the shrines of writers of the future are less and less likely to be either urban or rural. They will not be brought up in the Queen Anne rectories of Cotswold villages, or in half-timbered rooms projecting over the narrow streets of market towns or even in those neat Regency terraces on the edge of industrial cities, now denominated slums. They will be brought up, every one of them, either in cement tower blocks poised between earth and sky or in chains of semi-detached, chimneyless boxes of pre-constituted stone along by-pass roads, totally divorced from community life and from nature. It will be interesting to see what nostalgic effects these cradles of authorship will have upon their writings. For if this introduction has indicated anything it is that childhood surroundings and the mode of family life have an exceedingly important bearing upon an author's compositions. They may have little influence upon the purity of his prose or the nobility of his sentiments, but they will inevitably determine, judging by what the past has to teach us, the aesthetic consequences of a tree-less, flower-less youth and the dessicated vision of a drab grey world.

Wordsworth at Cockermouth and Allan Bank

Mary Moorman

Of the four great English poets who stand at the head of what we call the Romantic Movement, only one, Wordsworth, was the son of a professional man. Byron's father had been a dissolute captain in the Guards; Shelley's was a country gentleman and a baronet; Keats was the son of the 'manager' of an inn in London. But Wordsworth's father John Wordsworth was a lawyer (what we should call a solicitor, though in those days the term was attorney) and he was also 'law agent' and man of business to the chief landowner and political magnate of the district, Sir James Lowther, who became the Earl of Lonsdale, and controlled the parliamentary nominations to four borough seats in Cumberland and Westmorland and three county seats as well. Lowther was immensely rich, largely from the profits of the coal mines along the Cumberland coast, and also because he formed a habit of never paying his debts. Even Mr Wordsworth, who worked for him with great devotion for nearly 20 years, never received a penny of salary. Fortunately for the Wordsworths, this earl's heir, the second Lord Lonsdale, who succeeded in 1802, was of very different character, and paid all the claims of his predecessor's creditors without delay. Mr Wordsworth had a small estate of his own at Sockbridge near Penrith, and as he lived rent free in the fine house in the High Street of Cockermouth which Sir James Lowther had bought for his 'law agent' in 1765, he was able to bring up a family of five children in comfort, though not in luxury. William, the second child, was born at Cockermouth on the 7 April 1770. The Wordsworths kept no carriage; Mr Wordsworth rode about the country on horseback on his employer's business, which often took him many miles from home. His work was largely political, seeing that the freeholders were ready to vote the right way at election times, and buying up ever more freeholds to increase his master's influence.

The beautiful house with its panelled rooms meant little to Wordsworth – he never describes it – but it contained his father's library, classics, novels, poetry and books such as *Don Quixote* and *Gulliver's Travels* in which Wordsworth revelled from his earliest days, learning by heart, at his father's behest, from Shakespeare, Milton and Spenser, while his favourite story-book was *The Arabian Nights*, a selection in a small copy which he sometimes took with him on fishing expeditions. Then, throwing himself down on the warm stones beside the Derwent, he forgot rod, line and fish, sometimes for hours together, till 'with a sudden bound of smart reproach' he remembered the real purpose of the expedition.

The Derwent ran through the town, past the ruins of Cockermouth Castle (which had been besieged by the Royalists during the Civil War) and on past the foot of the Wordsworths' garden, where there was a terrace walk. This terrace, said Wordsworth many years later, 'was our favourite playground. The terrace-wall, a low one, was covered with closely-clipped privet and roses, which gave an almost impervious shelter to birds that built their nests there'. Among these birds was the pair of hedge-sparrows whose nest gave rise to one of his most beautiful lyrics – 'The Sparrow's

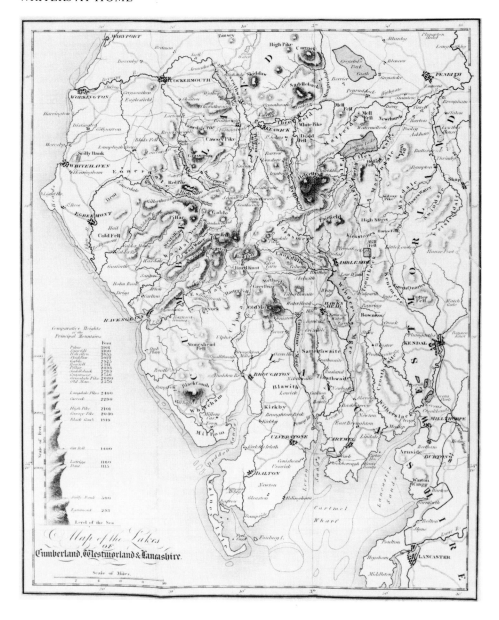

Map of the Lake District published as the frontispiece to the 5th edition of Wordsworth's *Guide to the Lakes* in 1835.

Nest'. The children playing are himself and his sister Dorothy: the poem gives us both a picture of her trembling joy at the discovery of the nest, and his famous tribute to what he believed she had given him:

> She looked at it and seemed to fear it;
> Dreading, tho' wishing, to be near it:
> Such heart was in her, being then
> A little Prattler among men.
> The Blessing of my later years
> Was with me when a boy.
> She gave me eyes, she gave me ears;
> And humble cares, and delicate fears;
> A heart, the fountain of sweet tears;
> And love, and thought and joy.[1]

Another playground for these two children of genius was in the ruins of Cocker-mouth Castle (colour plate V). Here William, descending into some stony vault, found himself face to face with 'soul-appalling darkness', and in a later poem called 'Address from the Spirit of Cockermouth Castle' he makes the Castle say:

> Not a blink
> Of light was there; – and thus did I, thy Tutor
> Make thy young thoughts acquainted with the grave;[2]

Other games were far from 'soul-appalling'. William clambered about the ruins in search of flowers – a 'golden progeny' he calls them. In their father's field beyond the river, or in the 'green courts' of the old castle, they rushed about chasing butterflies – William 'a very hunter' thinking only of the chase; Dorothy somewhat fearful of hurting the lovely creatures. Years afterwards, as he and Dorothy were sitting at breakfast in Dove Cottage, a chance remark of hers awoke his memory of those happy days, and, says Dorothy in her Journal for the 4 March 1802: 'he, with his basin of broth before him untouched, and a little plate of bread and butter, wrote the poem *To a Butterfly*. He ate not a morsel, nor put on his stockings, but sat with his neck unbuttoned and his waistcoat open while he did it. The thought first came upon him as we were talking about the pleasure we both always feel at the sight of a butterfly. I

Wordsworth House, Cocker-mouth.

The drawing-room, Wordsworth House.

told him that I used to chase them a little, but that I was afraid of brushing the dust off their wings.' This is the poem:

> Stay near me – do not take thy flight!
> A little longer stay in sight!
> Much converse do I find in thee,
> Historian of my infancy!
> Float near me; do not yet depart!
> Dead times revive in thee;
> Thou bring'st, gay creature as thou art!
> A solemn image to my heart,
> My father's family!
>
> Oh pleasant, pleasant were the days,
> The time, when in our childish plays
> My sister Emmeline[3] and I
> Together chased the butterfly!
> A very hunter did I rush
> Upon the prey:– with leaps and springs
> I followed on from brake to bush;
> But she, God love her! feared to brush
> The dust from off its wings.[4]

The Derwent, 'beloved Derwent, fairest of all streams' as he called it in 'The Prelude', provided two pleasures never to be forgotten; first, its own 'ceaseless music through the night and day', which seemed to give him even as a little boy, a composing peace, and which his adult consciousness saw as

> A knowledge, a dim earnest, of the calm
> Which Nature breathes among the fields and groves.

Secondly, it offered him the joys of bathing. He remembered how:

> Many a time have I a five years child,
> A naked boy in one delightful rill,
> A little mill-race severed from his stream,
> Made one long bathing of a summer's day,
> Basked in the sun and plunged and basked again,
> Alternate, all a summer's day, or coursed
> Over the sandy fields leaping through groves
> Of yellow ragwort; or when rock and hill
> The woods, and distant Skiddaw's lofty height
> Were bronzed with a deep radiance, stood alone
> Beneath the sky ... [5]

Cockermouth was a market-town at the confluence of two rivers; the Derwent flowing out of Derwentwater, and the Cocker which issued from Buttermere and Crummock. In the eighteenth century it prospered mainly on handloom-weaving and on country crafts such as tanning, basket-making and all the accompaniments of a cattle and sheep market. It had also a grammar-school, close to the parish church, and here Wordsworth and his brotheres were sent to be taught their earliest Latin. But the master, Mr Gillbanks, who also performed the Sunday duties at All Saints Church, was not a teacher of ability and Wordsworth afterwards said that he learnt more Latin in a fortnight from the undermaster at Hawkshead than he had learnt at Cockermouth in two years. For Hawkshead Grammar School, to which all the Wordsworths went as boarders as soon as they were nine years old, was a very much better establishment; its headmaster was always a Cambridge graduate and many of its scholars, including Wordsworth and his youngest brother Christopher, went on from there to Cambridge. It had been founded by Edwin Sandys, Archbishop of York in Queen Elizabeth's reign, who was born at Esthwaite Hall, a mile from the town. Hawkshead was about 30 miles from Cockermouth; the boys made the journeys on ponies with a groom who brought the ponies home and at the end of every term came over with the ponies to fetch the boys back for the holidays. Almost certainly, the Wordsworth children were taught to read by their mother, whom Wordsworth describes as 'the heart and hinge of all our *learnings* and our love'. Ann Wordsworth, who came from Penrith, indeed bestowed upon her brood of five children, for the short time that she remained with them, the priceless gift of peaceable and tranquil love that sustained and cherished them without interfering with their pleasures or imposing upon them schemes and activities of her own. His description of her in 'The Prelude', quaintly comparing her to a hen among chickens, well illustrates these qualities:

> Behold a parent hen amid her brood...
> And she herself from the maternal bond
> Still undischarged; yet doth she little more
> Than move with them in tenderness and love.
> A centre to the circle which they make.[6]

From her the 'brood' probably learnt the old fairy-tales and heroic legends of England which became so dear to Wordsworth and which he recommended as the best diet for children, rather than the 'moral tales' which were beginning to become fashionable, and were calculated to turn children into infant prodigies without imagination or joy.

Romance came to Wordsworth likewise from folk-stories and traditions of his own countryside. Cockermouth lies in the country to the north of Skiddaw and has affinities with the Solway Firth and the Border Country rather than with the Lake District. The Scottish shore of the Solway and the great mountain Criffel were as familiar a landscape to William Wordsworth as Skiddaw or the Ennerdale fells. He loved too the fragments of ballads and folk-talk that came from that exciting northern country. 'I own', he wrote to a friend in after years, 'that since the days of childhood, ... when I used to hear, in the time of a high wind, that

> Arthur's bower has broken his band,
> And he comes roaring up the land;
> King o'Scots wi' a' his power
> Cannot turn Arthur's bower,

I have been indebted to the North for more than I shall ever be able to acknowledge.'[7]

His mother's death in 1778 when he was scarcely eight years old was a tragedy for the 'brood', and for William it also meant separation from Dorothy who was taken away, perhaps rightly, by some relations of her mother's to be brought up with her cousins in Halifax. Her brothers all went off to Hawkshead as soon as they were old enough, so that had she remained at Cockermouth she would have been, for a great part of the year, a rather solitary child. She did not see William again for more than nine years.

Mr Wordsworth only survived his wife for five years, dying in the Christmas holidays of 1782-3 of a cold caught when he was out on Lord Lonsdale's business, and unable to get home before nightfall. William and his brothers John and Christopher reached home from Hawkshead only to find their father on his death-bed. Poor William thought it was a punishment on himself for having too eagerly looked forward to the joys of home.[8] The children were now left in the guardianship of their two uncles, Richard Wordsworth of Whitehaven, and their mother's brother, Christopher Crackenthorp Cookson of Penrith – 'Uncle Kit' – whom they all heartily disliked!

Cockermouth played no further part in Wordsworth's life until, in late middle age, he became convinced that the town needed a second church, the population having grown considerably. In 1835 he wrote letters to his friends, begging for contributions, 'until my arm ached', for the Cockermouth people did not want another church, and indeed none was built until some years after Wordsworth's death. But he was often in the neighbourhood, for his eldest son, John, became rector of Brigham and many family visits were exchanged. A few sonnets also were written at this time, the last of which, 'Address from the Spirit of Cockermouth Castle' (partly quoted above) shows how his thoughts were still lovingly centred on those early, happy days and the experiences they brought to him. They were fundamental indeed to the character and growth of his poetic genius – its concern with Nature and her beauty, with Romance and history, with 'high objects, with enduring things', with all that made him the poet of the human heart and its affections, as well as of the great world around him with its mountains and green valleys, clear streams, woodlands, birds and flowers.

By the year 1808 William and Mary Wordsworth had three children, John born in 1803, Dorothy (called Dora) in 1804, and Thomas in 1806. The cottage at Town End, Grasmere, which we call Dove Cottage, where they had lived for nearly nine years, had become altogether too small for the Wordsworths and their growing family. Wordsworth's sister Dorothy always lived with them, and Mary's sister, Sara Hutchinson, often paid long visits. Coleridge too, until his departure for Malta in 1804, was never long absent, and in 1807 Thomas de Quincey at last made his way to the cottage and was welcomed by Wordsworth whom he had long idolised at a distance. He became a great favourite with the children; 'Mr. De Quincey', said Johnnie proudly, 'is my friend'.

The decision to leave Town End was taken in 1807, but they did not move house until the summer of 1808. There were very few houses at Grasmere which were both available and suitable, and Allan Bank, a new house built by a Mr Crump of Liverpool, on the high ground behind the church, was the only possibility. The Wordsworths had been indignant when it was built. 'A wretched creature', Wordsworth had written, 'wretched in name and nature, of the name of Crump, goaded on by his still more wretched wife... this same wretch has at last begun to put his long-impending threats into execution and when you next enter the sweet Paradise of Grasmere you will see staring you in the face, upon that beautiful ridge that elbows out into the vale (behind the church and towering far above its steeple), a temple of abomination in which are to be enshrined Mr. and Mrs. Crump... The house... will entirely destroy the vale's character of simplicity and seclusion' (colour plate VI).

The Crumps, however, did not 'enshrine' themselves in it for the present but let it to Wordsworth, and allowed him to lay out the parkland below the house with well-

Grasmere Lake by Julius Caesar Ibbetson in around 1808, when the Wordsworths were living at Allan Bank – seen in the centre of the middle distance. *(The Faringdon Collection, Buscot House)*.

The view to the east from Allan Bank, towards Greenhead Gill.

spaced broadleaved trees, some of which still survive. Behind and above the house, woodlands covered the slopes of Silver How, as they still do, while in front the windows looked straight down the lake to Loughrigg Fell. The eastern view showed the great shoulders of Fairfield and Seat Sandal and the hollow of Greenhead Gill in which lay 'Michael's Fold', so that Dorothy, whose room faced that way, could watch the track of many a tramp with William, or of Coleridge when he came to them from Keswick 'over Helvellyn'. The house was spacious indeed compared to the cottage, and Dorothy was able to report soon after their arrival, 'We already feel the comfort of having each a room of our own'. The work of the move fell almost entirely on her shoulders, for Mary was expecting a baby (Catherine, born in September), Sara was

The room used by Coleridge as his study at Allan Bank. The photograph was taken while the house was owned by Canon H.D. Rawnsley, one of the founders of the National Trust.

unwell, and 'William you know is not expected to do anything'. But she had an invaluable helper in Mary's sailor brother Henry, who could turn his hand to anything, and, with Dorothy, 'worked body and soul' making carpets and curtains.

The house has undergone interior changes since those days, and there is now a spacious hall where before there had only been a narrow stone-flagged passage connecting the front of the house with the back. In 1810 Dorothy asked her eldest brother Richard, who was prospering as an attorney in London, to be so kind as to give them an 'oil-cloth' to cover this passage, thus saving the terrible labour of scrubbing the bare stones. Richard never even answered her letter. The Allan Bank years were indeed financially lean ones for the Wordsworths, for the larger house needed an extra servant and some new furniture; and Wordsworth, after completing a long poem called 'The White Doe of Rylstone' greatly disappointed Dorothy by refusing to publish it, in spite of great and successful efforts by Coleridge to get Longman (the publisher) to accept it on terms advantageous to Wordsworth. 'Without money what *can* we do?' she exclaimed, 'New house, new furniture! Such a large family! Two servants and little Sally [an orphan whom they had taken into the household until she was old enough to go into service]. Do, dearest William, overcome your disgust to publishing... and we shall be wealthy and at our ease for one year at least.' But 'The White Doe' remained unpublished until 1815.

Instead, in September 1808, Coleridge, now separated from his wife, who remained at Keswick with little Sara, arrived at Allan Bank to live permanently as a part of the 'large family'. The two older Coleridge boys, Hartley and Derwent, went to a small boarding school in Ambleside and spent every weekend at Allan Bank. Including the servants, therefore, the Wordsworth household often consisted of 15 people, for in September De Quincey also made his quarters there. Coleridge was not an easy inmate. He had long been addicted to opium and they had little joy of his company. He was also rather fussy about his food. Many years afterwards, Mrs Arnold of Fox How, the widow of Dr Arnold of Rugby and mother of Matthew Arnold, reported a conversation she had had with old Sarah Walker who had been a servant of the Wordsworths at Allan Bank. 'She said how well they lived and yet how plain; that they had not a bit of pride, and that Mr. Wordsworth always said, what was true; that all his friends were welcome who were content to live as they did. And she implied that all were, except *"that Mr. Colleridge,* he was a plague"*, and when I asked why, she said that he often wanted different things –... though it appeared that roast potatoes and cold meat at supper was what he desired – while she always laid for the Wordsworths small basins of new milk from their own cow and a loaf of bread'.

Their friend Southey likewise spoke of the shabbiness of the house during their tenancy. 'I am told', he wrote, 'that they make as dolorous an appearance in good rooms as you may suppose', and another friend, James Losh, thought that the house and grounds about it 'seemed neglected and far from comfortable'. The Words-worths were indeed incapable of being smart, either in their persons or their furniture.

The worst discomfort came from the 'smokey chimneys'. Almost every chimney smoked atrociously when the winds were high. 'I will not attempt', wrote Dorothy to Mrs Clarkson, wife of Thomas Clarkson the anti slave-trade pioneer 'to detail the height and depth and number of our sorrows in connection with smokey chimneys'. On one day the only room in which they could have a fire was William's study,[9] and they were at times 'a week together without a kitchen fire'. Workmen were in and out of the house at intervals for more than a year, and they were soon obliged to face the possibility of leaving Grasmere altogether as there was no other suitable house in the vale.

Coleridge was given the small room near the front door as a study, and there he began at once to produce his weekly 'Essay' which he called *The Friend.* The Wordsworths helped him in every way – sending out prospectuses and enlisting the interest of their friends – while Sara Hutchinson, the 'Asra' of his poems, decided that the best way to help him was to set him to work. So from September 1809, she became his secretary, and he dictated *The Friend* to her. It was a long and exhausting task, but she persevered for nearly six months and 26 numbers of *The Friend* were produced. She was by that time almost worn out, and in March 1810 she left Allan Bank on a long visit to her brother Tom in Herefordshire. Coleridge meanwhile had become a deadweight in the house, never appearing except for meals and then but briefly; above all never going out. 'This beautiful valley seems a blank to him', wrote Dorothy sadly, and they lost hope that he would ever do more than he had done. In May 1810 he returned for a time to Keswick, whence in October Basil Montague, Wordsworth's eccentric friend, persuaded him to go with him to London – a fatal move which resulted, through Montague's folly, in a serious breach between Coleridge and Wordsworth.

Meanwhile, Wordsworth had also been absorbed in writing. In the first year at Allan Bank almost all his writings were in prose – the most important being a long political essay which he called *Concerning the Convention of Cintra*. It was prompted by his anger – shared by most of his friends – at the agreement, made in 1808 by England's military leaders, by which Napoleon withdrew all his armies from Spain, leaving Britain with what proved a very valuable military base in Portugal. There was no consultation with the Spanish patriots who had risen against the French. Wordsworth was deeply indignant. He, with Southey and others, tried to convene a meeting of freeholders – the only people in those days who had votes at elections. But Lord Lonsdale, the Lord Lieutenant, would not consent, so Wordsworth, who had gone to Keswick to enlist support for the project, went home, as Southey said, 'to ease his heart in a pamphlet'.

Working closely with Coleridge, he began to compose what is in essence a prose version of the *Sonnets Dedicated to National Independence and Liberty* which he had written

Coleridge in 1804 by George Dance, *(Dove Cottage)*.

in 1802-3. He cared intensely about the patriotism and sufferings of the Spaniards under the rule of the French, and equally intensely about what he considered the unworthy spirit of most of his own countrymen. The power of his poetic view of man glows on every page, just as it had in the writings of Milton and Burke. De Quincey, who was now also an inmate of Allan Bank, went to London to see to the passage of the pamphlet through the press: Wordsworth constantly re-wrote or added many pages, and De Quincey had a difficult time. At last, in June 1809, the pamphlet appeared – but it fell almost unnoticed from the press. It came too late to catch the tide of indignation that followed the news of the Convention, and, as he himself said, 'the style of thinking and feeling is so little in the Spirit of the age'. Coleridge shared this view and thought that it was 'fitlier attuned to the oracular tone of impassioned blank verse'. One friend indeed said that 'the man of passion, of high moral enthusiasm, is the only man who will relish this work, and indeed to him it will be the Bible of his life'.

Wordsworth also wrote for *The Friend*, for Coleridge was not always furnished with enough material of his own for another number. Wordsworth's most important

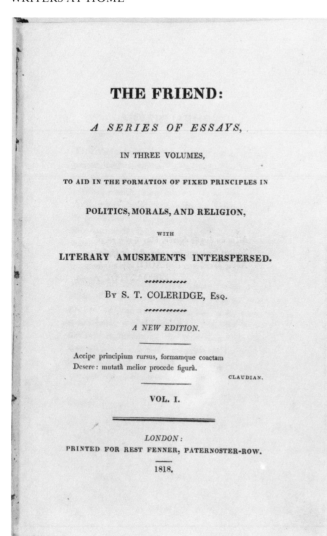

THE FRIEND:

A SERIES OF ESSAYS,

IN THREE VOLUMES,

TO AID IN THE FORMATION OF FIXED PRINCIPLES IN

POLITICS, MORALS, AND RELIGION,

WITH

LITERARY AMUSEMENTS INTERSPERSED.

By S. T. COLERIDGE, Esq.

A NEW EDITION.

Accipe principium rursus, formamque coactam
Desere: mutatâ melior procede figurâ.
CLAUDIAN.

VOL. I.

LONDON:
PRINTED FOR REST FENNER, PATERNOSTER-ROW.
1818.

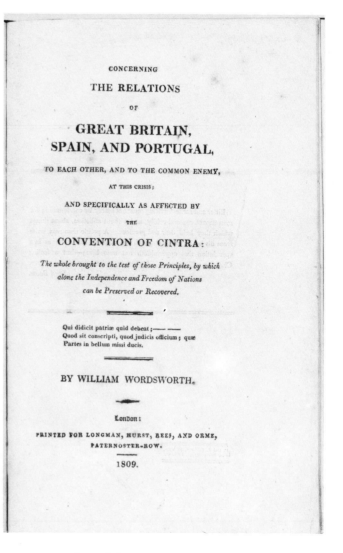

CONCERNING

THE RELATIONS

OF

GREAT BRITAIN,
SPAIN, AND PORTUGAL,

TO EACH OTHER, AND TO THE COMMON ENEMY,

AT THIS CRISIS;

AND SPECIFICALLY AS AFFECTED BY

THE

CONVENTION OF CINTRA:

*The whole brought to the test of those Principles, by which
alone the Independence and Freedom of Nations
can be Preserved or Recovered.*

Qui didicit patriæ quid debeat ;—— ——
Quod sit conscripti, quod judicis officium ; quæ
Partes in bellum missi ducis.

BY WILLIAM WORDSWORTH.

London:
PRINTED FOR LONGMAN, HURST, REES, AND ORME,
PATERNOSTER-ROW.
1809.

contribution was the 'Letter to Mathetes' – a reply to an urgent request from John Wilson ('Christopher North' of *Blackwood's Magazine*) that he would come forward as the teacher and guide of the young. Wordsworth's answer was, as we should expect, to turn to his own spiritual growth and experience, lovingly remembered and eloquently described. Finally, he told Wilson that the appropriate calling of youth was 'not to analyse with scrupulous minuteness, but to accumulate in genial confidence; its instinct, its safety, its benefit, its glory is to love, to admire, to feel and to labour'.

During this time too he wrote a number of sonnets, most of which are concerned with 'suffering Spain', but the background of some of them is not the world of men but of Nature:

> Hollow vale which foaming torrents fill
> With the omnipresent murmur as they rave
> Down their steep beds, that never shall be still:
> Here, mighty Nature! in this school sublime
> I weigh the hopes and fears of suffering Spain.[10]

Then, when the pamphlet and the writings for *The Friend* were completed he turned

(Left) The title page of the 1818 issue of Coleridge's organ, *The Friend*, and *(right)* Wordsworth's tract *Concering the Covention of Cintra*.

his mind once more to *The Excursion* – or as he used to call it, *The Pedlar* – begun long ago at Racedown in 1797. During the spring of 1810 he wrote the fifth, sixth and seventh books, in which the old Pastor describes the lives and deaths of some of his parishioners. Much of it has strong affinity with the *Essay on Epitaphs* – another contribution to *The Friend* – and also to those poems of the early Dove cottage days – 'Michael' and 'The Brothers'.

The birth of another child – Willy – in September 1810 interrupted his writing, but in the following spring he continued and completed *The Excursion*, nine books in all. He still regarded it as 'a portion of "The Recluse"', the long hoped-for philosophical poem which was never written, save for this 'excursion' and the 'poem on his own life', which we call *The Prelude*.[11] 'The Recluse' was a work which, he said, using Milton's words, he hoped that future times would 'not willingly let die'. But it was destined that it should owe its immortality to the two 'portions'. The rest was silence.

In June 1811, the Wordsworths left Allan Bank for the old Grasmere vicarage, a house close to the church which, though smaller and more manageable than Allan Bank, stood in what Sara Hutchinson describes as 'a bog' and whose chimneys smoked almost as badly as those at Allan Bank. Terrible sorrows befell them there, in the deaths of two of the children, Catherine and Thomas, in 1812, and great was their relief when in 1813 they were able to take a pleasant house at Rydal – Rydal Mount – where they spent the rest of their lives.

Notes

1. Lines 11-20, second verse of two. Composed 1801, published 1807.
2. Lines 8-10.
3. 'Emma', 'Emmeline' or 'Lucy' are names often used in his poems for Dorothy.
4. Composed on the 4 March 1802, published 1807.
5. *The Prelude*, I, 292-304.
6. *The Prelude*, V, 246-290.
7. W.W. to Alan Cunningham, 23 Nov., 1823.
8. In *The Prelude*, Book XII, there is a vivid account of this episode and the feelings it aroused in William, both at the time and afterwards.
9. This was the large room at the western end of the house, with a bow window looking up into the wood and another down the lake to Loughrigg Fell.
10. 'Composed while the author was engaged in writing a Tract occasioned by the Convention of Cintra'. *Sonnets Dedicated to National Independence and Liberty*, Part II, No. 7, November or December 1808.
11. One book, never published by Wordsworth, was published anonymously by Macmillan in 1888. It describes their earliest days at Dove Cottage in the winter months of 1800.

Coleridge at Nether Stowey

Ronald Blythe

The frantic circumstances which brought Coleridge to Nether Stowey, and which have long since made his cottage in Lime Street one of English literature's most potent addresses, were crammed with that worry and despair which is special to moving house, and which, even now, is instantly recognisable. Unbeknown to him, as he, his wife and baby son took possession of its cramped quarters on the last day of 1796, the year which was to follow would be his *annus mirabilis*. Never again would he write as he did then, never again, or so he later affirmed, would he be so happy. For in these small rooms, in the garden and in the Quantock countryside all around he was to write a dazzling succession of poems, which would include 'The Rime of the Ancient Mariner', the first part of 'Christobel', 'Frost at Midnight' and 'Kubla Khan'. When William and Dorothy Wordsworth were to rent Alfoxden, a country house some three miles distant in order to be near him, he was also to assist in launching from this spot the little book which was to redirect the course of English poetry, *Lyrical Ballads*. It is this cottage and the web of lanes between it and Alfoxden, rather than the Lakes, which is the birthplace of the Romantic Movement. To it came not only the Wordsworths, but William Hazlitt, Robert Southey, Thomas De Quincey and Charles Lamb; all of them, like Coleridge, young and made even more 'new men' by the ecstatic hopefulness released by the French Revolution.

The cottage was called Gilbards when Coleridge became Mrs Rendle's sub-tenant at £8 a year. It comprised two rooms downstairs and three up, a kitchen without an oven, a thatched roof and a huge garden, most of which has disappeared under subsequent buildings. After he left it became a manse and then a pub – 'Coleridge Cottage Inn' – but in 1892 a local clergyman saved it from the hazards of further development and possible extinction, and in the autumn of 1909 it became the property of the National Trust. Simple though it is, its profound associations give it an importance equal to anything which the Trust takes care of. Coleridge tumbled into it during a housing crisis, attained the peak of his genius while living in it, and was soon to find it unbearable. From Germany, where he was on a walking tour, he wrote to Tom Poole, the new friend whom he had wildly persuaded (against the latter's better judgment) to bring him and his family from Bristol to Nether Stowey: 'I must not disguise from you that to live *in* Stowey, and in that house... is to me an exceedingly unpleasant thought.' But more had happened at this time between the move and the flight than either Coleridge or Poole (or the Wordsworths) could possibly have anticipated. Coleridge came to the Lime Street cottage because marriage had tipped him into responsibilities with which he had little ability to cope, and he left it, partly because he and Sara's life together did not improve, and partly because, quite unwittingly, he and the Wordsworths stirred up a local hornets' nest.

He was 24 when he arrived, Wordsworth and his sister Dorothy a little older. All three were at the zenith of their literary powers, and astounding intruders they must

Samuel Taylor Coleridge aged 24, 1795, by Peter Vandyke *(National Portrait Gallery)*.

Coleridge Cottage, Lime Street,
Nether Stowey.

have appeared to the native eye. Moreover, the Coleridges were accompanied by an epileptic young man and the Wordsworths by a little boy. Both families walked about the countryside at all hours of the day and night. What was going on?

Troubles came thick and fast. Yet the intensity of everything which Coleridge experienced here, his domestic confusion notwithstanding, remained enviable to the last. Later, the Stowey Coleridge was to become for him his real but now unreachable self. As for the brave politics which made him and the Wordsworths so unwelcome here, they soon guttered out. Near to his death, he recalled this halcyon time, 'We [John Thelwall the reformer and himself] were once sitting in a beautiful recess in the Quantocks, when I said to him, "Citizen John, this is a fine place to talk treason in!" – "Nay, Citizen Samuel," replied he, "it is rather a place to make a man forget that there is any necessity for treason!"' Thelwall had touched on the double motive which had brought the poet to Nether Stowey. Its lovely neighbourhood and the enlightened mind of his dear protector Tom Poole had become the fused ideal which had lured him to this spot. Shortly after he had settled in Lime Street, Poole had written him a reassuring note: 'By you, Coleridge, I will always stand, in sickness and health, prosperity and misfortunes.' This comradely version of the marriage vows Poole was to observe to the letter, and the support which followed is reminiscent of that which John Fisher poured out to John Constable. Both benefactors had no doubt that they were duty-bound to protect genius.

Samuel Coleridge was the last of the ten children born to the Reverend John Coleridge, vicar of Ottery St Mary, Devonshire, and master of its grammar school, and his second wife Anne Bowdon. Before he was five the poet had headed off into a private realm of reading and dreaming which was to take precedence over the formal pattern of education provided by Christ's Hospital and Jesus College, Cambridge. Where books were concerned, he called himself a 'cormorant'. They, above anything, helped to carry him through the horrors of Christ's Hospital, with its bad food and violence. Southey, his future brother-in-law, had been sacked from Westminster School for daring to protest against the flogging there, but Coleridge, already lost in the reality of his imagination, came through the rough vicissitudes of his youth with impaired health but no great grudge. Much later, learning of the death of their brutal headmaster, he told Charles Lamb, 'Poor J.B. – may all his faults be forgiven; and may he be wafted to bliss by little cherub boys, all heads and wings, with no bottoms ...' He was still at school when he fell in love with Mary Evans, sister of one of the pupils. At Cambridge he continued on his wayward path, having long since devoured everything in the way of reading matter which the university required. He also ran into political trouble, being what he called 'an extreme democrat', into debt, and into deeper and deeper feelings for Mary Evans. In 1793, unable to cope with all this, he ran away and enlisted in the 15th Dragoons as 'Silas Tomkyn Comberbacke', an absurd name he had seen written up in the Inns of Court. As he was hopeless on a horse and nearly as hopeless on the parade ground, Coleridge's four-month military career was mainly taken up with writing letters home for his illiterate comrades and nursing them when they were ill. In the spring of 1794 his brothers bought him out and he returned to Cambridge.

A few weeks later, while visiting an old Christ's Hospital friend at Oxford, he was introduced to Robert Southey, whose father kept a draper's shop in Bristol and whose grandfather farmed in the Quantocks. The road to Nether Stowey, and to the shore of 'The Ancient Mariner', and the dreamland of 'Kubla Khan', begins here. During these Oxford days Coleridge, matchlessly eloquent, turned Southey into a Unitarian, and Southey, equally persuasive with another idea, began the process of setting up a utopian society in New England. Twelve young men and their wives were to live as a 'pantisocracy' on the banks of the Susquehanna River, Pennsylvania, a site chosen because of its pretty name. Here again we see Coleridge being drawn into youthful half-baked commitments which would soon have a profound effect on his art and future happiness. Much of the Susquehanna adventure was planned while he and Southey were on a walking tour of Wales that summer (1794). Southey then took him to Bath to meet a girl named Mary Fricker who was engaged to one of the Susquehanna River boys, Robert Lovell. Mary had four sisters and her mother was the widow of a bankrupt tradesman from Bristol. Soon these ladies were back in Bristol and so were the Susquehanna men, who were all sharing a house in College Street and saving up to emigrate.

Just before this Coleridge and Southey went on another of their great hikes, on this occasion tramping from Cheddar and the Mendips, and eventually to see Nether Stowey for the first time. Each had an undergraduate friend in this beautiful countryside, Southey's being George Burnett and Coleridge's Henry Poole. This latter introduced the poets to Stowey's most distinguished resident, his remarkable, self-educated and highly 'democratic' (a designation as suspect in late eighteenth century England as 'Marxist' is in the late twentieth) cousin, Tom Poole. The Pooles were the sons of the local tanner who had put one of his children through the local university and kept the other, Tom, at home to run the family business. This seemingly unfair treatment was to have astonishing results, for Tom Poole used the family money for the welfare of the whole town, set himself up in fine houses with an

extensive library, and became host to some of the greatest writers of his age.

It was through Tom Poole that Coleridge, after weeks of panic over housing, recovered his footing after a series of upsets which included his enlistment, his Cambridge failure, losing Mary Evans, marrying Sara Fricker, having the Pantisocracy plan quashed by Southey, running out of money and becoming very ill through anxiety. Poole gave in to Coleridge's implorings, brought him to Nether Stowey and steadied him. If he did so reluctantly at first, it was not because of any lack of love on his part or because of not wanting to have a young hot-head whom his family detested on his doorstep, but because the practical side of him told him that Coleridge simply would not be able to live the kind of life he had planned here. Tiny country towns do not support idylls. Coleridge's popular reputation in the West Country at this juncture was less that of a writer, although he had published a collection of poems and edited a magazine, *The Watchman*, than of a thrilling lecturer and preacher who made the Unitarian chapels ring with the new politics. But even where his writing was concerned, it was no gentle literary figure who was coming to dwell in Mrs Rendle's uncomfortable cottage, but a poet on the threshold of an unimaginable power. He arrived modestly, determined to make the best of his situation, 'I shall have six companions; my Sara, my babe, my own shaping and inquisitive mind, my books, my beloved friend Tom Poole, and lastly, Nature looking at me with a thousand looks of beauty', and he left having completed everything necessary for him to be seen as one of poetry's most extraordinary masters.

No sooner had he settled his family and arranged their meagre belongings, and then begun his self-imposed regime of early morning gardening, reviewing, and preaching on Sundays at Bridgwater (he was still thinking about becoming a Unitarian minister as a way out of the precariousness of his existence), than his entire being caught fire. Never before and never later was he to know such joy. He filled the house with guests who could not but notice the drudgery to which Sara was reduced.

(Left) Robert Southey by Peter Vandyke, 1795 *(National Portrait Gallery)* and *(right)* Tom Poole, whose benevolent patronage brought Coleridge to Stowey.

The Unitarian Chapel in Dampiet Street, Bridgwater, where Coleridge preached while at Stowey.

Charles Lloyd, Coleridge's disciple-pupil, and son of one of the founders of the bank of that name, had a bed-sitting-room, and Nanny the maid also slept in, so these months could not have been anything but a crush. There was also Hartley, the adored baby son 'Like the moon among the clouds,' wrote Coleridge, 'he moves in a circle of light of his own making. He alone is a light of his own. Of all human beings I never saw one so utterly naked of self.' Hartley was cradled by his table as he worked, sometimes finding his way into the poetry.

The cottage contains an indelible imprint of the first years of this 'strange, strange boy', as his father described him, and even of the short-lived Berkeley, his second son. For a sleeping child usually accompanied him in the room on the right where he worked when everybody else had gone to bed. One February at midnight in 1798 he shared the room thus:

> The Frost performs its secret ministry,
> Unhelped by any wind. The owlet's cry

Came loud – and hark, again! loud as before.
The inmates of my cottage, all at rest,
Have left me to that solitude, which suits
Abstruser musings: save that at my side
My cradled infant slumbers peacefully...
"Dear babe"... all seasons shall be sweet to thee,
Whether the summer clothe the general earth
With greeness, or the redbreast sit and sing
Betwixt the tufts of snow on the bare branch
Of mossy apple-tree, while the high thatch
Smokes in the sun-thaw; whether the eave-drops fall
Heard only in the trances of the blast,
Or if the secret ministry of frost
Shall hang them up in silent icicles,
Quietly shining to the quiet Moon.[1]

An amazing literary toil had been taking place, not only in the small hours in this parlour with its cot and writing-table side by side, but seemingly everywhere within walking distance from the cottage, during Coleridge's every waking moment. The event which carried him to such heights of creativity was the arrival of the Wordsworths at Alfoxden in the summer of 1797, where, as Coleridge was to put it in his *Biographia Literaria*, they were to re-direct the mind from the lethargy of custom 'to the loveliness and the wonders of the world before us'. To the young poets this meant both life in the ordinary village world and life which was 'romantic' and supernatural. Wordsworth was to deal with nature and Coleridge with what lay beyond it. 'With this in view I wrote The Ancient Mariner' – and in this low room. This terrifying ballad for which he hoped to get £5 and thus begin to pay the bills which, in spite of Poole's generosity, were themselves a nightmare, was in fact to mark a lasting turn in his fortunes, for no sooner had he completed it and gone off to preach at Shrewsbury (where the 20-year-old William Hazlitt walked ten miles to hear him), than he heard that the rich Wedgwood brothers were to offer him an unconditional £150 a year for life. It would be wrong to omit from the various factors which made 1798 such a matchless time for Coleridge, his inspiration, his friendship with the Wordsworths, his discovery not only of where he should go but where he could go, his new and modest financial security.

Hazlitt encountered the headiness of this brief moment as soon as he arrived in Lime Street that spring. So sublime was it to be invited there that he had prepared himself for the Quantocks, now made paradisal by the presence of 'my first poets', by tramping all the way to Llangollen. 'In the outset of life our imagination has a body to it. We are in a state between sleeping and waking, and have indistinct but glorious glimpses of strange shapes, and there is always something to come better than what we see.' Hazlitt hints at the theme of Alain-Fournier's *Le Grand Meaulnes*. He crossed the threshold of the cottage, believing himself to be at this stage an artist, but already taking notes which were to make him Britain's finest essayist. Two days later Wordsworth arrived, gaunt and looking like his own Peter Bell. After wreaking havoc with the cheese, he looked through the window and said 'How beautifully the sun sets on that yellow bank'. The next day the poets told their guest how they wrote. 'Coleridge has told me that he himself liked to compose in walking over uneven ground, or breaking through the straggling branches of copse-wood; whereas Wordsworth always wrote walking up and down a straight gravel-walk, or in the same spot where the continuity of his verse met with no collateral interruption... Thus I passed three weeks at Nether Stowey and in the neighbourhood, generally devoting the afternoons to a delightful chat in an arbour made of bark by the poet's friend Tom Poole, sitting under two fine elm-trees, and listening to the bees humming around us, while we quaffed our *flip*.' Coleridge took him 'for miles and miles on dark brown heaths' through Minehead and on to Linton, the seascape of 'The Ancient Mariner', and told him that in *Lyrical Ballads* he and Wordsworth were going to 'use only such words as had probably been common in the most ordinary language since the days of Henry II'. It was a language which neither critic nor ordinary reader associated with poetry and the book was a failure. Besides 'The Ancient Mariner' and other great poems, it also contained Wordsworth's 'Tintern Abbey'.

The starry conjunction of Coleridge and Wordsworth in the Quantock Hills occurred because each young man had drifted into Somerset about the same time. Some might call it destiny, others accident. After searing political experiences in revolutionary France and a love affair with Annette Vallon which resulted in the birth of their child, Wordsworth had returned to the demands of his family to enter either the church or the law, and settle down. He was then suddenly freed from either of these unwelcome occupations by a legacy of £900, and on top of this good fortune, invited to tutor the son of a widowed friend in exchange for £50 a year and a rent-free farmhouse near Crewkerne. Coleridge had already read some of Wordsworth's early poetry, and Wordsworth had heard of Coleridge's glorious republican oratory when they met in Bristol. Each immediately recognised in the other a personification of all that they longed for and the power to achieve it. Visits to Stowey and Racedown, Dorothy and William's village, were made and a thrilling new language for their mutual beliefs and emotions discovered. All three were intoxicated by what could happen – by what must happen – and during the hot summer of 1797 the Wordsworths decided that they must join Coleridge and went house-hunting

Interior of Coleridge Cottage.

around Nether Stowey. They found Alfoxden, a country house standing in a picturesque park near the sea, and below which lay a glen with a roaring waterfall. With Tom Poole as reference, they were able to rent it for a year. This move inaugurated for each of them, and for Coleridge especially, a season of fulfilment and pleasure such as would never be repeated. They had scarcely decided on how they would use the extraordinary freedom which Alfoxden promised them, with its many rooms and spacious grounds, when the three-mile journey between it and Coleridge's home in Stowey began to establish a regular pattern of daily walking and talking in their lives. But although they constantly immersed themselves in the same scenery of 'that dear and beautiful place', as Dorothy was to refer to it when she and her brother were driven from it by busybodies, they viewed it in three separate and distinctive ways. For Wordsworth, fresh from France, it was a paradise where simple labouring people, orphans and common soldiers half-starved; for Dorothy, it was a paradise of plants, creatures and geographical colours and shapes; for Coleridge it was both a paradise and an earthly territory for the limitless thrust of his imagination.

This walking and talking had hardly begun when an interruption far more grotesque (although less damaging in the long run) than that of the 'person from Porlock' occurred. A combination of local tittle-tattle, genuine mystification and 'patriotism' reached the ears of the Home Office, which sent a government spy down to Nether Stowey to see what was going on. With rumours of French invasion and even of a possible French-style revolution by the 'people' of Britain, Pitt's administration was taking no chances. Here was an unorthodox group in a key position by the Bristol Channel made up of a man who prevented his countrymen from burning Tom Paine's *The Rights of Man* (Poole), a Unitarian minister preaching democracy and other heresies (Coleridge), and a man (who had come from France) and a woman who called themselves brother and sister, who, although they had rented a mansion, spent all their time wandering about having conversations with peasants. Walsh, the government spy, put up at the Globe Inn in Castle Street, almost next door to Tom Poole's house where the poets met, and watched them. The result was that the Wordsworths had not been at Alfoxden for more than a month or two when they were given notice to leave after their year's lease had run out. If they were upset and disturbed by all this suspicion, there is little evidence of it in either Dorothy's Journal or in *Lyrical Ballads*, or, indeed, in all that we know about the way in which they continued to live, roofless for the most part, whether it shone or poured, whether it was morning or midnight. Dorothy and Coleridge, especially, were during these months ceaselessly exploring the combes and woods, she quietly in love with him, he, experiencing for the first time the companionable glories of a mind such as hers, and now bitterly convinced of his wife's inadequacies.

There was one famous walk which Coleridge took on his own. It was from Porlock to Culbone where, just above the church, he found an old house, Ash Farm, where he hid himself away after a row with his difficult lodger, Charles Lloyd, had made him both physically and emotionally ill. He had brought with him some opium and an old book called *Purchas his Pilgrimage* which contained 'a history of the world in sea voyages and land travell by Englishmen and others'. Seated downstairs in the farmhouse he took two grains of opium and, while he waited for it to take effect, read the following:

> In Xamdu did Cublai Can build a stately Palace, encompassing sixteene miles of plaine ground with a wall, wherein are fertile Meddowes, pleasant Springs, delightful Streames, and all sorts of beasts of chase and game, and in the middest thereof a sumptuous house of pleasure.

'Alfoxden Park, the seat of J. St. Aubyn Esq.' Lithograph from *Twelve Sketches of Somersetshire Scenery* by Miss Sweeting, 1850. *(Somerset County Record Office)*.

(Far left) William Wordsworth, painted in 1798 for Joseph Cottle by W. Shuter, 'an artist then at Stowey' *(Cornell University Library, Ithaca, New York)*.

The 'Valley of the Rocks', Linton, visited on the 'Ancient Mariner' walk by Coleridge and William and Dorothy Wordsworth in November 1797. Lithograph by Francis Nicolson.

Ash Farm, Porlock, Devon, reputedly where Coleridge composed 'Kubla Khan'.

Coleridge then slept for three hours, had what he called a vision, woke up with a complete recollection of it and was in the act of putting it all down on paper when the most notorious interruption in English literature occurred when 'a person on business from Porlock' called, stayed for an hour, and caused the poet's marvellously remembered dream to vanish. Only 50 of what he believed would have been a poem of some two to three hundred lines had been caught on the page. He returned to Lime Street with them in his pocket, the peerless fragment 'Kubla Khan'. It was only published many years later at Byron's insistence.

An equally propitious ramble, and one taken in far happier circumstances, had occurred a few months earlier than this, when Coleridge and the Wordsworths had suddenly taken it into their heads to walk to Watchet and back. They started late on a dreary November afternoon and so it was nearly dark when they descended West Quantoxhead and looked for beds in the seaside town. For some time Coleridge had been visiting the shore north of Nether Stowey to stare at a ship just as it came into sight on the open sea. It seemed to him an immense moment. The landfall of a ship manned by ghosts was a scary notion with which seafaring people had long frightened themselves, and a friend of Tom Poole's had told Coleridge such a tale. Coleridge was engrossed at this period in a book called *A Voyage Round the World, by the Way of the Great South Sea* by George Shelvocke, a rascally sea adventurer who, in 1719, while steering a ship named the *Speedwell* round Cape Horn, was driven as far south as latitude 61° 30' by appalling weather until 'We all observed that we had not had the sight of one fish of any kind since we were come to the southward of the Straights of Le Maire, nor one sea-bird, except a disconsolate black albatross, who accompanied us for several days; hovering about us as if he had lost himself, till Hartley, my second captain... imagining that from his colour it might be some ill-omen, after some fruitless attempts, at length shot the albatross, not doubting, perhaps, that we should have fair wind after it.' After the death of the albatross, the *Speedwell* suffered dreadful gales for six weeks until at last it sighted the coast of Chile. It was Wordsworth who had first read this story and who drew his friend's attention to it. Between the walk to Watchet in November and his journey to Shrewsbury in January (and his meeting with Hazlitt), Coleridge had embodied in 'The Rime of the Ancient Mariner'

Shelvocke's anecdote and everything which Nether Stowey's vicinity to the sea had taught his imagination. This became his chief contribution to *Lyrical Ballads* which was to be published, but not understood or much bought, in 1798.

The months of collaborative genius at Nether Stowey came to an end when the Wordsworths were obliged to return the keys of their beloved Alfoxden. They left, as they had arrived, after a short stay with the Coleridges in Lime Street. Coleridge found life without them intolerable and caused concern by temporarily abandoning Sara for a tour of Germany with John Chester, a young neighbour, Dorothy and William. While they were away, poor Sara and the children went back to Bristol to live with her mother. When Coleridge returned from Germany he had no intention of resuming life in a Wordsworth-less Nether Stowey, and in June 1800 he followed them to Grasmere, there to become estranged from one Sara and to begin a hopeless love for another, Sara Hutchinson, Wordsworth's sister-in-law. Soon the Quantock Hills and the cottage in Lime Street were to be recognised by Coleridge as the landscape and home of his most splendid achievements. For the remainder of his life he waited for the lost lines of 'Kubla Khan' to come to him, but they never did. Similarly lost for ever was that spontaneous mastery which, through all the hardships, accompanied him everywhere at Nether Stowey. The place itself remains essentially as he and his friends saw it; scores of the buildings which line its streets, its brook and, of course, its views are those which he and the Wordsworths knew. One does not have to be over-fanciful to see Coleridge hurrying through Castle Street and Lime Street with his zig-zag gait, a thin, dark-haired man in his mid-twenties with clear grey eyes and wide mouth with bad teeth. A confession written by his son Hartley when he was seven might almost apply to the poet himself.

> I see it – and I saw it, and tomorrow I shall see it again when I shut my eyes, and when my eyes are open, and when I am looking at other things. But... it is a sad pity, but it cannot be helped, you know, but I am always being a bad boy when I am thinking my thoughts.

Thomas Carlyle

Ian Campbell

Thomas Carlyle's house is number 24 Cheyne Row today, though number 5 when he moved there in 1834. To approach it from either end of Cheyne Row today is to go back in time. The street runs towards the river at the Albert Embankment, though it is separated from the river and the busy road by a small garden with Boehm's famous statue of the seated Sage of Chelsea. Turn from the steady roar of London's traffic into Cheyne Row, and the years fall away, as they do for a pedestrian turning from the commercial bustle of King's Road towards Cheyne Row, each step taking him further from the traffic and the pressures of the twentieth century into quiet streets, diminutive gardens, white paint and polished brass, and small houses of individual character. Approaching Carlyle's House, the visitor finds that the excitement grows with the sense of peace and silence.

Carlyle chose 5 Cheyne Row for this very reason. In 1834 Chelsea was an unfashionable suburb, far from London's din, and a suspicion of dampness from its close proximity to the river kept many from considering it as a suitable address. But then it was quiet, and it was inexpensive, and both things mattered to Carlyle. Following his marriage to Jane Welsh in 1826 these had indeed become major priorities in their planning. Two comfortable years in an Edinburgh suburb had been stimulating enough for two clever and very sociable young people, but they had been expensive. Cheaper by far were the following years in Craigenputtoch, a hill farm in Dumfries-shire, far from towns and company and costing next to nothing to live in, since the property belonged to Jane's family. However, this was so quiet as to be frankly boring for both. Holidays were a relief, whether spent with their families in nearby farms, or better still in Edinburgh or in London, where both spent the exciting winter months of 1831/32 seeing something of the political ferment which accompanied the Reform Bill.

In 1834 the Carlyles made a significant choice. Though both of them Scots born and bred, both accustomed to life in Edinburgh, they came to see, with that acuteness of vision which makes them invaluable commentators on their century, that as a cultural capital it had had its day. In 1832 they were writing to friends from Edinburgh that it had much of the character of a village – quiet, friendly, charming, uninteresting. In 1834, the solitude of Craigenputtoch finally proving too much for Thomas (Jane had had enough years before) they decided they required city company. And their choice, seemingly without hesitation, was for the excitement of London.

Yet their requirements had changed little. Thomas was, and remained, thin-skinned and hypersensitive to noise. Jane was fussy about cleanliness, and though she had a genius for managing on small budgets, she liked to be able to hold her own with her acquaintances. Nor were they rich by 1834 – they had not been affluent at any time during their marriage, and the early 1830s saw their finances seesaw from comfort to near-penury.

Thomas Carlyle (1795-1881). A photograph of *c.*1860 by Julia Margaret Cameron.

Carlyle had written *Sartor Resartus*, his first major independent work, but he was better known for his essays (including the seminal 'Signs of the Times' of 1829 and 'Characteristics' of 1831) and translations from German, particularly his work on Goethe and Schiller. He was a largely self-taught genius, a man who had passed through Edinburgh University and gained from it a keen general education (in particular professional qualifications in languages and the natural sciences) and a restless appetite for books which saw him through 20 years of lonely self-education, first in English then in Continental literature. Carlyle did more than anyone in the 1820s to bring German literature and thought to public notice, and as the 1830s progressed he was to help give a major new impetus to social and historical thought in his time and his country. He led people towards the hidden meanings behind surface appearances, to an awareness of the inter-dependence of society now and in the past, to the dangers that the Industrial Revolution imposed on a society whose mechanisation had come too rapidly and with too little attention to human consequences. What is more Carlyle had done this largely on his own, in correspondence with Goethe (and later with Emerson), in the friendship of a small band of brilliant men like Francis Jeffrey of the *Edinburgh Review*, but most of all from the solitude of his study, largely in the hill farmhouses of his native Dumfries-shire. He was known in the cities by the mid 1830s, by Emerson in Boston and Mill in London, as a coming man. And he was supported through it all by his wife who understood his complex and lonely personality better than anyone. Jane had fascinated Carlyle from their first meeting in 1821, and had eventually married him in 1826 despite his lack of money or social standing. They had courted one another, appropriately, by letter, for together they formed a partnership in correspondence unrivalled in their century. Thomas was to become a major force in British literature as the Sage of Chelsea; Jane was to remain his wife, often overshadowed, often embittered, but always fascinating, always his severest critic.

The early years in Scotland were an apprenticeship. The Carlyles remained a Scottish enigma to many of their English friends, and indeed the recent publication of the *Collected Letters* (a co-operative venture between Carlyle's *Alma Mater*, and Duke University, North Carolina) shows the full extent to which each was indebted to their earliest years for ideas which followed them through adult life. Without his Scottish roots, his Scottish education, and the experience of his Scottish years, Carlyle is meaningless. He came to Chelsea at 39, fully formed, his ideas rapidly maturing towards the writing of *The French Revolution*, the book which made him famous in 1837. By then he was part of Chelsea. Until Jane's death in 1866, they were one of the everyday sights of Cheyne Row. When Carlyle himself died in 1881, it was the end of an era. The reporters who hung around the doors, the very messenger from the Queen who came regularly to enquire, the people who scattered straw on the streets to quieten the traffic noises for the old man dying inside were aware that London was losing a major figure. For years American visitors had been sheltering behind trees and round corners in hopes of meeting the Sage of Chelsea. In 1881, it was all over. Refusing a place in Westminster Abbey, Carlyle stipulated that he should be buried beside his family in his native Ecclefechan, and today the statue at the end of Cheyne Row, and the plaque on the wall of No. 24, seem small reminders of so dominating an intellectual force.

There is little to suggest an exceptional house from the street, nor indeed is there much exceptional about it; it is a terraced brick building of three stories and a sunk basement, dating from the first decade of the eighteenth century. The top storey was much altered because of Carlyle's wish to build his famous sound-proof study, and some internal walls were moved in the Carlyles' time, but they were tenants, not owners, and such major changes were few. Initially they did not have the money for

Cheyne Row in 1875, from a photograph by Robert Tait. No. 5 is in the centre of the photograph.

more than running repairs. They had ingenious ways of appearing to be better off than they were; carpets were turned, and patches sewn on to them, blankets were dyed, furniture used and re-used, the original wainscotting painted and turned to advantage as a decorative feature – and one that saved wallpaper. As times became easier for the Carlyles they became less and less disposed to endure the earthquakes which builders necessarily brought with them, and which both of them found hard on the nerves. The work of incorporating the first-floor closet into a large drawing-room, and of adding the 'sound-proof' room (which, alas, was anything but proof to the sounds of London as it spread rapidly to engulf Chelsea) were the only important alterations they made.

That fact gives the clue to one of the major attractions of Carlyle's house to visitors today. It has changed remarkably little from the house that Thomas and Jane first saw in 1834. Change came slowly and carefully; Jane was a canny housekeeper, and saw little sense in piping in gas lights everywhere when useful light could still be had economically from candles and patent lamps. Piped water was available long before it was actually provided in the basement kitchen. When Jane died in 1866 Carlyle naturally had little inclination to change the house as they had known it together, and after his death in 1881 it was not occupied for long as a dwelling-house. Thus the fabric of the house remained surprisingly little modernised in their lifetime, and remarkably little had to be done to restore the Carlyle's house to the condition in which he would have known it.

The years after Carlyle's death were not happy ones for the house. The tenancy passed to an eccentric lady with a love of pets to the extent and number that the property became unhealthy and squalid. These conditions continued till 1894, and in 1895 the efforts of a large number of people on both sides of the Atlantic resulted in the purchase and opening of the house as a memorial to the Carlyles; from late July 1895 onwards 24 Cheyne Row has been preserved as such.

To pull the ancient bell, to be admitted, to look around the hall and take a first look at the house is to be struck by the extent to which not only the fabric but the atmosphere has survived. Robert Tait's famous painting *A Chelsea Interior* (see front cover) which hangs in the front parlour, the Carlyles' breakfast room, shows Thomas, wearing his flannel dressing-gown, filling a pipe by the fireside in that same room. The room is bright and sunny with Jane seated nervously and self-consciously by the fire, Nero the dog on a nearby sofa, everything in its place. Today, everything is still thus, the same furniture in the same place, similar carpets and hangings where the originals were not available, the very sofa is there, though without Nero, buried decades ago at the foot of the garden. Over the fireplace in Tait's picture there is a mirror; next to the fireplace now Tait's picture freezes a moment in the Carlyles' lives for posterity. It *is* the same room; furniture and tone are alike. In fact the furniture is to an astonishing extent as genuine and unchanged as the fabric of the house. After the purchase in 1895 the committee set about reassembling the dispersed belongings of both Carlyles, items which had been claimed by members of the family, or given away, or sold, at or before Carlyle's death. Slowly, the interior was reconstituted with the original items, the books replaced on the same shelves, the wallpapers renewed where possible with similar patterns, essential modernisation tactfully done. Taking stock, the visitor is transported into the nineteenth century. Only the host, filling his pipe, the hostess eyeing the artistic intruder, and Nero the dog, are missing.

To descend into the basement is to enter the Victorian era. Here a succession of maidservants battled against heavy odds. The basement was poorly lit by day, and frugally by candlelight at night. The cupboards were deep and we know were infested with insects. Jane was fanatical about bedbugs, and both Thomas and Jane shower-bathed and washed scrupulously; but against cockroaches in the basement there can have been very little defence. There was only a small fireplace, a limited water supply, and meals had to be carried up the steep stairs to be served, and crockery down to be washed. Thomas used the basement as a place to escape, to walk when he was irritated and could not go out, or to smoke late at night, for smoke irritated Jane, and he refrained from indulging in the habit in her company. The maid had to live there, to eat, sleep, keep herself and it clean, and to produce meals on time for two exceptionally demanding people. Small wonder that so many maids came and went. Thea Holme's *The Carlyles at Home* seems mostly to be about maidservants, so numerous were Jane's stories about them.

The food that came from this basement was largely for the family, as the Carlyles seldom entertained or gave dinner parties, whether through inclination or financial necessity. Their own needs were relatively modest, conditioned partly by habit and partly by the supplies their families loyally sent from Scotland – bacon and ham, oatmeal, potatoes, butter, even whisky. Carlyle's digestion and his lifelong complaints of dyspepsia, are topics that Victorian scholars have tended to over-stress. Yet even today it is easy to see some of its causes. From the basement kitchen came breakfasts of scalding coffee (Carlyle would drink no other) and toast with perhaps eggs and bacon, but mostly a simple breakfast sufficed. The main meal, served in mid-afternoon, would always follow the same formula; boiled or grilled meat (mutton was a great favourite), boiled vegetables and old potatoes. Perhaps there

The back dining-room from a photograph of *c.* 1880.

might be pudding, also boiled. We know Jane herself had certain party pieces she would cook, such as pancakes or marmalade. She made bread, but infrequently. Brandy and water might occasionally be served, and invariably in the late evening a bowl of porridge. Such items as fruit and salad were then regarded as luxuries and out of the question. Variety was totally lacking, but that simplified the catering. Here is Jane writing to a servant while she was on holiday:

> You know his ways and what he needs pretty well by this time. Trouble him with as few questions as possible. You can ask him what he will take tea or coffee to breakfast? – and whether he would broth, or a pudding to dinner. You must always give him one or the other with his meat and either an egg to breakfast or a slice of bacon... He takes oftenest boiled fowl, mutton broth, chops and bread and ground rice puddings.

The ground floor of the house was a sunny place in the mornings, and the parlour the natural choice for breakfast. The Carlyles were both nervous people, neither a cheerful breakfaster. Each slept ill and complained well, and breakfasts we know could be tense. This sunny ground floor suited well, its front windows looking into the street through venetian blinds, its back windows into the garden. Folding doors separated front from back, and in Tait's famous painting they stand open, revealing a deep, narrow house. The garden is an extension of this plan. When the Carlyles came in 1834 the front looked on to a row of antique elms and open ground beyond, and the back on to more open ground with a very distant view of Westminster Abbey and perhaps even the Houses of Parliament.

The maid had many more stairs to tackle than those from kitchen to ground-floor parlour. The first-floor drawing-room, with a bedroom behind (connected by a folding door), required constant attendance, to bring the master's books, to carry up and serve tea to the guests who visited constantly, and keep the fire supplied with coal. The first floor was the powerhouse in many ways. For this house was not only the home of Thomas and Jane Welsh Carlyle; to it, attracted by their personalities, their conversational power, their aptitude for making and keeping friends, literary London flocked.

The roll of the Carlyles' friends is impressive, and would fill pages. The most successful Victorians counted themselves fortunate to know and to visit the Carlyles at Chelsea – Dickens, Forster, Thackeray, Ruskin, Tennyson, Browning, George Eliot, Harriet Martineau, Mill, Froude – men and women, rich and poor, writers and readers. Jane had a gift for befriending the helpless (Mazzini) and those who needed a mother-substitute (Geraldine Jewsbury). Thomas was attracted to members of the aristocracy, much as he lamented their power in society; Lord and Lady Ashburton were family friends, so intimate as to put the Carlyles' marriage under strong pressure at one time. Thomas had his particular friends, Jane hers; shared friends came at all times. The front room upstairs on the first floor must have witnessed many memorable evenings of conversation.

Both Carlyles knew how to talk to amazing effect. Carlyle enjoyed reminiscing –'he liked nothing better than to hear of the old companions of his boyhood... His long residence in London had not touched his Annandale look, nor had it – as we soon learned – touched his Annandale accent'. As for his conversation, it was '... never for an instant commonplace. The whole diction was always original and intensely vivid, and it was more saturated and interlaced with metaphor than any other conversation I had ever heard'. Jane's was a more piercing style, mocking, satiric. She had a tendency to sit quiet in front of her husband till he over-reached himself, then deflate him with a word. After her death people tried to put her attraction into words; 'the brilliant mockery, the sad softness with which the mockery alternated, were both gone'. And when Carlyle was out (which he often was, walking alone in the London streets, or at social gatherings where he was much in demand), she had her own resources:

> I never sit down at night, beside a good fire, *alone*, without feeling a need of talking a little, on paper, to someone that I like well enough, that likes *me* well enough to make it of no moment – whether I talk sense or nonsense, and with or without regard to the rules of grammer.

Anyone who has edited Jane's letters will ruefully agree with that last sentence. She had an enormous fund of words pent up. She could have written well; indeed, her one sustained piece of writing to survive, her journal of a visit to Haddington in 1849, is brilliant. Instead, she chose to write incomparable letters, and to talk.

Jane and Thomas were magnets which drew people down Cheyne Row, walking or driving from London, coming out to visit them from the metropolis, visiting them as neighbours (as did the Leigh Hunts from Upper Cheyne Row), or staying with them as guests (as Carlyle's brother John did frequently). Talk flowed incessantly from late afternoon to late evening. Carlyle, once stoked up to conversational pressure, was unstoppable, and delivered a monologue for many minutes brooking no interruption. His conversation was vivid, full of denunciations, unforgettable. It is plain that he practised the anathemas which would later appear on paper. He railed against the degeneracy of the times, its politicians and institutions, comparing them unfavourably with the more fixed and rigid institutions of the past. He ridiculed contemporary men of science, letters, religion and politics. He pointed to an all-pervasive spiritual emptiness and want of guidance in his times, a degeneracy compared with the rigid and pious men and women of historical times – above all to Cromwell and the Covenanters in England, and the Presbyterians of Scotland from whose stock he himself had come.

There was much that was self-indulgent in these tirades, and much that was mere rhetoric, for most of them ended in uproarious laughter. Heard for the first time, however, they were unforgettable, and the appeal survived many hearings. Even though habitual visitors like Allingham and Gavan Duffy make testy asides that they have heard some line too often, or are appalled by the Sage's unwillingness to listen to the other side, or even admit he is quite wrong, the spell cannot be broken. Carlyle came from a family of good talkers much given to denouncing their enemies, and, as his *Reminiscences* makes quite clear, he realised he had inherited and refined their gifts. In his drawing-room, they gathered him an enormous circle of friends. Transmuted into a unique style on the printed page, finding form in *The French Revolution*, *Heroes and Hero Worship*, *Chartism*, *Past and Present*, *Cromwell*, *Latter-Day Pamphlets*, and the back-breaking *Frederick the Great*, the style made him world-famous.

To meet the renowned Mr Carlyle and his entrancing wife at their Chelsea home was an honour often recorded in Victorian diaries. Young men were excited to be brought to visit, and tourists and visitors from America were fascinated. Some were received and encouraged to become quasi-disciples (Allingham, Froude, Duffy, Espinasse), while others with less stamina came only rarely. Herbert Spencer left an astringent diary which exemplifies that response. But no one could deny the importance of the Carlyles' home as one of the conversational powerhouses of London.

The room behind the drawing-room on the first floor, like the bedrooms on the floor above, changed character and occupancy from time to time and was altered when the drawing-room was enlarged. The various bedrooms were occupied and re-occupied as the Carlyles fitted in guests, or themselves changed rooms in an effort to attain quiet undisturbed nights.

All the rooms at the back of the house shared a pleasant sunny small dressing-room with a view on to the garden. In more modern times these closets would have provided a bathroom on each floor. In the Carlyles' time, a hip bath and a home-made shower-bath (for cold showers) had to suffice, and hot water had to be brought up the many stairs from the basement. The bedrooms looked on to the back garden, and as such were vulnerable to all the noises which the neighbours made, including such horrors as bantam cocks (for eggs were much in demand and hens a luxury). Nor were the walls between the houses thick; the Carlyles were often disturbed by their neighbours playing their pianos. Jane enjoyed playing hers and the neighbours seem to have accepted her music meekly. But let one of their neighbours play a scale, and Carlyle was frantic. Sleeping was difficult for him at home, nearly impossible when travelling. Small wonder he changed bedrooms and wandered restlessly round the house at night seeking peace and a place to smoke – the garden in summer, the basement in winter.

The staircase runs right up the house; its wainscotting, dark today, was surely doubly dark by candlelight in the Carlyles' time. One of the most striking ways in which the house retains its Victorian character is in the very sparing fitment of electric light; at the top of the stairs it is very dark indeed as the visitor prepares to broach the famous 'sound-proof' study.

The study is really just a large room with a corridor running round it to form a

double wall, a large skylight (with a roller blind to control the amount of daylight) and a fireplace. The double construction of the skylight was intended to be sound-proof, while allowing light (and fresh air through patent ventilators) so that the occupant could work insulated from the offending world outside. Alas, it did not work. The materials were poor, the design hopeful rather than effective, and London had crept much closer. The railway age had brought steam locomotives and whistles, coach traffic was increasing on the embankment, shopmen and pedlars of every variety advertised their wares and in the nearby gardens pets barked or mewed or sang or

The attic study today, and in three photographs of *c.* 1857 by Robert Tait. Carlyle's unusual writing desk is today still in the same position in the room. The historical maps and prints which hung in such profusion in the attic study were his working documents.

howled. Carlyle was never a good worker. When he was doing well, a small interruption (such as an unwelcome guest) would throw him badly. When he was doing badly (and to believe his letters, he did badly a great deal of the time) any interruption, however tiny, assumed the proportions of an earthquake.

The attic study supplanted the drawing-room as a working room, and it was principally here that Carlyle did the research and writing for *Frederick the Great*, the completion of which in 1865 effectively marked the end of his career as a major writer. After that, the attic became a maid's bedroom. But it is inseparable from the eccentricity which brought it about. Robert Tait again provides the evidence, in the form of a photograph which hangs framed in the study. The desk is now a museum piece, but seated at it in the photograph, in exactly the same position in the same room, littered with books and slips of paper and scattered references, sits Carlyle, his head in his hands, miserable. He hated writing. He did it messily, patching it together from notes, and changing his mind constantly. When he reluctantly sent copy to the printer, it was to change proofs, alter the revises, change the page proofs, revise the revises – printers found him very trying indeed. If the walls of the first-floor drawing-room heard some memorable conversation, the walls of the attic study must have heard many curses.

Tait's photographs are the most poignant of all the reminders that 5 Cheyne Row was a working man's working home, whether of Carlyle seated outside under an improvised canopy, or at his desk. The camera points at corners, at the untidy reality of books lying, furniture misplaced, the mess which every writer makes and tidies away before the world can intrude. Tait's *Chelsea Interior* is nature methodised, and Jane appears in the painting taking good care that order prevails. The camera shows something closer to the truth of everyday life.

By day, the house was organised rigidly around Carlyle's personality and occupation. The maidservant cleaned early, then left the house quiet while the master worked. He often rang for books to be fetched to him. Visitors were tactfully excluded during his working hours. He loved fresh air – the back door stood ajar most of the day in fine weather to create the draught he loved, and which Jane was convinced caused her neuralgia. He enjoyed smoking, and smoked up the chimney in the drawing-room, out of doors in fine weather, in the kitchen at other times. He longed for peace at night, but thought nothing of banging round the house when he himself could not sleep. He loathed the smell of paint (Jane always had the painters in when he was travelling alone and she had the house to herself) and hated having workmen in the house hammering and sawing and upsetting his ordered normality. He loved order. He kept little things in order, maps tied neatly in bundles, timetables and guides always to hand. He liked meals on time, servants quiet and unobtrusive, mail on time.

Number 5 Cheyne Row obviously affected Carlyle positively. It was very well adapted to his love of orderly quiet, and Jane, sensing his wishes, made sure that it suited his temperament. The result, whenever Carlyle was in a mood to work, was a good clear space of working day from mid-morning to mid-afternoon. The geography of the house was ideal, allowing Carlyle to immure himself in first-floor drawing-room or attic study, while Jane entertained or merely sat downstairs.

Given Carlyle's increasing dependence on historical research from *Cromwell* to *Frederick*, the need for bulky books and above all for dates, references and stray facts on slips of paper (the way Carlyle always worked), a room free from interruption, where he could leave his work on the floor and set out from session to session, was invaluable. Had Carlyle had a smaller house, where he had had to tidy up from day to day, and go through the labour of setting out his notes before each fresh start, it is hard to see how *Frederick* (difficult enough as it was) could ever have been written.

Carlyle seated smoking beneath an awning in the garden at the rear of the house. The photograph was again taken by Robert Tait.

Moreover, Carlyle found it exceptionally difficult to work in libraries. He loathed the British Museum library and its curator Panizzi, he agitated for years to have the London Library formed for people like himself who were not at home in a large public reading room, with an inadequate catalogue. He was an impatient and intolerant worker, and needed a lending library from which he could take books as he needed them, and use them in his private premises. Increasingly, as he became able to do so, Carlyle employed research assistants to do the library work for him, and retreated more and more to the privacy of his attic study.

The order and privacy of his Chelsea house as a basis for his working life are therefore of the first importance. But what of Chelsea itself? Surprisingly, many of the same things can be said. Chelsea was neither in London, nor out of it. Visitors could walk there and stay for an afternoon without inconvenience, but notwithstanding Carlyle's complaints about noise and pollution, it remained a village outside London. Carlyle could be available when he wanted and hidden when he preferred. He loved to walk for hours with friends (though he quite liked walking alone), seeing his visitors back to Sloane Square or Hyde Park Corner. When he could afford it, he loved nothing more than to ride over the river to Battersea, and out into the leafy lanes which still lay very close by, repairing the damage to his nerves, putting

MR. CARLYLE'S LECTURES
On Heroes and the Heroic.

LECTURE-ROOM,
17 EDWARDS STREET, PORTMAN SQUARE.

TUESDAY	May 5	FRIDAY	May 15
FRIDAY	— 8	TUESDAY	— 19
TUESDAY	— 12	FRIDAY	— 22

Each Lecture to commence at Three o'clock precisely.

130

T. Carlyle

Among the memorabilia preserved in the attic study are tickets for Carlyle's lectures and *(right)* the only fragment of the first draft of *The French Revolution* to escape accidental burning while in the care of John Stuart Mill.

his mind in order for further writing or for lecturing (he prepared for *Heroes and Hero Worship* largely on horseback). He liked being within an easy omnibus-ride of the busiest commercial parts of London, while not being in London itself. Chelsea, in short, was just far enough away from London to suit Carlyle, yet close enough that both he and Jane could make use of shops and libraries, offices and friends' homes without inconvenience. Neither really enjoyed dining out, though when they did they could use the Darwins' carriage, or a hired fly, or simply the omnibus. Jane rode alone on omnibuses, even on the top deck, and dined alone in restaurants – her attitude was far in advance of her times. Being in Chelsea was no barrier to her; what she needed was talk, company, stimulus, and Chelsea brought her plenty.

So much for the obvious advantages of geography. But Carlyle's House has a deeper significance in the understanding of his writing. When Jane died suddenly in 1866 of a heart attack while she was riding in her carriage through Hyde Park, she had lived at the same address for 32 years. In that time, apart from her domestic earthquakes, little had been done to the house. When Thomas himself died 15 years later, virtually nothing had been changed. Carlyle had long notice of his death. The lonely years without Jane gave him much time to think, and to plan posterity's view of him. In the first instance, to dull the maddening lonelinesss of the first few months without Jane, he wrote what became the most attractive and approachable of his works – the *Reminiscences*. In Chelsea, and on holiday in the South of France (kind friends hustled him off to Mentone for the winter after the shock of her death) he scribbled down memories of his years with Jane, a photographic memory combining with his anecdotal, vivid style to bring back years of their life together with painful accuracy. 'Jane Welsh Carlyle' in the *Reminiscences* is a full record of these years, little incidents swimming back to Carlyle's mind, the incident of the burning of the first volume of *The French Revolution* in manuscript, the adventures of visitors, the terrible series of accidents and attacks of neuralgia and migraine which disfigure Jane's last years. '... *Here* we spent our two-and-thirty years of hard battle against Fate; hard but not quite unvictorious, when she left me, as in her car of heaven's fire'. There was only one *here* for Carlyle in London, and the walls of 5 Cheyne Row focused for him all the experiences of London and his adult writing life.

Blind and deaf that we are: oh think, if thou yet love anybody living, wait not till

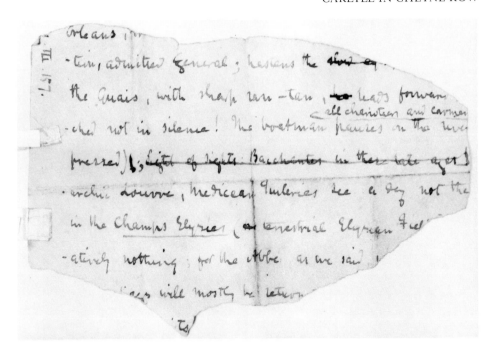

Death sweep down the paltry little dust-clouds and idle dissonances of the moment; and all be at last so mournfully clear and beautiful, when it is too late!

Too late perhaps to bring Jane back to Chelsea, but these mournful years gave Carlyle the opportunity to write out in *Reminiscences* an autobiography unparalleled in English literature for freshness and vividness. A wise artistic impulse made him stop when he had run out of material. The *Reminiscences* are chaotic, untidy, painful – they gave offence when published – but vibrant with life. They illuminate the life of Cheyne Row as no guidebook can.

His memories thus recorded, Carlyle turned to some other occupation, some way of prolonging the contact with Jane. He began the project of gathering together her letters and memorials, editing them himself. In marginalia, in introductory essays and tailpieces, he added many more reminiscences, explanations of private jokes and 'coterie speech' by which they communicated so much. He wrote round to his friends, asking for Jane's letters. Amazingly many had survived, as did extraordinary numbers of his own.

The Carlyles had lived in the same place since 1834, and, as far as we know, they had not thrown away any letters in that time. Thus with Carlyle's gathering-together of Jane's letters after 1866, and the collection of his own after 1881, it became possible to put together an astonishing jigsaw of correspondence. These archives, the fruit of Carlyle's own industry in the first place, but later of biographers such as Froude and Carlyle's nephew Alexander, are the basis of today's editorial labours, the future *Collected Letters* of the Duke-Edinburgh edition, the archives of the National Library of Scotland, the Berg, and the Beineke. They owe their existence to the never-cleared cupboards of Chelsea, and to the extraordinary quality of the letters written at Cheyne Row which led their recipients to preserve them.

The marvellous reminiscences and biographical documents which emerge from Carlyle's late years make the biographer's work easy, since the material was self-confessedly written at speed and with defences down in bereavement and loneliness. But the need for tactful editing was obvious, and was not applied by his first official biographer, James Anthony Froude. Froude, a protégé of Carlyle's, was painfully honest in his desire to depict the whole man, and by publishing the *Reminiscences* very soon after Carlyle's death (the edition had been ready for some time), and the monumental four-volume biography in 1882 and 1884, he revealed the secrets of Chelsea for all the world to see while the obituaries were still fresh.

Froude's biography is a masterpiece, though badly flawed by little inaccuracies and large errors of fact and judgement, and prejudiced in favour of Jane and against Carlyle himself (particularly Carlyle's Scottish working-class background). It painted a picture whose vividness has not been superseded, but it was not the picture the age expected. Nurtured on the image of the Sage of Chelsea, a white-bearded prophet (for Carlyle had achieved that status 40 years before, and had achieved something of the character of a national institution by his death), the readers were not prepared for the revelations of the *Reminiscences*, the evidence throughout the biography of marital strain between Thomas and Jane, the biting sarcasms both could use on their friends as well as their enemies. Stories flew around London of Carlyle's supposed impotence, his wife-beating, his infidelity. The thin-skinned judgements of the *Reminiscences* offended many. The outer calm of Chelsea was shown to have concealed a vivid, exciting, noisy, sometimes tempestuous marriage. Those who had known him personally, and who remembered the good years when Jane and he were younger, an enchanting host and hostess in Chelsea, were outnumbered by those who knew him only in his writing, who knew nothing of the self-deprecating laugh, the personal kindness, the moderation in private life to offset the violence of public utterance. People remembered rather the growing invective of the later public writing, the *Latter Day Pamphlets*, *The Nigger Question*, *Shooting Niagara*. The earlier work, on the Germans, on the French Revolution, on the early effects of the industrial changes of Carlyle's own youth, seemed increasingly irrelevant. Whether because of the revelations about his private life or a sense that he was less and less relevant to the present, Carlyle began to lose his status as hero, and he was rapidly relegated to the position of fallen idol. This may explain why his house was given over to dogs and cats after his death, and over 14 years elapsed before it was taken over and re-opened as a monument.

When Carlyle's house opened in 1895, his reputation was still in decline. The Carlyle Society in London was to struggle on into the twentieth century, but with little success while its Edinburgh counterpart (which flourishes and grows today) was to wait until 1929 before the time seemed propitious for a new start. An academic revival (largely in America) in the 1930s petered out in the Second World War, particularly when Nazi doctrine came – quite wrongly – to be identified with Carlyle in the popular mind. It took until the mid 1960s and later for Carlyle to be reassessed fairly, and the work of establishing him as an eminent Victorian to commence.

There is no denying him this position. If only because of the great practising writers of the nineteenth century with whom he associated, Carlyle would have to be remembered. But the author of *Heroes and Hero Worship* left an obvious and indelible mark on his century, and at least half a dozen of his works are necessary reading for the understanding of a period spanning many years. For Carlyle's working life spanned many decades, and from 1834 onwards he was a living stimulus to his London society. He lived to old age, and changed as he aged; his early interests altered as Victoria's reign extended. The nature of his contribution to his age changed as his position did, as he became famous, became the Sage of Chelsea. Increasingly, visitors came to hear him and he responded to this homage.

The visitors still come. A cosmopolitan visitors' book bears ample testimony to the appeal Carlyle has all over the world, and many come from great distances – Japanese visitors with obvious satisfaction at fulfilling a long-held ambition are a

The Sage of Chelsea, bronze statue by Joseph Edgar Boehm on the Albert Embankment and *(right)* an anonymous photograph of Jane Welsh Carlyle.

notable feature. Carlyle's house is no cold museum; here he can still be felt to be writing angrily upstairs, stalking the corridors by night, and talking, ever talking. He had a lot to say, and he believed in the urgency of his message. 'Mans' Unhappiness, as I construe, comes of his Greatness', he wrote. He was never to relax and be at ease with the complacency, slack moral values, and limited vision of a whole generation. The survival of his house as a place of literary pilgrimage offers some indication of the importance of his task, and the measure of his success.

Thomas Hardy at Bockhampton and Max Gate

Desmond Hawkins

In March 1882 Thomas Hardy wrote to the Earl of Ilchester's land steward 'I am requiring a freehold site on which to build a dwelling-house', and went on to enquire about a building plot on Stinsford Hill, owned by the Earl, in the Dorset parish of Stinsford where Hardy was born and reared. The letter was written from Wimborne where Hardy had been living temporarily while he conducted his search for a permanent home of his own building.

The search had begun at least a couple of years earlier, when Hardy was living in London at Upper Tooting. At that time a Dorchester solicitor, Mr Lock, was making enquiries on his behalf about available sites owned by the Duchy of Cornwall. There appeared to be two possibilities. On April 20, 1880, Hardy wrote to his brother, Henry, asking him to talk it over with 'Young Lawyer Lock'. It was Henry who carried on their father's business in the building trade and would undertake the construction of the house that Thomas, with his architectural training, proposed to design.

Neither of these possibilities came to anything but the continuing contact with the Duchy bore fruit at last. In 1883 Hardy acquired a site of 1½ acres in Dorchester, on the Wareham road. Here he erected Max Gate, the permanent home of the second half of his long life – within walking distance of his birthplace at Higher Bockhampton. It is difficult to think of any other writer whose home-life was so deeply rooted in one locality. To the 45 years of his residence at Max Gate must be added the 34 earlier years when his parents' 'homestead' at Bockhampton continued to provide him with his only home until the day he finally departed to embark on married life.

Bockhampton is a hamlet within the parish of Stinsford, little more than a couple of miles from Dorchester on the southern side of the main road to Puddletown and London. The Hardys first appeared at Puddletown in the latter part of the eighteenth century in the person of John Hardy, a mason who reputedly brought with him little more than the tools of his trade. In 1777 he married, and in the following year his son Thomas was born. Like his father, Thomas was prompt to assume the roles of husband and parent and by the turn of the century he needed a home of his own. Fortunately John Hardy had prospered sufficiently to give his newly married son a modest but adequate start in life.

In the County Record Office at Dorchester there is a map of Kingston and Bockhampton Farms which bears no date but can be confidently assigned to about 1800. This map shows the genesis of a new development. At Bockhampton Farm's boundary with Bhompston Heath the words 'The New Street' are written, and a single named plot is indicated. The name is J. Hardy. Many years later his daughter-in-law, Mary Hardy, described to her grandchildren the first years of her married life in the cottage built on this plot, that we now know as 'Hardy's Birthplace'. John Hardy and his son Thomas could employ their own skills to erect the simple two-roomed building, so no great capital outlay was required. The property was

Thomas Hardy (1804-1928) in the garden at Max Gate.

leasehold, at a modest annual rent for the term of three named lives, in accordance with local custom. Its 1¾ acres provided sand and gravel to be dug for Thomas's work as a mason as well as a productive small-holding to supply food. To a young wife with no great expectations it offered a secure home, but it was undeniably in primitive and isolated surroundings: her nearest neighbours were the moorland ponies grazing on the adjacent heathland – the 'heathcroppers' that Hardy describes in the *Return of the Native*. Her husband was involved with the smugglers who came by night across the heath from a coastal landing: the flick of a whip on the bedroom window meant that he must hurry downstairs to stow away some casks of brandy until they could be safely collected. It was a secret task for which the loneliness of the place was well suited.

> Our house stood quite alone, and those tall firs
> And beeches were not planted. Snakes and efts
> Swarmed in the summer days, and nightly bats
> Would fly about our bedrooms. Heathcroppers
> Lived on the hills, and were our only friends;
> So wild it was when first we settled here.

In that extract from the earliest of his poems to survive, 'Domicilium', Hardy recorded his grandmother's description of the cottage in the first decade of the nineteenth century. In due course other plots of land were taken up for the building of small houses or cottages, and the Ordnance Survey map of 1811 gives to the vicinity of 'The New Street' the designation of 'New Bockhampton'. With the passing of the years the original Bockhampton became Lower Bockhampton, to distinguish it from the new hamlet, which is now known as Higher Bockhampton.

Hardy never saw his grandfather, the first Thomas, who died in 1837. The tithe map of 1838 shows the Hardy property as plot number 75 in the occupancy of the widow, Mary. Her three surviving daughters had married, and one of her sons, James, lived opposite on plot 77. The only child still at home was the youngest and favourite son, the second Thomas, who presented her with a formidable daughter-in-law when he married Jemima Hand in the following year, 1839. Jemima was already pregnant with the third (and last) Thomas, and gave birth to him in the cottage on the 2nd June, 1840. Among the influences on the character and genius of the future author the powerful personalities of these two women – Jemima, his mother, and Mary, his grandmother, were to have dominating importance.

What first brought Jemima to Stinsford was her employment as cook in the household of the vicar, the Rev. Edward Murray. Sitting in church on Sundays her attention was drawn to the handsome young violinist in the musicians' gallery:

> She turned in the high pew, until her sight
> Swept the west gallery, and caught its row
> Of music-men with viol, book and bow
> Against the sinking sad tower-window light.
>
> She turned again; and in her pride's despite
> One strenuous viol's inspirer seemed to throw
> A message from his string to her below,
> Which said: 'I claim thee as my own forthright!'

In those opening verses of 'A Church Romance' Hardy described in suitably romantic terms the dawning acquaintance which led to his parent's marriage. Years later Jemima recalled her impressions of her future father-in-law and his two sons, Thomas and James, hurrying over the brow of the hill to Stinsford Church with their

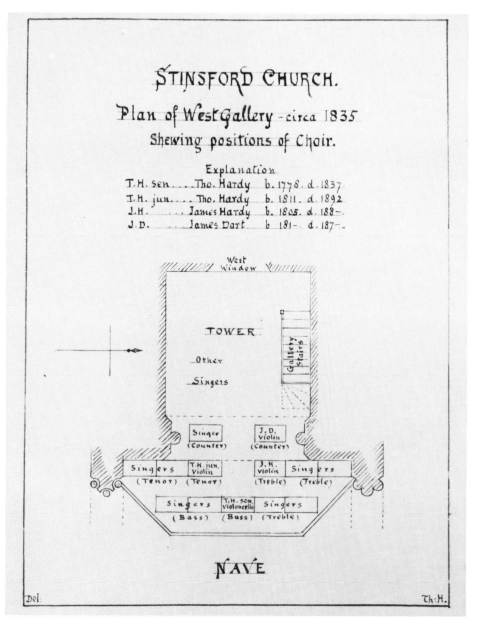

STINSFORD CHURCH.

Plan of West Gallery - circa 1835
Shewing positions of Choir.

Explanation

T.H. sen.	Tho. Hardy	b. 1778. d. 1837.
T.H. jun.	Tho. Hardy	b. 1811. d. 1892
J.H.	James Hardy	b. 1805. d. 188-.
J.D.	James Dart	b. 181-. d. 187-.

West Window

TOWER

Other Singers

Gallery Stairs

Singer (Counter)

J.D. Violin (Counter)

Singers (Tenor)

T.H. jun. Violin (Tenor)

J.H. Violin (Treble)

Singers (Treble)

Singers (Bass)

T.H. sen. Violoncello (Bass)

Singers (Treble)

NAVE

Del.   Th:H.

Thomas Hardy senior's plan of the choir at Stinsford Church, near Dorchester *(Dorset County Museum)*.

fiddles and cello in green baize bags tucked under their arms. They wore top hats, stick-up shirt collars with black silk neckerchiefs and the blue swallow-tail coats with gilt embossed buttons that were typical of the period: the older man retained the breeches and buckled shoes of his generation while his sons wore French-blue trousers. For the origins of 'the Mellstock Quire' there is no need to look further.

Music, both sacred and profane, was a major preoccupation in the Hardy household and a key component in Hardy's writings. The first Thomas had played the cello in Puddletown church before he married and moved to the newly built cottage at Bockhampton. The standard of music in his parish church, Stinsford, so appalled him that he undertook to form a proper 'quire' of instrumentalists. His two sons, James and Thomas, were taught the violin and took their places in the church-gallery as soon as they were old enough to do so.

Nor was it only the music for church services that engaged them. Carols at

Christmas and dances at all seasonable times in barns and farmhouses extended their repertoire. They were also in demand to accompany wedding processions, such as the one in Hardy's poem 'The Country Wedding':

> I bowed the treble before her father,
> Michael the tenor in front of the lady,
> The bass-viol Reub – and right well played he!
> The serpent Jim; ay, to church and back.

Hardy grew up in this musical tradition although the family connection with the church music ended shortly after his birth. When he was four he was given a small accordion and he could fiddle competently at an early age. While still a boy he used to go with his father to dances where together they played the dance tunes of the period.

If the keenest of ears can detect a ghostly sound in the Hardy cottage today it must be the sound of a viol. For half a century and more that was the distinctive keynote, bass or treble, of this household. The scenes and sounds of dancing constantly recur in Hardy's novels and poems; so do the songs and ballads of an ancient peasantry; and so too do the liturgy, the psalms, the anthems and hymns of the Church of England. Two pictures of that cottage interior in the 1840s come to mind – of the child Thomas dancing in the evenings to the accompaniment of his father's violin, and in a different mood pretending to be a parson with 'Granny' as his congregation. The outlines of the future author were drawn early within the homestead.

There were two annual festivals at Bockhampton to be noted. One was the Christmas carolling, when it was the custom of Hardy's grandfather, as Hardy describes it

> to assemble the rather perfunctory rank-and-file of the choir at his house; and this necessitated suppers, and suppers demanded (in those days) plenty of liquor. This was especially the case on Christmas Eve itself, when the rule was to go to the northern part of the parish and play at every house before supper; then to return to Bockhampton and sit over the meal till twelve o'clock during which interval a good deal was consumed at the Hardy's expense, the choir being mainly poor men and hungry. They then started for other parts of the parish, and did not get home till all was finished at about six in the morning.

Hardy's father continued the custom and Hardy finally turned it to good account in *Under the Greenwood Tree* where the Christmas gathering of the Mellstock carollers in the 'long low cottage with a hipped roof of thatch, having dormer windows breaking up into the eaves' invites us to enter the home of Hardy's boyhood. The liquor consumed on this occasion was home-brewed cider and it was this which provided the year's other festival – the harvesting of the orchard and pressing of the apples. Until he married Hardy liked to be at Bockhampton in the autumn to assist at his father's cider-making. Among the 'great things' of life, along with dancing and lovemaking, the poet included cider:

> Sweet cyder is a great thing,
>   A great thing to me,
> Spinning down to Weymouth town
>   By Ridgway thirstily,
> And maid and mistress summoning
>   Who tend the hostelry:
> O cyder is a great thing,
>   A great thing to me!

The cider-making scene in 'Desperate Remedies' seems to recapture personal childhood memories of picking up the fallen apples; and in *The Woodlanders* the character of Giles Winterborne epitomises the itinerant cider-maker described in the poem 'Shortening Days at the Homestead':

> It's the cider-maker,
>   And appletree-shaker,
> And behind him on wheels, in readiness,
>   His mill, and tubs, and vat, and press.

For Hardy this was clearly the outdoor climax of the year at the family home. The 'sweet smells and oozings in the crisp autumn air', he wrote, 'can never be forgotten by those who have had a hand in it'.

A convivial temperament, a love of music-making and resignedly philosophical attitudes to life were strong characteristics in Hardy's father and they helped to mould young Thomas. Very different was the influence of the two Hardy wives, his mother and grandmother, in their contributions to the later complexity of the novelist and poet. Both had lived through harsher conditions in their youth than their husbands had known. The war against Napoleon had brought the added fear of an invasion of the Dorset coast and Mary saw her husband in the uniform of the local defence volunteers – the Green Linnets – deployed to defend Weymouth. The post-war years brought increasing unrest at home, culminating in the agricultural riots of the 1830s, when ricks were burned and farming machinery destroyed at Puddletown, and at Tolpuddle the 'martyrs' of later fame were transported to Botany Bay. A dread of poverty and a defensive clannishness fuelled the close-fisted ambition that sent young Thomas to work in an architect's office in Dorchester, where his own inner drive to self-improvement opened wider horizons.

From his grandmother particularly there came another strand of inheritance, richly imaginative and further augmented by parents, relatives and neighbours. This was the corpus of legend, folk-tale, local history and superstition which acquired the potency that comes from successive distillations. While young Thomas and his sister Mary sat by the open hearth in the downstairs room, their grandmother told them tales of long ago – of maypole dancing and public whippings of poor children and threats of war:

> She told of that far-back day when they learnt astounded
>   Of the death of the King of France;
> Of the Terror; and then of Bonaparte's unbounded
>   Ambition and arrogance.
>
> Of how his threats woke warlike preparations
>   Along the southern strand,
> And how each night brought tremors and trepidations
>   Lest morning should see him land.

It is scarcely necessary to add that the boy listening intently by the cottage fireside was the future author of 'The Dynasts', 'The Trumpet-Major' and other stories and poems that sprang from his unquenchable interest in the Napoleonic Wars. Many years afterwards he paid a moving tribute to the visionary quality of the old woman's recollections:

> With cap-framed face and long gaze into the embers –
>   We seated round her knees –
> She would dwell on such dead themes, not as one who remembers,
>   But rather as one who sees.

The vividness of such moments persisted through his life. When he was 75 Hardy recalled in one of his best-known poems, 'The Oxen', how as a boy he had sat 'by the embers in hearthside ease' and listened to the legend of the oxen kneeling at midnight on Christmas Eve; and he commented wryly:

> So fair a fancy few would weave
> In these years! Yet, I feel,
> If someone said on Christmas Eve,
> 'Come; see the oxen kneel
>
> In the lonely barton by yonder coomb
> Our childhood used to know',
> I should go with him in the gloom,
> Hoping it might be so.

The first stage of his emancipation from the close intimacy of the family circle in the Bockhampton cottage began in 1862 when he set off to London. The capital city was always his cultural Mecca, the arena in which he wanted to triumph, and he must have relished the contrast between the family homestead and the office in the Adelphi where he worked for the eminent architect, Arthur Blomfield. For a dozen years in his young manhood he lived intermittently in lodgings or at home while he worked for architects in London, Dorchester and Weymouth. His early novels were written out of office hours or in the intervals between periods of employment. When possible he liked to write at home. While he was working on 'A Pair of Blue Eyes', for instance, he noted that he could not get on with it in London 'and late in September went down to the seclusion of Dorset to set about it more thoroughly'.

By this time the original one-up-one-down design of the cottage had been developed by partitioning and by incorporating outbuildings to produce something nearer to the 'seven-roomed rambling house' of Hardy's later description. He could use his bedroom as a study and write there without disturbance, or he could write out of doors in the homestead's peaceful surroundings. While he was writing *Far from the Madding Crowd* he found a particular drawback in the outdoor method, as described in *The Life of Thomas Hardy*:

> He would occasionally find himself without a scrap of paper at the very moment that he felt volumes. In such circumstances he would use large dead leaves, white chips left by the wood-cutters, or pieces of stone or slate that came to hand.

This novel was to be the last one written at Bockhampton. When it was published in 1874 he was already married and living with his wife, Emma, at Surbiton – one of several brief residences during their early years together. Hardy was evidently torn between the rival attractions of Wessex and London as a permanent home and moved restlessly between them until a serious illness in London brought him to the decision that his health needed the Dorset air. Emotionally too he seems to have needed to preserve his links with the family circle and the family home at Bockhampton. He was the senior and most conspicuously successful of Jemima's children – a position which implied certain obligations. To build a home of his own in the vicinity of Stinsford, but to be in London each year for 'the Season' was a practical blending of opposed impulses. Like the heroine of *The Hand of Ethelberta* whose fashionable success as an authoress was troubled by a 'sense of disloyalty to her class and kin', Hardy never found it easy to reconcile his public achievements with his private context.

These fluctuating tensions are a persisting element in his writings and they are epitomised monumentally in the contrasting buildings of his birthplace and Max

Portrait of Thomas Hardy *c.*1883
and *(below)* his visiting card.

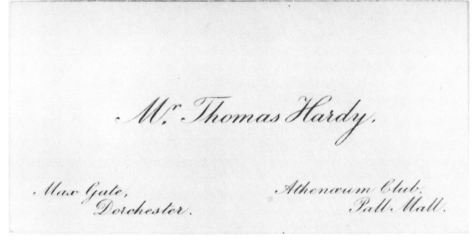

Gate. The Bockhampton cottage sits plainly in the vernacular tradition of the villages of Egdon Heath, unemphatic, serviceable, of local provenance. Max Gate, by contrast, associates itself with the pervasive urban affluence of its time. It is akin to the well-finished, commodious and modestly assertive villas that every Mr Pooter hoped to acquire in the new city suburbs. It was Hardy's hostage to the level of society in which he now found himself – 'only a cottage in the country which I use for writing in' was his defensive description of it. In his cherished concept of a Wessex–London axis, Max Gate was to supply the writer's workshop end, while London provided the social and cultural stage on which his achievements would be expressed and acclaimed.

Work began on the site at Max Gate on November 26, 1883 and took about eighteen months to complete, under Hardy's personal supervision. One of his first actions was to plant two or three thousand small trees, mostly Austrian pines, to provide seclusion in later years.

> I set every tree in my June time,
>   And now they obscure the sky.

So he wrote in the poem 'At Day-Close in November'. The trees grew so thickly that they emphasised the impression of melancholy gloom which recurs in his visitors' descriptions of Max Gate in the 1920s. Not only was the house screened almost completely from the road, but in summer it appeared – in Hardy's words – 'as if at the bottom of a dark green well of trees'.

Hardy's elevations for the entrance front of Max Gate *(Dorset County Museum)*.

(Above) Max Gate when first built, around 1885, *(Dorset County Museum)* and *(right)* in about 1900 *(Dorset County Museum)*.

He was by no means confident of the wisdom of his undertaking as it progressed. When Lady Portsmouth urged him to settle in her neighbourhood in Devonshire he noted 'She says they would find a house for us. Cannot think why we live in benighted Dorset. Em would go willingly, as it is her native county; but alas my house at Dorchester is nearly finished.' A few months later, on June 29, 1895, Hardy and Emma slept at Max Gate for the first time, but by the year's end Hardy was wondering 'whether building this house at Max Gate was a wise expenditure of energy'. Nor was this a passing mood: he subsequently commented that for himself and Emma the move to Dorchester was 'a step they often regretted having taken'. Its most redeeming feature was the bracing air and, he concluded, 'in the long run it proved not ill-advised'.

The name 'Max Gate' is all of a piece with Hardy's practice in his novels of coining cryptic or thinly disguised place-names. A local landmark near his building-plot was a tollgate operated by the Dorchester & Wool Turnpike Trust. Its official name, according to Professor Ronald Good in *The Old Roads of Dorset*, was Loud's Gate, but for many years the gate-keeper had been Henry Mack and presumably therefore the gate became known locally as Mack's Gate. The simple change from Mack's to Max added a superior social resonance and provided Hardy with a whimsical sideways glance at Roman Dorchester when he used 'Porta Maxima' in a letter to Edmund Gosse.

Hardy could have had several reasons for feeling a degree of pride, or at least of satisfaction, in the creation of Max Gate. It was an incontrovertible witness to his success in the hazardous career he had chosen. It outshone the Bockhampton property which he might, in less prosperous circumstances, have expected to inherit. It gave full play, moreover, to whatever impulses of architectural design he may have developed during the employment of his earlier years. When his original London employer, Sir Arthur Blomfield, came to visit in 1892 he 'liked the design of the Max Gate house', according to *The Life*, which notes this approval as 'contrary to Hardy's expectations'. Such enthusiasm as Hardy himself may have felt for the project is muted, however, and matter-of-fact in tone. The period of planning, construction and first occupancy finds remarkably little expression in his letters or personal papers. One senses a deliberate intention to subordinate the matter to the nuts-and-bolts level of life's humdrum necessities. A 'country-headquarters' was required: Max Gate provided it.

The larger strategy into which Max Gate fitted is clearly stated in *The Life*: 'several months of each spring and summer were to be spent in London during the ensuing twenty years, and occasionally spells abroad'. In realistic terms what Hardy had constructed on the fringe of Dorchester was a workshop and a base-camp, in which he took little pleasure. 'Life here is lonely and cottage-like' he wrote to Gosse in 1886. One might expect the spending of the following spring and summer in Italy and London to have been succeeded by a contented homecoming but Hardy was soon writing once more to Gosse 'I am quite frantic to go off somewhere again – but must not'. It was a pattern of life that came to an end with the death of Emma and the outbreak of the Great War.

Through the nineties and the Edwardian years Max Gate saw its owner as the prolific writer in the solitary confinement of his study, like a hermit in his devotional cell, drafting the successive masterpieces – *The Woodlanders*, *Tess of the d'Urbervilles*, *Jude the Obscure* – that concluded his career as a novelist; and then launching himself publicly as a poet and addressing himself to the mammoth task of *The Dynasts*. As for the house itself:

> 'That is a quiet place –
> That house in the trees with the shady lawn'.

Hardy in his study at Max Gate.

'–If, child, you knew what there goes on
You would not call it a quiet place.
Why a phantom abides there, the last of its race,
    And a brain spins there till dawn'.

'The House of Silence' is the title of the poem from which that verse is taken. The silence of an intensely absorbed writer at work is easily understood, but there was another and grimmer form of silence deepening within Max Gate – that between husband and wife. Hardy and Emma had been married less than ten years when the foundations of Max Gate were being dug. To own this new home of their own creation must have seemed, to any casual observer, an auspicious start to a fresh chapter in their romantic history; but the reality was quite otherwise. Looking back, many years later, Hardy recalled a fleeting image of Emma in the happy mood of a garden-party, at Max Gate; but it is an exceptional moment:

How she would have loved
A party today! –
Bright-hatted and gloved,
With table and tray
And chairs on the lawn
Her smiles would have shone
With welcomings...

The mood that came to prevail at Max Gate was a sombre one. After her death the

Emma, the first Mrs Thomas Hardy. A photograph published soon after her death in 1912.

voice of Emma found its way into Hardy's poetry in unmistakable tones:

I play my sweet old airs –
  The airs he knew
  When our love was true –
  But he does not balk
  His determined walk,
And passes up the stairs.

I sing my songs once more,
  And presently hear
  His footsteps near
  As if he would stay;
  But he goes his way
And shuts a distant door.

The drawing-room at Max Gate.

The writing of this poem was an act of atonement. The figure of the author passing upstairs in silence and closing his study door crystallises the corrosive estrangement that was beyond their powers to alter.

It is not quite accurate to speak of Hardy's 'study' at Max Gate. At various times three different rooms served that purpose, the final one being part of an extension added in later years. All three were upstairs, out of reach of chance encounters and importunate callers. Some enlargement of the original house was also needed to accommodate visitors: in 1886 Hardy wrote to Gosse 'Next year we hope to have a regulation spare-bedroom for married couples: at present we have only a bachelor's room'.

While it remains true that a favourite view from Max Gate was towards Dorchester Station and the railway-line to London, the house had another appealing prospect in the direction of Stinsford and Higher Bockhampton. It was Hardy's custom, when he was at Max Gate, to walk or cycle each Sunday to his parents' home. The homestead with its childhood associations continued to nourish the deeper levels of his imagination. Scene after scene in the later novels, written at Max Gate, drew their vitality from Bockhampton – Grammer Oliver's dialect and the cider-making in *The Woodlanders*, Dairyman Crick's establishment in *Tess*, the boy Jude re-enacting Hardy's autobiographical poem *Childhood among the Ferns* – so that there is no mistaking where the tap-root of his genius enters the earth.

Hardy's father died in 1892, his mother in 1904. Technically the lifehold lease expired in 1892 with the death of Thomas Hardy senior but the owners allowed the widow and later the children to retain possession. By 1912 Hardy's brother Henry and his two sisters Mary and Kate had settled at Talbothays, in the new house Henry had built, and Hardy paid the final quarterly instalment of rent on his birthplace on the first day of 1913, thus terminating a family tenure which had persisted over more than a hundred years.

It was a period of change and uncertainty for Hardy. Emma had died only a few weeks before. In his grief he set off in March on a pilgrimage to St Juliot and Plymouth, seeking again the early romantic haunts of his 'West-of-Wessex girl' and thereby finding himself charged with a new poetic force. At Max Gate the normal household routines were in disarray. Emma's pets were neglected, strayed away, died or were killed. In the following year Hardy married again, and the outbreak of war in Europe emphasised the disappearance of the old lifestyle. Gone were the brilliant social events of the London season and the pleasurable trips to the Continent. The 'country-headquarters', perforce, became something more.

To the constraints of wartime were added the physical limitations of advancing age. In 1914 Hardy was 74. Fourteen years of life remained to him during which Max Gate increasingly became a sort of literary shrine to which the eminent and the humble were drawn to pay homage. The Prince of Wales came to tea; deputations of celebrated authors or university dignitaries brought suitable honours and addresses to one who was now the doyen of English literature. T.E. Lawrence, Siegfried Sassoon and Sir James Barrie were particularly welcome visitors to Max Gate. Doubtless many came because it was the thing to do: disparagement at first hand of the architecture of Max Gate was part of the table-talk of the Twenties.

Hardy continued to work daily up in his study, writing new poems, revising old ones, checking proofs of new editions and corresponding with editors and publishers. At tea-time he would meet his visitors with a mild courtesy, behind which he remained withdrawn – as Siegfried Sassoon described him in the poem 'Max Gate':

> Old Mr. Hardy, upright in his chair,
> Courteous to visiting acquaintances chatted
> With unaloof alertness while he patted
> The sheepdog whose society he preferred.
> He wore an air of never having heard
> That there was much that needed putting right.
> Hardy, the Wessex wizard, wasn't there.
> Good care was taken to keep him out of sight...

In his more private moments Hardy liked to walk from Max Gate to the railway-line to watch the goods trains passing with their cargo of huge blocks of Portland stone. Florence, his second wife, commented 'He seems never tired of watching these stone-laden trucks'. He also continued to visit his birthplace and to care for it, made possible by the owner, Cecil Hanbury's friendly recognition of Hardy's interest in the place, even though it was now based only on sentiment. As late as November 1926 Hardy noted 'Went with Mr Hanbury to Bockhampton and looked at fencing, trees etc, with a view to tidying and secluding the Hardy house'.

Some sense of filial obligation or respect for his ancestry had always led him back from Max Gate to Bockhampton. It grieved him to see the cottage neglected or the garden 'uncherished', and he particularly regretted the loss of the wide brilliantly white chimney-corner where he had sat as a child listening to his elders. In these last visits, when there were no longer any relatives to welcome him, his imagination conjured up conjectural dialogues with the ancient residents, the generations of Hardy men and women whose spirits might yet linger there. Max Gate was haunted by Emma, as several poems testify. At Bockhampton Hardy was with other and older

Tea in the garden at Max Gate with the Prince and Princess of Wales.

company, as in 'Night in the Old Home':

> When the wasting embers redden the chimney-breast,
> And Life's bare pathway looms like a desert track to me,
> And from hall and parlour the living have gone to their rest,
> My perished people who housed them here come back to me.
>
> They come and seat them around in their mouldy places,
> Now and then bending towards me a glance of wistfulness,
> A strange upbraiding smile upon all their faces,
> And in the bearing of each a passive tristfulness.
>
> 'Do you uphold me, lingering and languishing here,
> A pale late plant of your once strong stock?' I say to them;
> 'A thinker of crooked thoughts upon Life in the sere,
> And on That which consigns men to night after showing the day to them?'
>
> – 'O let be the Wherefore! We fevered our years not thus:
> Take of life what it grants, without question!' they answer me seemingly.
> 'Enjoy, suffer, wait: spread the table here freely like us,
> And, satisfied, placid, unfretting, watch Time away beamingly!'

Henry James at Lamb House

Frank Tuohy

In theory writers may live where they wish, where their talents flourish the most. But undercurrents always exist that make them drift towards some special area, unseen bonds can tie them to some particular social setting or bit of scenery. What looks like an individual choice may come at the end of a long sequence of choices made by other people. With Henry James and his encounter with Lamb House, Rye, we are at the end of such a sequence.

The first choice was made by his grandfather, the first William James we hear of, who set foot in America in 1789 at the age of eighteen. He came from County Cavan, and was a strict Presbyterian by upbringing and thus what the Americans refer to as 'Scots-Irish'. William James established himself in Albany, New York State, flourished exceedingly, gave his name to a town (Jamesville, N.Y.) and died in 1832, leaving a widow, eleven surviving children, and a fortune of $3,000,000.

William's fourth son, the first Henry, had rebelled against his father's protestant beliefs and adopted some unusual ones of his own – he was a Swedenborgian – and because of this he was disinherited. He brought a court action to contest the will, won his case and thenceforward had financial freedom. Henry James Senior could afford to live where he willed, and for much of the time his choice was Europe. His second son, Henry the novelist, referred to himself, his three brothers and his sister as 'hotel children.'

This second choice was by no means unusual: from the very earliest days of the Republic, Americans had been assiduous travellers. In 1835, Alexis de Toqueville turned his sharp yet unmalicious gaze on the inhabitants of the new country and observed that, when they arrived in Europe, they were anxious to project themselves as members of a just and democratic nation. At the same time, this involved being subordinate to no man, and so the visiting Americans congregated, ostensibly to pursue the arts, but often to escape the puritanical restraints and materialistic pursuits of their own rapidly developing nation.

In 1875, aged 32 and already well-known as a writer, Henry James lived in Paris, where he frequented the circle of Flaubert, Zola and the Goncourts; his most lasting friendship, however, proved to be with a fellow exile, Ivan Turgenev. The following year he made the choice that was to determine the remainder of his life: he settled in England. Much later he was to make two lengthy visits to his native land, but he never envisaged a permanent return.

Earlier visits to England had not been entirely happy. In London only a few years before he had felt 'a tiger-pounce of homesickness' for New York: 'London was hideous, vicious, cruel and above all over-whelming.' This time he settled in rooms in Bolton Street, near the corner of Piccadilly, with a sideways view of Green Park. From here he began his 'siege of London': he set about it with an entirely American dispatch and efficiency by means of letters of introduction. 'If you cannot be a duke with a large rent-roll in England,' a later writer was to put it, 'by all means be an

Henry James (1843-1916) about 1880.

agreeable American, for to one and the other all doors are open.'

The operative word, of course, is 'agreeable'. It certainly described the young American girls who appeared much in society at this time, and were celebrated in novels by English writers like Anthony Trollope, as well as in those of Henry James himself (Pansy Osmond, in *The Portrait of a Lady,* would make, we are told, 'a precious little pearl of a peeress'). To find Henry James, a single man in early middle age, so quickly in this category is to be reminded of his life-long power to charm and to arouse affectionate friendship in both women and men. Within a year of his solitary arrival at Bolton Street, he is dining at Lord Houghton's, where his fellow-guests include Tennyson, Gladstone and Dr Schliemann, the excavator of Troy.

Through the following years his social life continued to proliferate. One of his few popular successes, *Daisy Miller,* assisted in his becoming 'a highly developed diner-out'. Temporary memberships of several London clubs ended with his election to the Reform. Like many bachelors James had a tendency to keep his friendships in separate compartments but, like the American expatriates observed by de Toqueville, he did not like to feel excluded from any society that might be available.

This punishing regime was relaxed a little when, after nine years at Bolton Street, he moved to De Vere Gardens, a dark slot of a street on the eastern frontier of Kensington. Here he bought the lease of an unfurnished flat, took into his employment the Smiths, the boozy married couple who looked after him, in their fashion, for 16 years, and took to his heart the first of his dachshunds, Tosca. Henceforward his dining-out diminished, but he continued to make a round of country house visits, some of which left their mark on his writing: to the Roseberys at Mentmore and the Rothschilds at Waddesdon, for instance, and once, after an exhausting week at the Viceregal court at Dublin Castle, to his friends the Wolseleys, Lord Wolseley then being Commander-in-Chief of what James, remembering his Irish ancestry, referred to as 'the army of occupation.'

With interludes of travel on the continent, London remained his base of operations until two factors combined together to make him change his mind. His novels of the middle period no longer had the sales of his earlier work and he was forced to rely more and more on his private resources. More important was his misguided effort at playwriting and his ambition to conquer the London stage. Moderately successful at first, his plans were cut short by the disastrous first night of *Guy Domville.* George Alexander led the cringing dramatist on to the stage, to be greeted with jeers and catcalls. 'In three words' he wrote (a characteristic Jamesian miscalculation) 'the delicate, picturesque, extremely human and extremely artistic little play was taken profanely by a brutal and ill-disposed gallery...' Sharing his life with no-one, he was peculiarly vulnerable to defeat. After this traumatic experience, he fled from London as soon as he could. He spent the summer at Torquay.

The following winter he noticed a watercolour that attracted him in the house of an architect friend, Edward Warren. The work of Warren himself, it showed the Georgian facade of the annexe to Lamb House, in the 'Antient Town' of Rye ('Antient Town' was a title bestowed on Rye and Winchelsea, linking them to the Cinque Ports). Later, in the subtly deprecatory style James employed when his emotions were aroused, he wrote of Rye and Winchelsea as 'the pair of blighted hill-towns that once were sea-towns and that now draw out their days in the dim after-sense of a mere indulged and encouraged picturesqueness.'

Henry James was not indifferent to appearances or historical background, but he winced away from providing a more exact picture. A modern writer, Jan Morris, is more precise in observing Rye with its

> Hobbitesque silhouette on a hill above the sea, its tumbled streets falling away
> from the tower of St Mary's precipitously through the town gates to estuary

The watercolour of the garden room at Lamb House by Edmund Warren, dated 2 September 1895, which first prompted Henry James's interest in the house. The drawing is now in the Houghton Library, Harvard University.

Henry James circa 1898 (from *Henry James at Home* by H. Montgomery Hyde).

below. It is a crannied, pebble-cobbled, weather-boarded, low-beamed, tangled kind of town, like a knobbly protrusion of its own hillock . . . It is a genteel tea-shop town now, but it used to be very rough indeed: a community of fishermen and smugglers.

Falling for a mere watercolour, Henry James set about wooing and winning the object of his desire: a lengthy process which has been described for us by H. Montgomery Hyde in his *Henry James at Home.*

In 1896 James took a cottage at nearby Point Hill. Already in his fifties and endowed with the figure that tailors describe as 'short, portly', he could nevertheless write: 'I must (deride me not) be somewhere where I can, without disaster, bicycle.' It was the new fashion: according to Chamber's Encyclopaedia of the period, 'Royalty disports itself upon it, and the nobility and gentry make no secret of their love of the wheel.' James himself went on: 'It seems to give me a glimpse of the courts of heaven.' And so he spent the summer bicycling through the countryside, with occasional interruptions when he went up the steep cobbled street, then grass-grown, and made what he facetiously called 'sheep's eyes' at Lamb House. He even enquired at the local ironmonger if it might ever be to let, and had the forethought to leave his London address.

During the summer, he moved from his cottage to the Vicarage at Rye. Next year neither was available, and he went off to Suffolk with some American friends. On his return to London he received the information that Lamb House was to let. With Edward Warren's advice, he procured a long lease at £70 a year.

(Right) the façade of the garden room; (far right) the hall at Lamb House as it is today and (below right) an old photograph showing the interior of the garden room before its destruction in the Second World War.

Lamb House, Rye. An old photograph showing, to the left, the garden room, destroyed by a bomb in August 1940.

Though his passion for Lamb House was genuine, Henry James lacked the aesthetic vocabulary to express it. The masterly analyst of motive, nuance and velleity found difficulty in picturing his new residence to friends and family. In any case, he was living at a turning point in educated taste. Early Georgian houses appear frequently in the illustrations to Dickens's novels, but as the gaunt, gloomy and forbidding residences of unsympathetic personages. But now, together with their contents, they were beginning to be appreciated once more. In James's novel *The Spoils of Poynton,* the actual spoils are never depicted, but were presumably Elizabethan and Jacobean. Now people were bringing down Georgian furniture that had been consigned to the attics at the beginning of the Victorian era.

As his friend Edith Wharton was to remark, Henry James's was the pride that apes humility. In his letters he talks of a 'smallish, charming, cheap old house' with 'a little parlour' and 'a little vista' on to 'a small old street'. All the same he must have been aware that, in spite of the limited size of the rooms, typical of the 1720s, Lamb House was (and is) the most imposing house in Rye. As for prospective furnishing, James

tells his sister-in-law Alice, he is developing 'the most avid and gluttonous eye and most infernal watching patience in respect of lurking "occasions" in not too-delusive Chippendale and Sheraton.'

The house's historical connections came from it having been the residence of the Lamb family, who had provided a succession of town mayors. Royalty had slept there: in his enthusiasm, Henry James announced that it had been George II, then both George I and George II. Finally he settled for historical accuracy: the ship carrying George I from Hannover to England in 1726 was driven ashore on Camber Sands. The Mayor of Rye, James Lamb, gave His Majesty his own bedroom, a panelled room on the first floor overlooking the garden, which became known as the King's Room. Next to it is the Green Room, where Henry James chose to work in the winter months.

The small size of the ground floor rooms must have prompted James Lamb when he was Mayor to build the spacious annexe which had attracted the writer's attention in the first place. Known as the Garden Room, it became Henry James's work place in the summer. The German bomb which obliterated it in 1940 thus deprived us of the scene of some of the most extraordinary labours of the creative mind. There were, however, compensations: money for war damage was wisely used by the National Trust, not to rebuild the Garden Room itself, but to provide bathrooms, without which modern conveniences the Trust would hardly have been able to attract the distinguished tenants who have occupied Lamb House up to this day.

Henry James surprised his early visitors by his ready adaptation to provincial life. Already, according to A.C. Benson, he seemed to know 'everyone to speak to – an elderly clergyman in a pony carrriage, a young man riding. Three nice-looking girls . . . the dogs also bounding up to him'. He refused the Vice-Presidency of the Cricket Club, but joined the Golf Club, not to play but to have tea there. On one subject his attitude changed fairly rapidly. He had complained that about gardens he was 'densely ignorant – only just barely know dahlias from mignonette.' The garden at Lamb House is about one acre in extent, and though according to his lease he was meant to keep it up, he was prepared to do the minimum. He must soon have realised that such an attitude is barely tolerated in England, where the remark 'they let the garden go' carries the strongest moral opprobrium. And so George Gammon (a name to delight his employer) was set the task of conjuring up miracles. Henry James grew progressively more enthusiastic: in the end he was winning prizes at the Flower Show.

James had intended to occupy Lamb House from May to October. He moved in during June 1898 and a mild autumn made him linger on. A stream of visitors occupied his first months, but, since he never saw them in the mornings, they did not interfere with his work. Later he confronted the two enemies always to be confronted, until they finally vanquished him: solitude and the English winter. But there was a new element in his life which detained him at Rye for longer than he might otherwise have wished.

He had enthusiastically welcomed the bicycle; now he discovered the typewriter – not on his own account, but with one of the new breed of stenographers. His brother William, the Harvard philosopher, advised him to dictate his letters, but very soon he was using dictation for everything except his most intimate correspondence.

His first typist was a dour young scot, William MacAlpine, whom nobody seems to have liked. His two successors, Miss Weld and Miss Theodora Bosanquet, were far more sympathetic. They have left accounts of the Master at work. There were limitations: typewriters were not yet portable, and so he could only work at home. The Reform Club would not admit women on the premises: when he stayed there, he could not continue with whatever was in progress. And he could no longer go on

Henry James's typist Theodora Bosanquet and *(right)* his valet Burgess Noakes.

The garden in 1955 shortly after the restoration work on the house was completed by the National Trust. The new brickwork in the wall to the right marks the former extent of the garden room.

extensive visits without ceasing to work altogether.

Often, when we visit the residence of a famous man, we do not see the scene of his labours but the symbol of his success, the manner in which he informs the world that he has 'made it'. At Lamb House we are in a true 'cave of making', a place where the art of fiction was pushed to one of its utter limits, where the air ought still to echo with the explosions of those great 'raids on the inarticulate', as Henry James gave his genius free range.

Other novelists, their attention bound by the physical constrictions of writing – the scratching quill and guttering light, or, later, the jammed tape, the lost eraser, the fudged carbons, the grey detritus that accumulates in odd corners of the machine – have flinched from undertaking the numerous drafts and revisions from which comes command of form and structure. The three novels completed at Lamb House – *The Ambassadors, The Wings of the Dove,* and *The Golden Bowl* – achieved standards which his contemporaries, like H.G. Wells and Edith Wharton, were forced to find good reasons for not pursuing. Even if today word-processors lighten the novelist's burden, who can emulate James's dedicated apprenticeship in hotels, in *pensiones,* in boarding houses, in gentlemen's chambers? He had earned his freedom, and his right to create the standards by which he wished to be judged.

Lamb House was never just the country home of a distinguished personage. The seven people who attended to the needs of a single elderly bachelor were in charge of a power house. Apart from the typist, who lodged in the town, the rest of the staff included the Smiths (the married couple from De Vere Gardens, who spent the generous tips of American visitors on whisky, and were finally washed away), and their successor Mrs Paddington, an unsmiling woman and, in James's words, 'an absolutely brilliant economist.' There was Gammon the gardener, a parlourmaid and a housemaid, and, early in the new century, Burgess Noakes the 'apprentice', who joined the household at the age of 14. Burgess Noakes later became James's valet and travelled with him on his last visit to America in 1910. Encouraged by his employer, he enlisted in 1914, was wounded and rendered partly deaf; invalided out, he held James's hand when he was dying. Burgess Noakes lived on to become one of the last to remember Lamb House in the days of Mr James.

There were resident dogs: Tosca, who accompanied him from De Vere Gardens, was followed by a terrier, Nick, and then Max another dachshund, 'the best and gentlest and most reasonable and well-mannered as well as the most beautiful small animal of his kind to easily come across...' Max's social grace made it feasible for him to remain in residence when in 1905 his master visited America. 'If he is taken for walks', the prospective tenants were informed, 'all the latent beauty of his nature will come out.' When Max died in 1909, he had no successor.

Two crises were to be surmounted before Henry James was finally established in his 'great good place'. In February 1899, writing letters in the Green Room late at night, he noticed smoke coming through the floor. Transatlantic standards of comfort had been too much for the old house. Firemen found the beams between the floorboards smouldering, and downstairs the dining-room and the oak parlour were damaged. James summoned Edward Warren to undertake repairs and restoration, and fled to France and Italy. Today Warren's work in the house looks coarse and clumsy, especially the thick glazing bars on the upstairs windows, and the curious carving recess in the dining-room.

By him, and by others, Lamb House was under-appreciated. Edith Wharton called it 'an unadorned cube'. Even more derogatory was William James, basing his judgment on a mere description given by a third party. In 1900 Henry James was offered the freehold for £2000. He expected William to 'fraternize over the pleasure of my purchase' but instead received 'a colder blast than I could apprehend.'. William ridiculed the intention of paying $10,000 (the rate at the time) for a mere *pied-à-terre*. He had rarely given his approval to his brother's fiction; now he tried to deny him his effort to find a home. William James was an equally vulnerable character, in spite of his breezy manner; in February 1905 Henry was elected to the newly established American Academy of Arts and Sciences, William's election came up a month or two later but he declined the honour, giving the reason that 'my younger and shallower and vainer brother is already in the Academy'.

Nevertheless, Henry James went ahead with the purchase, taking on a couple of mortgages to mitigate the outlay needed. A year later, in a local bank, he was shown a golden bowl, presented by George I for the christening of James Lamb's child who had been born on the night the King landed in Rye. James wrote to a descendant of the Lambs expressing his admiration of the bowl (it was to give him the title of his last complete novel) and added that he felt:

> personally indebted to your peculiarly civilized ancestor who kindly conceived and put together to my benefit, so long ago, exactly the charming, braceful, sturdy little habitation (full of *sense*, discretion, taste) that suits alike my fancy and necessity, and in which I hope in time (DV) to end my days.

Henry James celebrated the new century by shaving off his beard: he became the stately figure we see in the Sargent portrait, reminding some of a Renaissance cardinal, others of a successfuul American entrepreneur. He spoke, in England at least, without an American accent, but those attending his 1905 lectures in America reported differently.

Though his earlier passion for dining out had diminished, he was assiduous in keeping up his social contacts. The solitude he experienced at Lamb House was a problem of the winter months. The fine weather brought plenty of visitors. Mornings remained sacred to work, and the cadences of his dictation resounded from the Garden Room. Afternoons were devoted to his visitors. There were bicycle rides, long walks accompanied by Max, and later motor trips. His friends included fellow writers, social figures from London, visiting Americans, and those of the younger generation on whom he fixed his affections. After his usual fashion, he kept his

Henry and William James, circa 1901 (from *Henry James at Home* by H. Montgomery Hyde).

friendships in compartments, according to their categories. Local residents were at first merely acquaintances but later he made several good friends – perhaps more interesting people had come to live in Rye.

Already this part of Kent and Sussex was attracting writers. Lodging at Rye Vicarage in 1895, James gave lunch to one of the first of them, Ford Madox Hueffer, then a rather pushy unconvincing young man, with a passion for literature and a reverence for its practitioners. Ford (the surname he later adopted) has contributed much that is amusing, if apocryphal, to the legend of the Master. Of this occasion, he has a convincing description of James's distress as the drunken butler, Smith, endeavoured to serve lunch.

James bore with, but scarcely encouraged, this persistent admirer (he refused to read Ford's perceptive book about his novels, the first full length study). When Violet Hunt, whom James had liked for years, went to live with Ford, who had deserted his wife, James felt 'compelled to regard all agreeable and unembarrassed communication between us as impossible'. Violet was barred from Lamb House at short notice. Ford himself may have had the last word: one of his best books, *The Good Soldier*, portrays a sexless puritanical New Englander misinterpreting the amatory intrigues of the English upper class.

James was distressed by bohemianism among writers because he believed that it prejudiced the chances of getting good work done. An example was Harold Frederic, author of *The Damnation of Theron Ware*. Frederic died after his mistress, a Christian Scientist, had refused him medical treatment, and left one legitimate and one illegitimate family. James (whom Frederic had described as 'an effeminate old donkey') came to the financial aid of the orphaned children.

But he was more closely concerned with Stephen Crane, whom he admired both as a man and a writer. Crane and his common-law wife Cora, former Madam of the Hotel de Dream, Jacksonville, Florida, rented Brede Place, a mediaeval manor house some eight miles from Rye. They gave lavish entertainments but, in spite of his concern and admiration, James was rarely present though once, accompanied by Cora, he was photographed eating an American doughnut with apparent distaste.

Soon afterwards, Crane's death from consumption brought to an end this encounter with the forerunners of the 'tough guy' school of American fiction. Cora went back to Florida and to brothel-keeping; when she reappeared in England some years later, Mr James was 'not at home'.

Other literary neighbours fitted in more closely with his idea of the dignity of the profession. Together with Edmund Gosse, he bicycled over to Sandgate for his first meeting with H.G. Wells. In spite of their increasingly different conceptions of the novel, Wells and James remained on friendly terms – with the result that Wells's violent attack on everything that James stood for, incorporated in *Boon* published in 1915, came to the victim as a devastating surprise.

With the most distinguished of his neighbours, Joseph Conrad, there was less divergence in aim. Conrad had written of the man he called 'the historian of fine consciences', and James was unambiguous in his praise of *The Nigger of the Narcissus*, though he privately referred to Conrad's later novels as 'wastes of desolation'. Socially, though, James felt ill at ease. For him, Conrad was 'the mariner-novelist', a man of uncertain provenance and morbid temperament, burdened with an uneducated wife who made a fuss if sufficient attention was not paid to her. When Ottoline Morrell wished to meet Conrad, James warned her: 'He's never met a lady in his life'. At that time only Edward Garnett knew of Conrad's background in the Polish nobility.

Henry James and Joseph Conrad spoke to one another in French, each elaborately courteous in a language in which formality can easily supplant authenticity. Conrad's reiterated 'Cher Mâitre' is a title which in England could surely never be without a touch of humorous irony. Nor, one thinks, would Henry James have wished it to be.

For some reason, once established in his 'great good place', James's thoughts returned more frequently to his native land. Unlike his fiction of the nineties, his three Lamb House novels show a preponderance of American characters, and he followed their publication with his triumphant visit to America in 1905.

Since he could now offer extended hospitality, it is not surprising that his most persistent visitors should be Americans. Some, like his niece and two nephews, William's children, learned as part of their European education a growing respect and admiration for the uncle they had only too often heard disparaged at home. Others were permanent expatriates like himself, such as the crippled Jonathan Sturges, 'the little demon', who told him all the scurrilous London gossip. No relation, and a less frequent visitor, was Howard Overing Sturgis, who had made his own 'great good place' at Queen's Acre, Windsor. James's judgement of this friend's entertaining novel *Belchamber* was a good deal too ruthless: Sturgis went back to *petit point* and did not publish again. He was, as E.M. Forster put it, 'a bit of a muff, and far, far, from a fool.'

Far the most important among his American friends was Edith Wharton. In this gifted complicated woman he met his match. The numberless ironies in their comments on each other make it difficult to decide how much affection was involved. Their candid criticism of each other's work often caused well-concealed pain. Yet James knew all the complexities of Mrs Wharton's love affairs, details of which have remained hidden from the rest of the world until quite recently.

Mrs Wharton was the type of talented American lady whose cisatlantic arrivals are presaged by an exchange of groans before they are welcomed with open arms. When James first got to know her, she already lived in great style in America and France. Herself a member of the old New York aristocracy, she had many English friends but was less at home here. 'She never forgot she was a Rhinelander and a Jones', one of her friends, Raymond Mortimer, wrote, 'and we never remembered'.

Henry James in front of the french windows from the dining room, which were among Edmund Warren's alterations to the house.

A pastel drawing of Joseph Conrad by William Rothenstein, 1903 *(National Portrait Gallery)*.

Edith Wharton was in many ways James's guardian angel, though he called her 'the angel of devastation' and later 'the Firebird' after seeing the Ballet Russe.

In letters to friends James referred to her as 'the Angel of Devastation', he wrote of her 'eagle pounce and her eagle flight' and deplored the expense involved in following her trajectory. After his death, she revenged herself in writerly fashion in *A Backward Glance*. Alone among the visitors to Lamb House, she complained of the hospitality received; commenting on his (or Mrs Paddington's) 'anxious frugality', on puddings served up on successive days 'with their ravages unrepaired'; describing the flower borders as 'unkempt', and even criticizing his ability to deal with servants (although something of a martinet, James seems to have been served with loyalty and devotion to the end of his life).

She could not shake his affection for his home. It was, after all, the place where time was never wasted, where the true purpose of his life became clear. When in 1907 she captured him for a long and luxurious tour of France in her new Panhard, driven by an American chauffeur, James looked back to Lamb House 'so russet and humble and so British and so pervaded by boiled mutton and turnips; and yet withal so intensely precious and so calculated to rack me with homesickness.'

Indeed, these years at Rye were among his happiest: the age of the telephone and motor car was in full swing, and he had many visitors. He made friends among the residents, and from one of them, Sydney Waterlow, he heard of a whole new generation of admirers at Cambridge. One of these was E.M. Forster, who wrote of a visit to Lamb House: 'It is a funny sensation going to see a really first class person. I felt all that the ordinary healthy man feels in the presence of a lord.' Leonard Woolf described his own and his friend Lytton Strachey's reactions to the novels:

> The strange, Jamesian, convoluted beauty and subtlety of them act upon those who yield to them like drink or drugs; for a time we became addicts, habitual drunkards – never, perhaps, quite serious but playing at seeing the world of Trinity and Cambridge as a Jamesian phantasmagoria...

In the end Henry James was invited to visit Cambridge by the undergraduate Geoffrey Keynes and a friend. The visit had its awkward moments: a falling punt pole struck the Master on the head, and, among what he described as 'the queer little all juvenile gaping group', he rather annoyingly fastened his attention on a marginal figure, a young poet of astonishing beauty. He claimed to be relieved when Desmond Macarthy told him that Rupert Brooke as a poet was 'no good', 'for with *that* appearance if he had talent it would be too unfair'.

There were other young men whose charm outweighed the limitations of their talent. An early visitor to Lamb House was the young Norwegian-American sculptor, Henrik Anderson, whom James had met in Rome. Of megalomaniac ambition but mediocre gifts, he nevertheless aroused a warm affection: James confessed a longing 'to put my arms around you and make you lean on me as a brother and a lover.' Later Jocelyn Persse, an Anglo-Irish gentleman of great charm and no personal ambition, uninterested in literature, came closest to reciprocating these feelings; for him, Henry James was 'the dearest human being I have ever known'. More articulate and unashamedly ambitious, Hugh Walpole was always welcome in Rye. Letters to him began 'belovedest little Hugh' and ended 'I am yours, dearest Hugh, *yours* H.J.'. All the same, Walpole reported that 'he told me gently that I was an idiot and that my novels were worthless'. Fortunately for Walpole's later career, the world was not peopled with Henry Jameses.

James may have believed that Persse and Walpole destroyed his letters. He was, however, a man of infinite caution. He had closely followed the Oscar Wilde scandal, in which a stolen letter featured prominently; he had helped Mrs Wharton's lover to recover correspondence with which he was being blackmailed by an ex-mistress. James surely knew that because his affections did not transgress the laws of the day, he had nothing to fear.

Surrounded by friends, he could look forward to a calm old age. His physical health was good, but a shadow of despair lay in the way, despair that was to cause his separation from the house he had loved. Since his American tour of 1905, his creative energy had gone into the revision of his novels and tales for the New York edition of his works. The project turned out to be a disaster with the reading public – though his complaint 'it has landed me in bankruptcy' was metaphorical, or rather, psychological. (Later readers too have voted against the New York edition by seeking out, wherever possible, the unrevised versions.)

Disappointment and depression brought on heart trouble and renewed attacks of gout. That he was greatly overweight would have troubled Edwardian doctors less than it might today. In 1909 he made a big bonfire of letters and private papers in the garden at Lamb House, a proceeding designed to obstruct future biographers. The conflagration offered only temporary relief from his melancholy. His nephew Harry arrived to find him in deep depression, facing the frustration of all his hopes and ambitions: 'there was nothing for me to do but sit by his side and hold his hand while he panted and sobbed for two hours until the doctor arrived.'

By the following year, occasional periods of elation broke through the gloom. William, himself a sick man, came over with his wife Alice to stay at Lamb House. The three of them travelled in Europe together, staying at Bad Nauheim, where William took the cure. Then Henry decided to accompany them back to America – 'I am wholly unfit to be alone' he wrote – and they sailed on the 12 August. William died on the 26 August at his country home in New England.

Overwhelmed by grief for his brother, and still fearful of solitude, Henry James lingered on in Boston and Cambridge until late the following year. He saw many old friends, he was given an honorary degree by Harvard, but he was bored. 'This is a hard country to love', he wrote, and 'better fifty years of fogland!' Mrs Wharton, herself undergoing a crisis while she decided whether or not to divorce her husband, diagnosed his plight and hurried him back to England. 'What a woman! Her imagination boggles at nothing! She does not scruple to project me in naked flight across the Atlantic!'

Throughout his life he had adored his elder brother and sought for his approbation which was only rarely offered. Now, intermixed with his grief, was a certain liberation and his creative powers returned to him with the planning of his two autobiographical memoirs. At the same time he decided to change the pattern of his life. In London he was to live at the Reform Club and go daily to Miss Bosanquet's flat to dictate *A Small Boy and Others* and *Notes of a Son and Brother*. Around this time he told Sydney Waterlow: 'Little Rye – poor little Rye – I find life there intolerable – has had to be deserted – no, not *permanently* deserted, heaven forbid, – but I have had to make a nest – a perch – for myself in London, which involves the desertion of Rye for the winter – only temporarily, *hibernetically* speaking.'

Late in 1912 he found a flat, 21 Carlyle Mansions in Chelsea, and brought up books and furniture, as well as his servants, from Rye. Henceforward Lamb House was for the summers only. His loud and hyperbolic lamentations only remind us that this was what he had intended to do in the first place, over ten years before, until the exigencies of his creative life had obliged him to hang on through the winter months.

Returning to London, he re-entered the glittering network of his social relationships. For his seventieth birthday, in 1913, after managing to frustrate a plan of Edith Wharton's to provide him with a substantial sum of money, he received a golden bowl of his own – a Charles II silver-gilt porringer and dish – for which his friends in London, Rye and elsewhere had subscribed. The balance of their donation went to pay for the portrait by John Singer Sargent, which James insisted should be the property of the National Portrait Gallery. He was pleased with it, as most people have been since: 'Sargent at his very best and poor old HJ not at his worst... I am all large and luscious rotundity – by which you may see how true a thing it is.' This anniversary found him at the height of his fame, and even if it was a fame which owed as much to his gift for friendship and his effulgent social presence as to the diffusion of his writings, it must have given him great satisfaction.

With his London life restored, he could spend the warm days at Lamb House – with the usual explosive irruptions of Mrs Wharton (since the arrival of the Russian Ballet, he had re-christened her 'the Firebird'). Another regular, and rival, companion was his niece Peggy, who spent the winter with him in London. Famously, the year 1914 offered 'the most beautiful English summer conceivable'

John Singer Sargent's portrait of Henry James of 1913, painted to celebrate his seventieth birthday. James remarked 'Sargent at his very best and poor old HJ not at his worst ...' *(National Portrait Gallery)*.

but after the beginning of August he was aware only of 'the shining indifference of nature', and of 'a nightmare from which there is no waking save in sleep.' Work became impossible. Burgess Noakes joined up: 'It was like losing an arm or a leg'. Henry James left Rye in September, just as the first Belgian refugees began streaming through the little town.

James and Edith Wharton, with their American generosity of spirit, immediately involved themselves in wartime activities, Mrs Wharton with the Red Cross in France, and James, following the example of his great compatriot Walt Whitman during the Civil War, began visiting the wounded in hospitals. First the Belgians (who were surely troubled by his Parisian French) and then the English soldiers as well. One of his last pieces of writing was a memoir of Rupert Brooke, who died in April 1915.

That summer Henry James learnt that as an alien, even if a friendly one, he would require a police permit whenever he visited Rye. Until now he had hardly considered his nationality to be a problem (this was before the days when the IRS pursued American citizens to the ends of the earth). His love for Lamb House, together with his passionate involvement with the Allied cause, impelled him to seek naturalization. With the Prime Minister, H.H. Asquith and Edmund Gosse as sponsors, he took the oath of allegiance on the 28 July. Congratulations poured in from England, condemnation from the United States. There the blight on his reputation was to last for at least 30 years, until the academic study of American literature took off as a major industry.

Henry James did not reach Lamb House until October of that year. In the garden he saw for the first time the gap left by the great mulberry tree, brought down by the storms of the previous winter: 'Once the fury of the tempest really descended, he was bound to give way because his old heart was dead, his immense old trunk was hollow.' James spent much time in burning papers and photographs, until recurrent heart trouble forced him to return to London to be near his doctor. This, physically at any rate, was his final visit to Lamb House. But his transforming imagination, so much the most significant part of his being, was to return him there in the last days of his life.

On the 2 December, his maid, Minny Kidd, found James lying on his bedroom floor at Carlyle Mansions, and heard him say, 'it's the beast in the jungle, and it's sprung'. A second stroke threw his unremittingly active mind into tragic confusion. Sometimes he believed himself mad, and feared visitors would notice. Then he thought himself on board ship or in a hotel, or visiting Cork, Dublin, Edinburgh or New York. Sometimes he was Napoleon: he dictated to Miss Bosanquet a letter giving instructions to his sister and brothers for the redecoration of the Tuileries.

Meanwhile at his bedside a situation was developing which would have delighted the author of *The Bostonians* and *The Spoils of Poynton*: hastening from America, Alice James and her daughter Peggy reacted with marked hostility to the continued presence of Theodora Bosanquet. Unaware of the niceties of English life, they treated her as a servant; in addition they knew her to be in constant touch with Mrs Wharton, concerning whose moral reputation they had heard distressing reports.

Mrs James had, at this late date, become aware that her ineffectual and eccentric brother-in-law was a great and important figure. However when the Order of Merit was awarded him in the New Year's Honours of 1916, it was to Minny Kidd that he whispered 'Turn off the light so as to spare my blushes'. When Mrs James intervened while he was talking to Burgess Noakes, she was quelled by 'What is this voice from Boston, Massachusetts, breaking in with irrelevant remarks in my conversation with Burgess?'

Nevertheless, Mrs James magnanimously reported back to Boston that: 'he very especially likes Burgess. Burgess James he called him yesterday. It is a touching sight to see little Burgess holding his hand and half kneeling in the chair beside him, his face very near to Henry trying to understand the confused words that Henry murmurs to him.' Burgess, invalided out of the Army, was now almost totally deaf.

It may have been the constant presence of Burgess and Minny which caused him to believe, six weeks before his death on the 23 February 1916, that he was once again back at Lamb House. What memories, what images might have returned then to the secret chambers of consciousness? Perhaps of that first summer when he pushed his bicycle up the steep street, where grass sprouted between the cobbles, to make 'sheep's eyes' at Lamb House; that same street which saw disaster overtake Rudyard Kipling's brand new £2000 car, so that it became a total loss, and the Kiplings had to return home ignominiously by train; the two visits of Hendrik Anderson, the handsome defeated sculptor, so like one of his own early creations; the old garden walls, over which he had been horrified to see his brother William, perched on the top of a ladder, trying to catch a glimpse of the grotesque figure of G.K. Chesterton; the long delayed departure of the Smiths, his cook and butler, by then 'two saturated and demoralised victims'; the intrusions of Ford Madox Hueffer, least welcome among his admirers; Mrs Conrad at tea, taking offence because she was not served first; the child Borys Conrad bursting out on his first sight of the Master 'Oh, isn't he an elegant fowl!'; Stephen Crane's hectic and tragic sojourn nearby; Bernard Shaw shocked when his host kissed him on both cheeks... But much of this we know from the recollections of others, which have gone to make up the legend of the Master. In his own mind the beloved house would have glowed in a rather different light. Although a place of friendships, it was also the scene of some of his greatest labours, the arena of his unrelenting struggle to give aesthetic form to the chaos of experience. Lamb House had seen the culmination of his lifetime's effort to breach the walls of solitude and make from them the foundations of the palace of art.

Rudyard Kipling at Bateman's

Jonathan Keates

'The King and I', ran Queen Mary's telegram, 'are grieved to hear of the death this morning of Mr Kipling. We shall mourn him not only as a great national poet, but as a personal friend of many years.' The Prince of Wales, more economical, begged the writer's widow to 'accept my sincere sympathy in the sad loss you have sustained by the death of your distinguished husband', while his great-uncle the Duke of Connaught, never a man to waste words, telegraphed simply 'Deepest sympathy in your sad loss.'

Everyone – but everyone – was at the funeral in Poet's Corner, and Westminster Abbey was so packed that the vergers had difficulty in opening the doors. The famous 'Recessional', with its sinisterly equivocal refrain of 'Lest we forget, lest we forget', had been given no less than 28 different settings, but it was the strains of John Bacchus Dykes's version from *Hymns Ancient and Modern* which floated over the Union Jack-draped coffin, whose pall-bearers with a nice appropriateness, included Kipling's cousin the Prime Minister Stanley Baldwin and his literary agent A.P. Watt.

Literature doffed its hat in the persons of Laurence Binyon, Alfred Noyes and E.V. Lucas; the visual arts were represented by Sir William Rothenstein; music by the critic of the *Morning Post*; the stage by Lady Tree; the press by Lord Beaverbrook; and the Tory party by the Chancellor of the Exchequer, Mrs Chamberlain and 'Mr A. Duff Cooper, Secretary for War'. Stalky and M'Turk materialized as G.C. Beresford and Major-General Dunsterville, and a Sussex workman sent a wreath of oak, ash and thorn. Rubbing shoulders with the ambassadors of France, Brazil, Belgium, Italy, Holland, Denmark and Finland were mourners from the Imperial War Graves Commission, the Boy Scouts, the Athenaeum and the London Library.

Yet despite the encyclopaedic nature of this official despatch to eternity, we may wonder what Kipling himself would have thought of it all. His was the fatal gift of being universally accessible: the vast range of his achievement in poetry and prose suggests that there was hardly an area of human life he had failed to probe. The nature of his artistic success was unique among contemporary writers in that it was gained not simply among a self-consciously literate public but in areas where books were otherwise thought of either as subversive or boring or else never read at all. Practically everyone knew *The Absent-Minded Beggar* and *The Road to Mandalay*, the cliché of empire had absorbed *The White Man's Burden* and *Gunga Din*, two generations of children and adults had taken *The Jungle Book, The Just-so Stories* and *Puck of Pook's Hill* to their hearts, and 'If' was graven in stone, inscribed on vellum or burned in poker-work everywhere from Pitcairn Island to Port Swettenham...

Rudyard Kipling (1856-1936) at Batemans. An unpublished photograph from a family album.

If you can keep your head when all about you
Are losing theirs and blaming it on you,
If you can trust yourself when all men doubt you
But make allowance for their doubting too;

No one, however, laboured more strenuously to escape from the scourge of his own popularity. His horror of being interviewed was notorious, exacerbated as it had been by the buccaneering tactics of some American journalists during his years in Vermont. His cousin Angela Thirkell, recalling life at The Elms, Rottingdean, where the Kiplings lived from 1897 to 1902 notes that they were 'obliged to have the gate boarded over in self-defence, leaving a little hole with a sliding shutter through which you put your hand to open it... Not once or twice did Aunt Carrie [Mrs Kipling] have to ask a kneeling crowd of sightseers to move aside and let her go into her own house.' Neighbours were often helpful in deflecting the faithful, either by simple ruses of ignorance or through more magisterial measures: a Mrs Ridsdale, for instance, would always answer tourists' enquiries for directions with 'Have you read anything of his?' and if the response was 'No' they were inevitably dismissed with a 'Then I won't tell you' as she sailed on down the village street.

Provoked beyond endurance Kipling could be awesomely, unforgettably rude. One well-meaning New York hostess, indulging her fancies in a manner she supposed would captivate the creator of Mowgli and Bagheera, decked her salon with jungle exotics and enlisted the aid of real monkeys to re-enact the 'flung festoon' of the Bandar-Log. As the guests of honour arrived a popular baritone sang *Gunga Din* to orchestral accompaniment. The Kiplings left before the dinner was over.

Among the paradoxes of his life, however, was that the ideal retreat from the world's prying and adulation should not have been discovered until Kipling, at 36,

The approach to Batemans from Burwash Village.

Rudyard and Carrie Kipling by the front door.

was already at the height of his fame. Life at Rottingdean had implanted in him a fondness for Sussex which was to grow into an enduring passion. Still exclusively rural and without that cosmetic blandness of aspect which recent decades of commuter settlement have brought to its villages, the rolling country, with its downlands, forests and fat pastures watered by Arun, Rother and Glynde, took on for the writer the role of an essential paradigm of the English experience. True, this was subsequently to be vulgarized by poets in the 'Chesterbelloc' mould, reflected at its worst in the Georgian anthologies of Sir Edward Marsh and J.C. Squire, but to Kipling it offered a profound fascination. And at the heart of this, visually and spiritually, lay Bateman's itself.

The house had captivated him from the very first. In one of those gleaming motor cars, his passion for which so bemused his fellow author Henry James, he recalls in *Something of Myself,* '"That's her! The Only She! Make an honest woman of her – quick!" We entered and felt her Spirit – her Feng Shui – to be good. We went through every room and found no shadow of ancient regrets, stifled miseries, nor any menace though the "new" end of her was three hundred years old.'

In its shape and colours Bateman's is so archetypally the small English manor house of fantasy, legend and tradition that an initial encounter with it hardly seems real. It is almost as if Kipling had imagined it into existence in order to give body to his particular notion of what it meant to belong to Sussex, a notion founded to some extent on his awareness of himself as an alien observer. The boy who was born in India, the man who had settled happily enough in New England and South Africa, the restless globetrotter of *Captains Courageous* and *From Sea to Sea*, now became the colonist of his own dreams.

The entrance (east) front in 1908, six years after Kipling moved there.

Batemans at haytime, 1908.

The herbaceous border in front of the Oast House, from the north-east.

Completed in 1634, Bateman's was probably built for a prosperous ironmaster in the days when the Weald of Sussex and Kent smoked and clattered with metal-smelting forges. Though the discovery of Midland coal as a cheaper substitute for charcoal in the smelting process ultimately killed off this southern industry, Bateman's itself survived as a farm, with the addition of an oast house and the rebuilt mill at the end of the garden. On his arrival, Kipling installed his own electricity by laying a deep-sea cable in a trench from the mill to the house worked by a turbine from the nearby river Dudwell, and began refurbishing the interior in a manner befitting a nephew of Burne-Jones, the son of a professional artist, and a writer blessed with greater visual refinement than most of his literary contemporaries (Bloomsbury not always excepted).

The surprise of the house – for surprise there undoubtedly is – springs precisely from this background. Notice, for example, the plaster relief of Mowgli with the animals which hangs in the inner hall, and the sepia drawing for Kipling's bookplate above the bookcase in the study. These are the work of his father John Lockwood Kipling, Director of the Lahore Museum and an artist nurtured on the loftiest principles of Morris and Voysey, yet neither these nor the Whistler lithographs in the West Bedroom, nor Sir Edward Poynter's watercolours in the hall, nor even the scattering of Oriental *objets d'art* in brass and terracotta, are wholly out of keeping with the taste which animated the decor of Bateman's as a whole.

For this was the age of the Arts and Crafts movement, and the rediscovery of the traditional skills of English builders and craftsmen. This romantic ruralism, inspired by the English vernacular, aimed to reinvigorate architecture and interior design. Bateman's reflects this, not merely in the Kiplings' choice of it, but in the wealth of Jacobean and Caroline furnishings which bear witness to the crucial reappraisal of English decorative art taking place during the period when they first moved into the house. In one sense Bateman's *is* the English Kipling – a culture and a heritage not his by birthright and local association, but assumed, adopted, imagined.

The trouble with any writer's house is, of course, that feeling which we always cherish, however subconsciously, that somewhere or other among its staircases and corridors we shall push open a door and stumble upon genius at work. A corresponding awareness that this can never be so creates a species of haunted, tomb-like sadness comparable to no other: the lovingly-amassed rows of first editions, the display case devoted to the publications of the Society – dismal little altar of the cult – the caricatures and signed photographs, the lifeless array of manuscripts and letters, the terrible collection of personal objects like things tossed aside in a headlong flight from death, none of these can bring back what we have come to find.

Bateman's distills its own version of this particular melancholy, one which generates a curious allure. Some sadness there always was. The death of Kipling's son John during the Great War at the age of 18 was a blow from which the writer never fully recovered. It seems to have developed in him a type of rueful meditativeness which in itself was an extension of that essentially retiring quality in Kipling so puzzling to those who wanted continually to lionize him.

Visitors, approaching with whatever kind of trepidation, nevertheless recalled the spirit of the house and the quirks of Kipling in the guise of the country landowner, telling his secretary, Miss Ponton, 'You'll get on all right with the farm hands if you treat the men as boys of fourteen and the women as younger in intellect' and taking a pride in registering the markings and names – Bateman's Blizzard, Bateman's Bunting, Bateman's Butterpat – of his calves in the Guernsey Herd Book. Flattered by his absorbing interest in other people's 'shop talk', they responded naively to his willingness to listen, unaware that their plain narratives of life in distant outposts or

The hall and parlour in 1908.

on the trade routes of empire were being stored among the lumber of his restless imagination.

Children and young people especially were beguiled by Kipling's combination of unforced charm and instantly winning bluntness as master of Bateman's. Arthur Gordon, an American Rhodes scholar, arrived in respectful dread, only to be whisked off by his host to 'inspect my navy', a six-foot skiff on the garden pond.

Sir William Rothenstein's pencil drawing of Rudyard Kipling, *c.*1932 *(National Portrait Gallery).*

Kipling's study as it is today. Over the fireplace is Philip Burne-Jones's portrait of Carrie Kipling.

Gordon's nervousness made him break the hand-cranked paddle-wheel and the pair had to be rescued by the gardener with a long rake, but by then Kipling's unique ability to engage, 'something about him that drove the shyness out of you, a kind of understanding that went deeper than words and set up an instantaneous closeness', had got to work. Rupert Croft-Cooke, a pert 18 year old on a motorcycle, coming for tea and sound professional advice, noted that 'the grey bushes of eyebrow, the domed head, the thick lenses of his spectacles and the Great Name should have made him an awesome person, but with supreme tact he talked like a fellow adolescent, was enthusiastic or condemnatory of writers of the past, as though after a study tea at school we were smoking illicit cigarettes over a discussion of favourite authors.'

Yet it has often seemed to visitors to Bateman's since Kipling's death that the mellowness of weathered sandstone and handsome brick chimney stacks masks something destined to remain perpetually undisclosed. Some have even felt a distinct unease, brought about less by a haunting than by an awareness of what is not there. On the table in the study lie the writer's working tools, the lacquered pen tray, the paperweight said to have belonged to Warren Hastings, the 'inky foot rule and a Father of Penwipers, which a much loved housemaid of ours presented yearly'. There too is the wastepaper basket for discarded drafts and botched attempts, and on the wall hangs Philip Burne-Jones's creditable evocation of the man himself at work. In the end, however, it is all not much more than literary archaeology. Perhaps, in a last analysis, the real Kipling was neither interred in the Abbey nor gathered up at Bateman's but scattered instead across those immense portions of the globe where he had set his mark on the consciousness of an entire generation.

Shaw at Shaw's Corner

Michael Holroyd

On 5 October 1943, just over three weeks after his wife's death, Bernard Shaw wrote to the Secretary of the National Trust offering to bequeath his house to the Trust. 'I own the freehold of a ten room house in the village of Ayot St Lawrence in Herts', he wrote, 'where I have lived for the last 35 years – longer than in any other of my residences. I am now in my 87th year, and about to make my last will... The house stands in a plot of some two acres. There is a detached garage and greenhouse, and scraps of kitchen garden, orchard, and lawn, with a belt of trees... Has such a trifle any use or interest for the National Trust?'

An appointment was fixed for a member of the staff, James Lees-Milne, to visit the house on the afternoon of February 9, 1944. It made a dismal impression on him. 'Shaw's Corner is a very ugly dark red brick villa, built in 1902', he noted in his diary.

> I rang the bell and a small maid in uniform led me across the hall to a drawing room, with open views on to the garden and the country beyond, for the house is at the end of the village... There was a fire burning in the pinched little grate. Walls distempered, the distemper flaking badly in patches. The quality of the contents of the room was on a par with that of the villa. Indifferent water colours of the Roman Campagna, trout pools, etc. in cheap gilt frames. One rather good veneered Queen Anne bureau (for which G.B.S. had given £80) and one fake lacquer bureau. In the window a statuette of himself by Paul Troubetskoy. On the mantelpiece a late Staffordshire figure of Shakespeare (for which he paid 10/-), a china house, the lid of which forms a box. Only a few conventionally bound classics plus Osbert Sitwell's latest publication prominently displayed on a table. Two stiff armchairs before the fire and brass fender. A shoddy three-ply screen attached to the fireplace to shelter from draughts anyone sitting between the fire and doorway.

It was cold, raining and generally disagreeable. But Lees-Milne's spirits began to lift once Shaw appeared. His diary entry for that day gives the most vivid picture we have of Shaw in old age at Ayot St Lawrence:

> Presently the door opened and in came the great man. I was instantly struck by the snow-white head and beard, the blue eyes and the blue nose, with a small ripe spot over the left nostril. He was not so tall as I imagined, for he stoops slightly. He was dressed in a pepper-and-salt knickerbocker suit. A loose, yellow tie from a pink collar over a thick woollen vest rather than shirt. Several waistcoats. Mittens over blue hands. He evidently feels the cold for there were electric fires in every room and the passage. I had not expected the strong Irish brogue. This peasant origin makes him all the more impressive... G.B.S. said he wished to impose no conditions on the hand over, but he did not wish the

George Bernard Shaw (1856-1950) in the garden at Shaw's Corner on his ninetieth birthday in 1946.

Shaw's Corner, Ayot St Lawrence, Hertfordshire.

(Right) Shaw at work in the hut which he called 'The Wilderness'.

house to become a dead museum. Hoped it would be a living shrine. He wanted to settle matters now, for since his wife's death he was bound to re-make his will, and in three years' time he might be quite dotty, if he was alive at all... Took me into his study where he works at an untidy writing table. In this room is another Queen Anne bureau. The wall facing it is covered with reference books, and all the bound proofs of his own books, corrected by him. These, I said, ought to remain here... He ran upstairs, pointing admiringly to the enlarged bird etchings on the stair wall...

When he smiles his face softens and becomes engaging. He is not at all deaf, but comes close up to one to talk, breathing into one's face. His breath is remarkably sweet for an old man's. Having looked upstairs we descended. He tripped going down, and I was afraid he was going to fall headlong. He then said, "We will go out and have a look at the curtilage" – rolling the *r* of this unusual word. It was fearfully cold by now, and raining heavily. He put on a long, snow-white mackintosh and chose a stick. From the hall hat-rack, hung with a variety of curious headgear, he took an archaic rough felt hat, of a buff colour, high in crown and wide of brim. In this garb he resembled Carlyle, and was the very picture of the sage, striding forth, a little wobbly and bent perhaps, pointing out the extent of the "curtilage" and the line of the hedge which he had de-rooted with his own hands so as to lengthen the garden. The boundary trees of spruce were planted by him. "Trees grow like mushrooms in these parts", he said. We came to a little asbestos roofed summer house that revolves on its own axis. Here he also writes and works. There is a little table covered with writing material, and a couch. The summer house was padlocked. I said, "Do you sit out here in the winter then?" "I have an electric stove", and he pointed to a thick cable attached to the summer house from an iron pylon behind it. "This will be an attraction to the *birthplace*, if it survives," he said. We passed piles of logs, which he told me he had chopped himself. He showed me

his and his wife's initials carved on the coach-house door and engraved on a glass pane of the greenhouse. Took me into the coach house where there are three cars under dust sheets, one a Rolls Royce...

A collie puppy dog met us in the road and jumped up at the old man who paid it much attention... By the time we got back to the house I was wet through.

Tea was brought on a tray to the drawing room. A glass of milk only for him; but tea and cakes for me. I was given a mug to drink out of...

At 5.15 G.B.S. jumped up, saying it was getting dark and he had kept me a quarter of an hour too long. Thanked me for coming. I said I had enjoyed the afternoon immensely. He said he had too... He came out on to the road without hat or coat and stood until I drove off. In the mirror I watched him still standing on the road.

Shaw had turned himself at Ayot into a living advertisement for his vegetarianism, teetotalism, economic philosophy and hygienic clothing. The agility of his mind and body, the mixture of kindness and impersonality, modesty and self-advertisement and the cast-iron impeccable good manners that completely concealed his private grief over the recent death of Charlotte, his wife, were all essential parts of the paradoxical Shavian phenomenon. 'I am not neglecting the matter', he wrote to assure James Lees-Milne the following month, 'as I am in mortal dread of dying before it is settled.' He was trying to arrange matters so that, except for a few items that were to be personally disposed of, he could leave the entire contents of the house to the Trust. 'I shall transfer from London all the pictures and statuettes and busts

The drawing room at Shaw's Corner today. Shaw assembled the various images of himself prior to giving the house to the National Trust.

that are there to titivate Shaw's Corner as a showplace', he explained. 'The Trust can sell what is superfluous to pay for repairs.'

Shaw's Will is one of the most public-spirited testaments ever made. He had never believed in supporting private charities and relieving the ratepayers of their public duties – 'he wouldn't even give something to the lady in the village who collected for the Red Cross', a bewildered neighbour at Ayot St Lawrence remembered. Though he publicised himself as a skinflint, his letters reveal that for much of his life he had secretly given money to people, sometimes warning them that they would get no more if ever they made this information public. He was a collectivist and held that equality of income plus abolition of private property should add up to the socialist formula for a better way of life. The personal annuities he left to old servants and distant relatives were cautiously calculated and pretty well equal. His residuary legatees, who since his death have received almost all his royalties, comprised the three colleges of his university: the National Gallery of Ireland round which he used to prowl for hours when a boy; the Royal Academy of Dramatic Art representing the theatre from which he had made his livelihood; and the British Museum 'in acknowledgement of the incalculable value to me of my daily resort to the Reading Room of that Institution at the beginning of my career.'

Shaw's father had been an alcoholic and his mother, who had a low opinion of men, gave him little affection. Believing he had inherited a tendency to an addiction, he had transferred it from drink to work; and believing himself to be unlovable, he had replaced the need for love with a craving for public attention. In the Shavian philosophy the State becomes our parents, providing us with money and welfare as ideal parents are pictured giving their children care and protection. Shaw's humanity, beneath which move all sorts of subversive fantasies, was rigorously unsentimental. To his secretary, Blanche Patch, it seemed odd that he would each day 'soak bits of bread in some of the Marmite vegetable soup with which he began his lunch', but after scattering it from the french window on to the lawn never wait to watch the birds fly down.

He had scrupulously prepared his Will and it provoked a good deal of topsy-turvy confusion. He attempted to leave his initial royalties to the setting up of a new phonetic alphabet. By reducing the amount of print this would effect such huge economies, he had told James Lees-Milne, as to 'enable Great Britain to pay for another war as soon as the present one was over' – and if that did not appeal to the Government he did not know what would. In fact, the scheme was to lead to a huge expenditure of time and some Gilbertian antics in the Chancery Division of the High Court ('And who appears for the poor alphabet?' asked Mr Justice Harman. 'The Attorney-General, my lord'). Finally, seven years after his death, the alphabet was allocated a sum not in excess of £8,300. As for Shaw's Corner, it had been given, with its contents, to the nation, but Shaw had omitted to endow the house, believing that its upkeep should be met from the entrance fees of those who came to see it. This was his way of measuring a living shrine as against a dead museum. 'I never understood why Mr Shaw didn't endow the house instead of leaving all his money to that old alphabet of his', complained Alice Laden, his cook. She stayed on for a time as the Custodian. 'It was a completely different place without Mr Shaw', she said, 'and yet the same place. I almost felt I was seeing his ghost at times.'

Six weeks after Shaw's death James Lees-Milne went down again accompanied by the Secretary of the National Trust, Jack Rathbone, and Harold Nicolson. Everything was as G.B.S. had left it. They walked round the garden, down the sloping lawn, across the rough grass and around the elongated rose-beds. 'A bank, with a statue of St Joan', Harold Nicolson observed in his diary. 'A hut in which he worked... Postcards, envelopes, a calendar marking the day of his death, curiously enough a

Bible and prayer-book and Crockford's Directory, a pair of mittens... It will be essential to keep the furniture exactly as it is. All his hats and coats and nailbrushes etc are here. His long woollen stockings and his thick underclothes... Even the door-knocker is an image of himself.' The house, Nicolson decided, was wonderfully awful and he wrote of it ecstatically to his wife Vita Sackville-West.

> The furniture was lodging house. Not a single good piece... But darling, it was thrilling, Shaw was there. In the garden hut there he was still, in the shape of ashes, on the rose bed and garden paths, white ashes...

Harold Nicolson was not an admirer of Shaw. Ten years before, during the early stages of the Second World War, he had been responsible for banning G.B.S. from broadcasting: and Britain missed the chance of hearing her greatest pantaloon answer the weekly 'calls' of Lord Haw-Haw. Now, not realising that Shaw had deliberately assembled all the pictures, statuettes and busts of himself for the benefit of the Trust, and had tentatively offered his house as a 'trifle', to be sold in 20 years if it was 'found that his name was forgotten', Nicolson was aghast at the vanity of the man. How could he have supposed that so unprepossessing a place, crammed with self-images, should be immortalised? Yet he felt 'morally obliged' to accept it and warmly recommended its preservation by the Trust for all time 'as an example of the nadir of taste to which a distinguished writer could sink'. But why this 'amazingly brilliant contemporary' had chosen to occupy such a dull and undistinguished villa for 35 years was a puzzle.

> As a lady and gentleman were out driving in Henrietta Street, Covent Garden, yesterday, a heavy shower drove them to take shelter in the office of the Superintendent Registrar there, and in the confusion of the moment he married them. The lady was an Irish lady named Miss Payne-Townshend and the gentleman was George Bernard Shaw... Startling as was the liberty undertaken by the Henrietta Street official, it turns out well...

This notice, which appeared in the *Star* on 2 June 1898, was Shaw's method of announcing his marriage, emphasising the extraordinary spontaneity of the 'operation' in the face of those friends who for the past couple of years had insisted on taking the match for granted. To Shaw himself it did seem astonishing. He and Charlotte were both in their early forties and had little in common except (like the Carlyles) their determination never to marry. All one could say was that marriage was a fate better than death, and since he was then 'a wretch on crutches' fully determined to die, his proposal had taken the form of offering Charlotte widowhood. The Life Force, however, which may operate in such matters more keenly through women, knew better: and she calmly accepted.

With Shaw forever falling downstairs and off bicycles, the honeymoon developed into a year's convalescence which had the effect of postponing sexual intercourse between them until its absence became a positive part of their married life. They had, briefly, been lovers but that had been in another country (France) and, besides, they had not then been married. Now the relationship 'completely lost its inevitable preliminary character of a love affair.' Charlotte became G.B.S.'s nurse and, for a time, his secretary. She was, he boasted, 'a dragon'. She had a genius for worrying, registering his coughs and sneezes as a barometer registers the weather. Her mind ran largely on sickness and travel, diagnosing one, prescribing the other. A sprained ankle called for several weeks at Margate; a broken arm might need a month or more in Asia Minor; nervous exhaustion could be dealt with in Italy, while more serious illnesses still should be sent round the world on pleasure steamers. 'My curse on the wretch who invented holidays', Shaw cried out. He disliked travel and had no talent for resting. A contest quickly developed between the two of them. 'I don't really like work', Charlotte once admitted to Nancy Astor. But G.B.S. liked nothing better, especially the sort of 'creative work', Charlotte complained, 'that pulls him to pieces'.

They lived in Charlotte's double-decker flat on the south corner of Adelphi Terrace, overlooking the Thames and Embankment Garden. Apart from the occasional hooting of boats, it was a quiet place to work and, left to himself, that is what Shaw would have done there. But Charlotte insisted on his getting plenty of 'air' in the country. Sometimes she would rent a house in the Home Counties; at other times she would pack them both off to a hotel farther away. In the summer of 1904, as he was trying to finish *John Bull's Other Island*, she led him protesting round Scotland. 'The journey wrecked me; put me out of my stride...' he complained. 'Oh these holidays, these holidays.' The following year she planned to take him back to Ireland, though he felt (like Larry Doyle in his play) he would rather go to the South Pole.

Nothing would discourage Charlotte from misleading him on these trips abroad, but a house in the country would supply him with regular quantities of English air without the need to rush about. 'We are in the agonies of househunting', Shaw wrote to H. G. Wells on 5 April 1904. 'Now is the time to produce an eligible residence if you

Shaw with his wife, Charlotte, in 1905.

have one handy.' It was over two and a half years later that they found the Rectory at Ayot St Lawrence, not far from Wheathampstead in Hertfordshire. The Rector, who could not afford to keep up the grounds, had no need of such a large house himself, and Charlotte decided to rent the place for a short period. They were both tired of looking for houses and here was one of the few about which they could agree: neither of them liked it. In terms of Shavian paradox this was an advantage, since Ayot would interfere neither with Charlotte's passion for travelling nor Shaw's obsession with work. They had no intention of staying there long, though as it turned out they continued renting it for 14 years and then, shortly after the First World War, bought it.

What had pre-disposed Shaw in favour of the village was a tombstone in the churchyard inscribed in memory of Mary Ann South. She had lived from 1825 to 1895 and the inscription read: 'Her Time Was Short'. If the biblical term of three score years and ten was reckoned short for Ayot, then this must surely be a fitting place for the future author of *Back to Methuselah* to inhabit.

It was to take the villagers a dozen years or so to accept him. They 'didn't attach much importance to Mr Shaw's literary fame', Edith Reeves, who lived next door, calculated. Almost no one had read his books or seen his plays, though they knew he was a notable personality. But was he respectable? During the First World War he became such a hated figure in Britain because of his devastating pamphlet *Common Sense About the War*, that he was sometimes prevented by the threat of violence from speaking in public. The popularity he had begun to accumulate with *Pygmalion* in 1913 was not to be recaptured until more than ten years later with *St Joan*. This swing in public esteem was modestly if eccentrically echoed at Ayot. 'The villagers all thought he was a rum one – a *very* rum one', Edith Reeves reckoned. 'Later, during the first World War, everyone thought he was a German, because he kept a light burning in a window at the top of his house... and it was not until 1915, during the terrible Hertfordshire Blizzard, that the village in general got to know him more closely. He came out and worked hard with the other menfolk for days on end, sawing up trees which had been torn up by their roots and lay blocking the road.' He also made his cellar available to the neighbours as an air-raid shelter but few of them appear to have taken up this invitation, possibly because of their belief that German planes were aiming for the attic light.

Then, one day following the war, as Shaw was crossing the road in Whitehall, a policeman held up the traffic for him. It was rumoured that G.B.S. was one of the few people whom the metropolitan police had instructions to protect from traffic. A stray cameraman took a snap of the event to illustrate this rumour. The photograph appeared in several newspapers and, Shaw liked to claim, led to his greatness being finally established in Ayot. After this, the villagers began calling the Rectory 'Shaw's Corner', and in time the collector of rates did so too. Following Charlotte's death, Shaw employed the blacksmith at Wheathampstead to work this title into a new wrought-iron gate – and had himself photographed peering through it. He was, said Mrs Laden, 'a prisoner in his own house.'

Here was another conundrum. The red-bearded revolutionary writer who had so energetically promoted G.B.S. 'the pantomime ostrich', as a worldwide publicity phenomenon, was also this quietly-mannered fastidious gentleman who had chosen to live in a remote twelfth century village the size of a pocket handkerchief, with two churches, one shop and no bus or train service and where the last thing of real importance that had happened 'was, perhaps, the Flood.' People, he once told Mrs Laden, bothered him, and he had come to Ayot to hide away from them. Even in the 1930s the village was agreeably unwelcoming, having no gas, no water supply, no delivery of newspapers and no electricity – the Rectory itself using a private electrical

generating plant. The agricultural community at Ayot St Lawrence seemed to have withstood centuries of improvement. It was, said Shaw, 'a very wonderful thing.'

Such a statement by someone dedicated to social change, seemed oddly bewildering and helps to account for some villagers describing him admiringly as 'a real old hypocrite', 'the greatest leg-puller the world has ever known' and 'Conservative by temperament.' After all, how could someone with five servants, two cars (one a Rolls), a country house and an expensive London flat parade himself as a socialist? To such people, lacking perhaps some linguistic sense of irony, it was inconceivable that anyone could work from motives other than those of material self-interest – a point of view Shaw had specifically attempted to refute in *The Devil's Disciple*. The audiences that had converted that play into a romance (as *The Chocolate Soldier* and *My Fair Lady* were conversions of *Arms and the Man* and *Pygmalion* into musical romances) were composed of the same people who converted Shaw's socialism into humbug. It did not occur to them that the financial loss he would personally suffer as a result of his own policies being implemented was a measurement of his sincerity.

The Shavian advertising machine known as G.B.S. was a device for getting maximum publicity for his ideas on social reform. He wanted to write words that would lead to actions, to come up with thoughts that would be translated into our laws. If you did not write in an entertaining or even irritating way, he explained, if you did not play to the gallery, no one would listen to what you were saying. But the public's response, as in Ayot, was to cast him as an inspired clown who did not mean a word he said. He needed a public, despised this need in himself, but tried to turn it to something worthwhile. G.B.S., he said, was one of the most successful of his inventions. But it exasperated many people, particularly other writers. 'When you saw him last did he show you busts and pictures of himself?' Aldous Huxley once asked Sewell Stokes. And on being told that Shaw had indeed exhibited himself in this way, Huxley sighed: 'I can't understand it. He insists on showing them to everyone who enters that *theatre* of his. Why?'

One answer to this question derives from his early years. He had grown up in a ménage-à-trois, his mother sharing the house with two Georges: George Carr Shaw, a redundant civil servant; and George John Vandeleur Lee, a successful musician who had trained Mrs Shaw's singing voice as Professor Higgins trains Eliza's speaking voice in *Pygmalion*. Shaw's insistence that there was no romance between Higgins and Eliza reflects an anxiety he felt that he might have been illegitimate. Mrs Shaw had been contemptuous of her ineffectual husband and derived her happiness from Lee whom she followed to London on her twenty-first wedding anniversary. Though she took her two daughters to London, she left her son with his father. Shaw's method of overcoming this rejection was complicated and partly accounts for the conundrums in his character. He was loyal to his mother and argued that it was economic necessity rather than emotional (particularly sexual) preference that had made her come to London. He also saw that to win her admiration you had to be someone such as the mercurial Lee on whom, it is said, du Maurier based his character Svengali. 'G.B.S.' became Shaw's equivalent of 'Vandeleur', a name Lee had added in the days of his musical success in Dublin. But if G.B.S. was modelled on Lee, Shaw himself inherited all the diffident and retiring qualities of George Carr Shaw, his actual father. The name 'George', which he shared with the two men in the Dublin household became a symbol of his doubt and anxiety, and he eliminated it. 'Don't George me', he would tell people. The name he used on the title page of all his books and plays was Bernard Shaw. The name he used for signing letters and legal documents was G. Bernard Shaw. But still the public continued to George him.

Shaw called the picture of him by Augustus John, painted in 1915 when they were both staying with Lady Gregory in Galway, 'the portrait of my great reputation.' He knew the vulgarity that had gone into manufacturing part of this reputation. But when he showed people this portrait, or the bronze bust by Rodin, or any of the other images of himself, he was not indulging in simple vanity as Huxley and others may have thought. His great reputation was a screen behind which he hid. There had obviously been a psychological need to unite in his career images of the two men who had inhabited his mother's life. Since these two men were highly dissimilar he had to search for a method of reconciling opposites. It is from this search that the great debates in his plays proceed. He set about orchestrating the subtle themes of these plays for trumpet and big drum so that he might be theatrically effective, like Lee. Though its integrity was affected, this work gave him a new life. His display of pictures, statuettes and busts of himself had a dual purpose: to show off his success at having orphaned himself from his parents and become such a promiscuous author of himself; and to find an echo, in other people's reactions, of his own self-dislike.

Many thoughts came initially to Shaw as jokes. He would tell the joke then work out the meaning of it. His genius for comedy often obscured an emotional bleakness and intellectual pessimism as intense as that of Samuel Beckett. 'An Irishman has two

G.B.S. by Augustus John *(Shaw's Corner)*.

eyes', he once told a friend. One was for poetry, he explained, the other for reality. This is why, at his most serious, Shaw always seems to be winking: the eye for poetry is closed. Two experiences, both visual, influenced his early years. The first was the sight of the Dublin slums 'with their shocking vital statistics and the perpetual gabble of its inhabitants.' The second was the view from a cottage at Dalkey, ten miles south of Dublin, which Lee had rented. It overlooked two great bays between Howth and Bray Head, and its natural beauty intoxicated the boy. 'The joy of it has remained all my life', he was to write. His childhood, he told Ellen Terry, had been 'rich only in

129

dreams, frightful & loveless in realities.' Ireland represented to him a land of imagination, dreams and emotions. But coming to London at the age of 20 he turned his back on dreaming and, through his literary and political work in England, sought to make the realities of life less frightful. To his dentist in Welwyn Garden City, Shaw wrote: 'Far from contrasting occupations I often compare them. I spend my life cutting out carious material from people's minds and replacing it with such gold as I possess. It is a painful process and you can hear them screaming all through the Press.' His humour was a form of anaesthetic, but the quality of the gold he supplied for replacement had been diminished by years of emotional self-denial. When St Joan chooses death by burning rather than perpetual imprisonment, the inventory of sights she calls up ('the sight of the fields and flowers... the lark in the sunshine, the young lambs crying through the healthy frost') does not have the perspective of poetry – it is, in the words of Wyndham Lewis, 'thin journalese.' By the same token, there was nothing of Dalkey at Ayot. This deliberate eradication of beauty reflected a banishment of the inner life of the emotions by one who created at Shaw's Corner something of the imprisonment that St Joan describes as a form of death. But Shaw knew what he had eliminated from his life and how his writing, into which went so much vitality, was part of a device for transferring him into one of those intellectual voluptuaries he celebrated in *Back to Methuselah*. Some latent part of him continued to protest at this displacement of energy by supplying a continuous subversive and fantastical sub-text to his plays. 'Joey the Joker', as Mrs Patrick Campbell called him, loved to trip up G.B.S. the prophet. In some instances – the debate, for example, between the devil and Don Juan in *Man and Superman* – it is perhaps Shaw's natural pessimism rather than his moral commitment to optimism that unexpectedly triumphs.

One play in particular derives from Ayot St Lawrence: *Village Wooing*. This *Comediettina for Two Voices in Three Conversations* is one of Shaw's most delightful pieces for the stage, and through it runs an undercurrent that is curiously regretful and self-revealing. On 15 December 1932 Charlotte had persuaded him to embark with her on the *Empress of Britain* for a world cruise – 25 countries in 147 days. On 2 January 1933, while they were in the Sunda Strait having just left Cairo, Shaw began his play almost as an act of rebellion. He had developed the habit of labelling his people with a sequence of letters of the alphabet, from A onwards for the males, and Z backwards for the females. In *Village Wooing* he needed only two main letters, A and Z, which he retained as codenames for the characters. 'I do not see myself as the Man', he told Lillah McCathy; 'he is intended as a posthumous portrait of Lytton Strachey.' But A is as much Lytton Strachey as Marchbanks was De Quincey in *Candida* or Tanner the frock-coated Marxist H.M. Hyndman in *Man and Superman*: all use the notions of other men to camouflage a Shavian self-portrait. As for Z, she is not Charlotte but someone who lived down the road from them at Ayot: the village postmistress, Mrs Jisbella Lyth.

Mrs Lyth was a widow. She started her career as a kennel-maid; then spent a dozen years teaching in Hong Kong, followed this up by working as a nurse in America, then after some adventurous travel returned to England where in 1931 she and her husband took over the post office at Ayot. Almost immediately he died of a heart attack in the garden. Shaw and Charlotte came to visit the widow, and she told them her story. 'Oh! What a glorious death to die', G.B.S. complimented her. 'I hope I die like that in my garden underneath the stars.' 'Yes sir', Mrs Lyth replied, 'but not at fifty-four surely?' On leaving Shaw said: 'I hope we shall have you here in Ayot for many years.'

And they did. 'Mr Shaw wrote personally to me for every batch of stamps he needed', Mrs Lyth recorded over 20 years later. 'He wrote every request in his own hand, addressed the envelope himself, and had them delivered to me by hand – five or six pounds' worth each time, approximately once a month – not £100 worth at a time, as he could have done... He was exceptional in that he was so great that he was able to combine his artistic nature, his genius if you like, with being an ordinary man as well – at least, that's how I found him. Some would say, I suppose, that it was eccentric of him to order all his stamps by letter, but I prefer to regard it as simple kindness. I've sold almost all those letters by now of course – I believe he meant them to be a sort of legacy to me.' When she was ill, Shaw would send his car with the chauffeur to take her to hospital. When he died, 'I felt ever so much older all of a sudden – like a very aged woman', she said. '... Life didn't seem to mean anything any more at the time, and Ayot will never be the same place to me.'

It is this relationship that is transformed by Shaw's imagination into *Village Wooing*. In the first conversation on board the pleasure ship *Empress of Pategonia*, 'a literary looking pale gentleman under forty in green spectacles, a limp black beard, and a tropical suit of white silk' is crustily anxious not to be disturbed by Z 'a young woman, presentable but not aristocratic, who is bored with her book.' A is a self-sufficient intellectual obliged, for commercial reasons, to write the popular 'Marco Polo' series of guide books; Z, who insists on interrupting his work with her life story, is the daughter of a village postman using the money she has won in a newspaper competition to see the world. The second conversation takes place in a village shop and post office where Z is putting through telephone messages. A enters as a customer on a hiking holiday. He does not recognize Z. She describes the cruise they were on which has destroyed her romantic dreams of the world. 'Give me this village, any time', she says. But in half an hour it is A who (much to his surprise) has been persuaded to give up the occupation of literary gentleman and buy the village shop, putting on an apron and working with Z as her assistant. In the third conversation A has been the shop's proprietor for three months and learnt more, he realises, than he had in three years at Oxford. Z replies that he is not yet a real shopkeeper since the shop does not earn enough to keep three. The scene ends with the Rector's wife telephoning for vegetables. Z takes the order, asks to speak to the Rector, and tells him to put up the marriage banns.

The play contains, in miniature form, many Shavian themes and obsessions including the phonetics from *Pygmalion*, the Life Force of *Man and Superman* and the sense of literary futility engulfing *Heartbreak House*. Nowhere else did Shaw come so close to acknowledging the extent to which he had been maimed by the protected life, with its deprivation of sensory experience, he led with Charlotte.

Village Wooing is a tribute to Jisbella Lyth's awareness of the 'ordinary man' concealed within the G.B.S. framework. But she did not like the play much. It was not very exciting and it lacked, she thought, suspense. Nor did Shaw's barber think much of him as a dramatist. Ayot was a microcosm of Britain, with all the ordinary dullness and romantic folly that Shaw said he had been sent into the world to stamp on in thick boots. 'Let this illiterate country perish: it does not deserve your efforts', he wrote to Ebenezer Howard, founder of the Garden City Movement. Yet he subscribed very generously, investing many thousands of pounds in Ebenezer Howard's company. Though he did not love his neighbour any more than he loved himself, he believed all of them might improve, become more likeable at least, if their conditions were made better. Ebenezer's scheme of taking industries and people out of congested towns, rehousing them in well-planned buildings on low value new land, and financing the product out of the imposed rents seemed to him, pending the introduction of a socialist community – a sensible way of combining town and country life – a particular synthesis of opposites he had mentioned as a modest form of heaven on earth in *John Bull's Other Island*.

On a small scale, he made similar suggestions for the improvement of Ayot itself. His 'Plan for Ayot' included pressing the Ministry of Transport for a bus service and a fast new road from the new schoolhouse to the old St Peter belfry; the replacement of two obsolete old cottages without sanitation or water supply by a couple of modern 'gadgeted prefabs'; and the erection in the church meadow of a glorious 80-foot colonnaded water tower (not 'the miserable mushroom-and-stalk design of most towns in England') that would stand as an ornament of Ayot. These plans had no more success than his spelling reform, or political proposals for the coupled vote. 'I believe it was meant to be funny' pronounced Mrs Harding, wife of the licensee of the Brocket Arms, 'and we were all very serious.'

Only in the matter of a rubbish dump did Shaw have moderate success. It took him ten years and needed all his Fabian patience and persistence. In 1922 the Wheathampstead refuse had begun to be deposited about a mile south of his house. 'My famous neighbour, Mr Cherry Garrard, sole survivor of the worst journey in the world, after the horrors of which one would suppose that no discomfort possible in these latitudes could seem to him worth mentioning, has written a letter implying plainly that there is little to choose between midwinter at the South Pole and midsummer at Lamer Park when the dump is in eruption', Shaw reported. In 1931 he wrote to the district council telling it that he had recently been cruising in the Mediterranean 'where I was very strongly reminded of the dump by the fumes of the island volcano of Stromboli, which is believed by the islanders to communicate directly with hell, and to be, in fact, one of the chimneys of that establishment. I was able to assure them that this could not be the case, as our Wheathampstead volcano, which has no crater, is a much greater nuisance.' On his return he found the dump in full blast and giving rise to a further grievous nuisance that seemed beyond his literary powers to describe. He therefore quoted, for the benefit of the St Albans Rural Council and Islington Borough Council, verse 21 from the eighth chapter of the Book of Exodus: 'Behold, I will send swarms of *flies* upon thee.' This might have served Pharaoh right, he said, but was undeserved by the amiable citizens of Hertfordshire. Eventually in 1932 the Council agreed to make some changes, and four years later Shaw received a single enormous apple that had grown on a tree at the site. 'I swallowed some of it before I was told what it was', he wrote. 'I shall never be the same man again; but Mrs Shaw rather liked it.'

Such local jousting gave G.B.S. a chance of demonstrating 'How to Quarrel Properly' – which was the subject of a talk he delivered at the local Women's Institute. With his immaculately preserved Dublin accent, he had, as one resident put it 'a funny way of expressing himself sometimes.' For example, when invited to present a prize at the village school for the best conducted boy or girl, he responded with the alternative idea of starting a rival prize 'for the worst conducted boy or girl and we will watch their careers and then find out which really turns out best – the rightly or wrongly conducted boy or girl.' This proposal was not taken up. On another occasion following a visit to South Africa, he suggested that all villagers should dance to the hymns in Church 'as the black people do', and should add to their repertoire such offerings as: 'O, You Must Be a Lover of the Lord.' It was disconcerting, too, for the local chemist to be urged to 'try out' some of his own bottles of medicines on himself so that his customers could see how they worked; or, when greeting Shaw in the streeet with a 'How are you?' to be answered with: 'At my age, Sir, you are either well or dead.'

He had a funny way too of dressing: sometimes a Norfolk jacket, knee breeches, brown shoes, wide-brimmed hat and cape. For wood-chopping, to the delight of children, he appeared helmeted. In the street, clipping his hedge, he was often spotted wearing a battered panama hat, a darned tussore suit, a white shirt, and a collar and tie of conflicting shades of grey. A bright macintosh illuminated him at night.

He was at his most 'ordinary' with children and animals. 'He always stopped and spoke to my little dog, Judy', said Mrs Hinton to whom he did not seem to speak much. 'He always talked to my children as an equal, so they liked him and looked upon him as a favourite uncle.' Each year he sent the headmistress of the school at Ayot a cheque to be spent on sweets. She would pass the money over to the village shop and children were allowed to get their sweets, without paying, to the maximum of a shilling each.

With adults and neighbours 'he seemed on his guard'. 'He wouldn't, or couldn't let himself go. I felt he was shy', one of them observed. The local landowner Captain Lionel Ames whose 'outlook on life was completely opposed to his on almost everything' acknowledged that Shaw 'always put you at your ease, no matter how lowly you were, and made you believe you were the most clever guy. He was a most charming person.' The Conservative Party agent for the district, who received Shavian lectures on socialism, thought him 'friendly and unassuming, yet at the same time as remote as god.' He was less god-like with less grand people. He would mix with the poorest people in the village as well as with the 'top ten', said Albert Bedford; he was 'pally towards many local people', recalled W. Branch Johnson.

Those who knew him best were his and Charlotte's staff: Henry and Clara Higgs, head gardener and housekeeper; Fred Drury the assistant gardener; Margaret Cashin the parlourmaid; and Fred Day, chauffeur. The Higgses worked for the Shaws for over 40 years and 'never had a cross word.' Being childless themselves, Charlotte and G.B.S. treated a few special friends – T.E. Lawrence, Harley Granville-Barker – as surrogate children, and, in their fashion, the Higgses belonged to this category. 'Mrs Shaw looked upon my wife almost as a daughter', Henry Higgs said; 'they were like a father and mother to us.' G.B.S. inscribed one of his books for them: 'To Henry & Clara Higgs, who have had a very important part in my life's work, as without their friendly services I should not have had time to write my books and plays nor had any comfort in my daily life.' This sensitive statement of fact is echoed in the

tombstone he erected to them in Windlesham Cemetery: 'For many years they kept his house and garden at Ayot Saint Lawrence in the County of Hertfordshire thereby setting him free to do the work he was fitted for.' He was, however, criticised by the local stonemason for ending his sentence with a preposition.

Fred Drury's most persistent memory is of the Shaws walking round their garden by a special route one mile long. 'It gave him exercise without the need for going outside the gates.' Each time the Shaws passed the house they put a pebble on one of the windowsills to mark the number of circuits they had completed: then they would walk the other way round removing the pebbles. Several balanced miles were achieved in this way. Fred Drury used to watch them from the flower beds, wondering what they were talking about, and concluding that it was Mrs Shaw who *made* Mr Shaw. 'She used to help him a lot with his work. She used to read his drafts and proofs and make suggestions and criticisms. She was a real helpmate and constant companion in all aspects of his life. Theirs was that sort of marriage.' Shaw himself did not notice the flowers. Of the large red poppies at the end of the garden he merely enquired whether the seeds were poisonous ('We must get a packet and send them off to Hitler'). He was more interested in his fruit than flowers – especially the strawberry bed. 'He loved strawberries and cream', Fred Drury explained. He enjoyed bonfires too, tackled the log-sawing with great gusto and collected acorns which he sent in seven pound bags to Sidney Webb. 'Pruning with the secateurs was his chief interest', Fred Drury noticed, and '... He always had his notebook with him.'

Margaret Cashin remembered Shaw as a tidy man. 'He always put chairs back in place, and his pyjamas on his bed in his room, neatly folded.' He was particular about his appearance and held himself absolutely straight – 'proud of his person and figure' he was. He changed for the evening meal 'regardless of whether anyone was coming to see him or not' and was full of unsuspected kindnesses. She often came upon him slipping money into envelopes. He paid for her trips back to Ireland and he lent her his Rolls for her wedding which was grand. She remained with him 16 years until her marriage. 'He never said a cross word to me, nor I to him... He had no violent dislikes for anybody... If an article or play of his was criticised he'd only laugh at it... he was too big a person.'

Fred Day, the chauffeur, had the most adventurous time. When he came to the Shaws in 1919, G.B.S. was still then a fiery motorcyclist, eager to 'ginger up' his two-stroke machine which was frequently bucking him off and landing on top of him. He knew all about these machines except how to ride them. But he enjoyed his exploits. Mrs Shaw, however, did not. She was also rather nervous of the car and preferred to sit on the back seat which G.B.S. had specially upholstered for her, sealed from draughts and fitted with a heater. She, on the other hand, designed a front seat for him with a small cushion at his head 'which enabled him to sit bolt upright.' If he was not driving he liked to read or sometimes to walk or even to travel by train, sending Day along the route he had plotted transporting his suitcase. 'It seemed to me a funny sort of logic to use the Rolls merely for carrying the luggage', Day reflected. But most of all Shaw loved driving. He had started motoring in 1908 and 'it's a wonder we got anywhere', he admitted. That wonder stayed with him all his life, including the 31 years of Fred Day's employment. 'If ever anything happened on the road Mr Shaw was always ready to take the blame.' A great deal happened, and Day was often obliged to 'pull the wheel out of Mr Shaw's hand', or cry out 'Brake, sir', 'Stop! That will do sir.' Shaw would take the wheel in the mornings, Day in the afternoons. 'It was a very anxious time for me', Day acknowledged. 'I was fully occupied trying to keep him out of trouble.' Shaw drove more speedily than his chauffeur and seldom failed to find the narrow roads around Ayot impossible to negotiate. Cars travelling in the opposite direction were a particular hazard and were frequently bumped. Shaw's favourite mistake was to put his foot hard on the accelerator instead of the brake. 'I don't know why on earth they let me have a driving licence at my age. I'm not safe', he complained to Day when he was almost 80 and had just plunged into some hot water pipes at a garage. 'Besides I think too much of you Day, to risk your life by taking the wheel – you're a married man with children.'

Shaw did not drive much after 1937 (when he was 81). He had, Day noticed, a Bohemian streak in him and, if Mrs Shaw was not with them, might pick up a tramp and give him a lift and some money. Once, during a storm, he noticed Fred Day give a small wave to a woman and child at a bus stop. 'Who's that?' Shaw asked. 'My wife' Day answered. 'Stop' Shaw commanded '– turn round. We must take them home.' Day had schooled his family never to recognise him if they met him on duty in the street since 'in those days [1925] it was definitely not usual for the gentry to have anything to do with the staff socially. But Mr Shaw was different. He put his arm round her shoulders and helped her into the car. She was terrified...'

Shaw's 30 years of driving showed all his boyish love of gadgets and, what the local chemist called, 'his quite outstanding deficiency in mechanical sense.' Before cars, there had been a dozen risky years with bicycles. For most of his life too he was also an expert with the camera. He could talk jargon to the most professional photographers, but seldom got good results from his films. He was baffled also by the problem of a new ribbon for his typewriter – 'Could that typewriter type a play?' he had asked when buying it. His years of studying economics, too, had not prepared him for the business of household accounts. Mrs Laden noticed 'He had great difficulty in adding up the milk bill – he would make it a different total every time.'

It was Charlotte who superintended to the last penny these accounts, as she did G.B.S.'s life. She saw to it that his vegetarian and teetotal diet was as varied as possible, while she and their guests ate meat and drank whisky at the same table. They spent the middle part of the week in London, moving in 1927 to a flat in Whitehall Court that had been owned by the novelist Elizabeth von Arnim and where Shaw's secretary Blanche Patch worked typing 1500 words of copy each day plus his many letters. Nothing disturbed Shaw's disciplined rhythm of work. 'I had either to write under all circumstances or not to write at all', he explained; 'and I have retained this independence of external amenities to this day. A very considerable part of my plays has been written in railway carriages between King's Cross & Hatfield; and it is no worse than what I have written in the Suez and Panama canals.' At Ayot he worked at the bottom of the garden in his revolving hut, furnished like a monk's cell (and sometimes mistaken for a toolshed) with its desk, chair and bunk. Since this office was three minutes' walk from the house, Charlotte was able to inform callers with perfect honesty that her husband was 'out'.

He was up and ready for work before eight each morning, but latterly took a couple of hours over lunch, a silent meal (except, sometimes, for the radio) during which he went through his letters. There followed a siesta of an hour and a half, which started off with a book and ended, rather guiltily, with a nap. Then more work and, in the evenings, he would listen to the radio, play at the piano and sing to Charlotte. He was the last to bed, and liked to go into the garden to examine the stars, sometimes still singing. Then, forgetting to lock up, he wandered upstairs shortly before midnight.

He seemed to enjoy the air-raids at the beginning of the Second World War, and treated them as firework displays. Perhaps behind this frivolity, as with the characters at the end of *Heartbreak House*, there was a wish to end it all. Charlotte was growing increasingly ill and felt 'buried' at Ayot. 'This good and kind woman, whose love and devotion for her husband was unbounded, deserved a quieter and happier end than fate awarded her', wrote St John Ervine. She seemed to have tumbled into old age. 'Charlotte's *osteritis deformans* is incurable', Shaw wrote: 'she is often in pain, and moves about very slowly and not far.' He had placed the piano at the bottom of the stairs and would play to her, singing arias from operas and Irish airs he had heard his mother sing, while Charlotte lay in bed. On September 12, 1943, aged 86 she died. 'Her long illness had changed her greatly', Shaw wrote to their friend Sidney Webb, 'and was very distressing in some ways (she was troubled with hallucinations) but at the end the distresses cleared off; and her last hours were happy. As she lies now she is not a crippled old woman; she is just like the portrait Sartorio made in Italy when she was in her first youth. The change is inexpressibly touching...'

The service at Golders Green was simple. The organist played Handel's Largo, followed by 'I know that my Redeemer Liveth.' As the anthem neared its end, Blanche Patch noticed Shaw 'standing with hands slightly outstetched, sing the words softly, as though to himself.'

The Shavian armour which had twinkled so brightly for so long was suddenly pierced. He had barricaded himself against grief not because he was incapable of that feeling but rather because he knew too well its power to capsize him. After his mother left him in Dublin he had discharged his emotional energy into music; after Charlotte's death, he told Lord Alfred Douglas, 'I have not touched the piano.' Sometimes in public, he could not prevent himself from crying. A bookseller nearby noticed that for the next two or three years 'he seemed extraordinarily "caved in"... He looked very sad. I did not think he was capable of such emotional feeling, but he showed it quite obviously.'

He fought this enemy, grief, with every Shavian contrivance. He would sing hilariously and insist that he was indulging his gift for solitude so well that his health had very markedly improved 'since her death set me free.' He boasted of this freedom which allowed him at last to return to his bachelor habits of eating and dressing as he liked and going to bed after midnight. He had not forgotten Charlotte: in one mood he advised people to rejoice, as he did, in her memory; in another vein, after reading her correspondence with T.E. Lawrence, he confessed he had never really known her. His feelings fluctuated wildly. It was true that they had lived separate lives together, yet it was also true (as they had written to a mutual friend) that 'finally a marriage consolidates itself until the two lose all sense of separateness and the married life becomes one life.'

'So away with melancholy.' Though he looked sad he continued to speak very cheerily and to joke, people often felt, in the worst taste – as if grief has anything to do with taste. Charlotte's death, he explained, had been a great loss: a great *financial* loss as he had been obliged to pay tremendous death duties on the money she had left him. Money took an increasing hold on his imagination. As he had replaced emotion by money as the motive for his mother's decampment from Ireland, so now he covered his emotional loss by obsessively talking of his financial loss. He was paying over 20 shillings tax in the pound, he declared. Some people pointed to this as fresh evidence of his sham socialism; others found confirmation in it of his meanness. Only those who had lived at Ayot many years and remembered that it was Shaw who had put the Vitaglass into the school to improve the children's health, and Shaw who had largely restored the church roof, renovated the organ and meticulously supported the local tradespeople, could now put his fears of bankruptcy into a truer perspective.

'If you're after my money, you'd better see Mrs Laden – she'll probably give you some', Shaw told a party of carol singers one Christmas. Mrs Laden seldom saw him 'without a large chunk of cake in his hand', and sometimes caught him in the evenings seated eating sugar or honey from a bowl or jar in his lap.

Mrs Laden was almost as intractable a character as Shaw himself. 'You are the person I'm looking for', he had told her. She guarded him devotedly, keeping reporters, photographers and tourists at a distance. But a group of eccentrics had closed in on him, ruthlessly competing with one another for hand-outs of money and the spotlight of reflected fame. 'It always amazed me the way in which certain people could take advantage of Shaw', said his doctor. 'It seemed to me that he was surrounded by people who really took the most terrible advantage of his good nature.' Shaw watched them with amusement and some anguish: it was little more than he had expected. They almost deserved their old-fashioned alphabet. He completed his Will. He could hardly wait to be dead.

In September 1950 Mrs Laden went for a short holiday to Scotland and Margaret, Shaw's old parlourmaid, returned to look after him. Perhaps his wish to die was reinforced by Mrs Laden's absence. She had left him in the same week of the year that Charlotte had died and this may·have emphasised his loneliness. In any event, no sooner had she gone and it was dark than Shaw set out with his secateurs to prune the greengage tree, fell, and broke his thigh. 'It always was a bad tree that one', Fred Drury remarked '– its fruit was always hard, and it did him in, in the end'. In a sense he did die that evening in his garden, but less 'gloriously' under the stars than Mr Lyth.

Margaret heard him blowing the whistle he carried for emergencies. 'It was a terrible moment for me', she recalled, '...on my first day back with him... I ran out into the garden and found him on the ground. I had him sitting on my knees for fifteen minutes.' She would not put him on the wet grass but blew the whistle persistently until her husband came, and they fetched the doctor.

'If I survive this I shall be immortal' he told a doctor at the Luton and Dunstable

General Hospital. He was in great pain, but stoical; came well out of a first operation, but refused a second. 'I'm in HELL here', he told a visitor. 'Are you looking forward to dying?' he was asked. 'Oh, so much, so much', he said.

At the beginning of October he was released from the hospital so that he could end his days at Ayot. What he called 'this damned vitality of mine' kept him alive another month. Up to the time of his accident he had continued to absorb himself in work – if he did not stop soon, he had told Fred Day, he would completely ruin his reputation. His last work had been a *Rhyming Picture Guide to Ayot St Lawrence*, an endearing pamphlet of execrable photos and verses. Now he was unable to work at all and looked a different person 'as though he had shed his skin', one of his neighbours said, 'as some animals do.' He was a skeleton. 'It was pitiful to see him the last time I cut his hair...' his barber Mr Knight remembered. 'Formerly he enjoyed having his hair cut, but that last time he was completely miserable. I don't know how I got through it. He was a changed man – like a child.' But he still held on to his good manners, his battery of jokes: though hardly able to eat he took care to compliment Mrs Laden on her cooking and was alert enough to detect the Scotch whisky she had surreptitiously slipped into his soup ('You have been playing tricks on me, Mrs Laden'). To the hospital he sent a considerable cheque to be divided between the telephonists, porters and other staff.

'Shaw's last days were an agony for me', Mrs Laden recalled. The house was encircled by reporters as egregious as the journalist reporting the death of Dubedat in *The Doctor's Dilemma*. Shaw had asked everyone not to try to prolong his life. On Tuesday 31 October he spoke his last words: 'I am going to die'. His temperature rose to 108, he went into a coma and just before five o'clock on the morning of 2 November 1950 he died. 'When he was dead he looked wonderful – quite different' Mrs Laden said; 'clear of complexion and with a sort of whimsical smile on his face, as though he had had the last laugh.'

Others believed the last laugh was on Shaw. The author of *Back to Methuselah* had come to Ayot to live long but lived only to regret his longevity. In fact it was not greater age but a longer youth and span of vigorous maturity that Shaw wanted for human beings. 'We die because we do not know how to live' he wrote.

The crowd outside the house on Shaw's return from hospital in October 1950. The convalescent was hidden by a canvas screen.

For Shaw, as for Charlotte, there was a service at Golders Green. Their ashes were then mixed and scattered by his doctor on the garden they had circled so meticulously for so many years – those white ashes Harold Nicolson noticed on the rose beds during his visit shortly afterwards.

The following spring Shaw's Corner was opened to the public by Dame Edith Evans. In her speech, she recalled that at one rehearsal Shaw had without warning bent and very swiftly kissed her, 'I didn't get very much pleasure out of it because I was so surprised.' Lord Esher, chairman of the historic buildings committee, also spoke. Never had the National Trust, he said, possessed a house with the imprint of genius still so warm upon it. The six hundred visitors that day, some of them from China and India as well as from America and several European countries, were able to get in extraordinary detail an impression of Shaw's daily life – in the catholic selection of photographs of his contemporaries (from Sidney Webb and William Morris to Stalin and the boxer Gene Tunney); from the eccentric array of hats and sticks in the hall; the cameras and books, spectacles, fountain pen and gold propelling pencil; there too are the famous busts and pictures including the portrait by Sartorio of Charlotte; awards as various as the Nobel Prize for Literature and the Hollywood Oscar for the film of *Pygmalion* to the parchment scrolls recording Shaw's Freedom of Dublin and of St Pancras; and the filing cabinet with its drawers labelled by Shaw 'Ayot', 'Russia', 'Keys and Contraptions'.

Open a glass door at the back and you can step through to the verandah that Shaw called 'my Riviera'. From this verandah a path leads round the lawn and eventually reaches the small revolving summer house where he did so much of his work. As the sun circled the garden Shaw would leave his typewriter and move his hut to keep pace with it, until at last it vanished altogether.

John
To
Shaw
1935

T.E. Lawrence at Clouds Hill

Raleigh Trevelyan

What did Lawrence look like in the Clouds Hill days? We have no lack of impressions. Even in his forties he was still curiously boyish. Bernard Shaw said that he had the grinning laugh and artless speech of a schoolboy. His height was five foot five and a half inches, and he had a body long for his legs. He had fair hair, a ruddy complexion and pale blue eyes that could 'burn'. He had a large jaw and a mouth that some people thought cruel. He had small hands and feet, and a trick of holding his hands loosely in front of him. At first impression you might have thought him insignificant. He did not like being touched, and had a bad handshake. Was he shy then? Bernard Shaw did not think so, but others did, to begin with anyway. He had a gift for putting you at your ease, and extraordinary powers of encouragement; 'When we talked about the Arab revolt', E.M. Forster said, tongue in cheek, 'he made me feel that I could almost have taken Damascus myself'. Most people soon became conscious of what Winston Churchill called Lawrence's magnetic power, discovering that the 'insignificance' was a mask. His humour was described as puckish, at times grim, at times teasing, at times bawdy, though Forster said that there was no 'low talk' at Clouds Hill. But if Lawrence was a tease, he did not like being made fun of.

Churchill said, 'He looked what he was, one of nature's greatest princes'; while Shaw observed 'He was a very strange fellow, a born actor and up to all sorts of tricks.' But then, as Osbert Sitwell remarked, Lawrence was at his best with the Shaws; when they were present, there was a sort of 'audacity of mischief about his attitude and conversation that was enchanting'.

It had been some years since I had last seen Clouds Hill, but its curious atmosphere and the strong sense of Lawrence's presence in his 'earthly paradise' had always remained with me. 'The cottage is alone in a dip on the moor,' he had written in August 1924 to his RAF friend Jock Chambers, who was planning to visit him. 'Very quiet, very lonely, very bare. A mile from camp. Furnished with a bed, a bicycle, three chairs, 100 books, a gramophone of parts, a table. Many windows, oak-trees, an ilex, birch, firs, rhododendrons, laurels, heather. Dorsetshire to look at. No food, except what a grocer & the camp shops provide. Milk. Wood fuel for the picking up. I don't sleep here, but come at 4.30 p.m till 9 p.m nearly every evening, & dream, or write or read by the fire, or play Beethoven or Mozart by myself on the box. Sometimes one or two Tank-Corps-slaves arrive and listen with me...'

The heath is Hardy's Egdon Heath and Lawrence liked to imagine that Clouds Hill was Eustachia Vye's cottage, even if Eustachia Vye, with that 'raw material of divinity' and her 'pagan eyes, full of nocturnal mysteries' was far from the sort of woman with whom he evidently felt at ease. Already in Lawrence's time the tanks from Bovington Camp were churning up the bell-heather and the gorse, behind his barrier of rhododendrons. As I drove from Wareham on the A352 I looked down on the

T.E. Lawrence (1888-1936) in RAF uniform, by Augustus John, 1935 inscribed 'John to Shaw 1935' *(Ashmolean Museum, Oxford)*.

Lawrence in about 1935, one of the last photographs to be taken of him.

muddy runways and the ruin of Hardy's 'home of strange phantoms' and saw the red brick huts of Bovington which Lawrence had hated so much – 'the army is muck, stink and desolate abomination'. I fancied that both he and Hardy would have seen fewer pine trees. I stopped for a ploughman's lunch at the Ship Inn, Wool, one of the pubs where Lawrence's grander guests, such as Forster, used to stay. I also found what must have been the post office where Lawrence had sent the telegram to Henry Williamson before roaring back on his motorbike to his death-crash only a couple of hundred yards away from Clouds Hill.

The pub was packed with soldiers. Lawrence never drank alcohol, or smoked, so he probably avoided that bar. In any case if he ate at Wool, he would have gone to one of the cafés for fish and chips or bacon and eggs. I found Wool very much a main-road village, and the railway did not help to improve it. As Clouds Hill would not be open for a while, I decided to go first to Moreton and see Lawrence's grave. It was a relief to reach what he had called the 'clean emptiness' of the real Dorset, the narrow lanes with blue views of hills. An obelisk pushed up through a wood; it had been built in 1784, so I discovered, in memory of one of the Framptons, squires of the area and, oddly enough, kinsmen of Lawrence's father.

I was no longer in heathland. The cow parsley and nettles were rampant in the ditches, on that perfectly English May afternoon. As I approached the village and the Framptons' manor house in its park, there were several old beeches, their leaves fresh and young. I could not help thinking of a contrasting description in *The Seven Pillars* of the arrival at the sandstone mountains and tamarisk valleys of Rumm, in that familiar almost photographic Lawrence style: 'We entered Rumm at last, while the crimson sunset burned on its stupendous cliffs and slanted ladders of hazy fire down the walled avenue.' I also thought of the film *Lawrence of Arabia* and of Peter O'Toole as 'Lurens' leading his horde of yelling Arabs across the desert wastes to massacre Turks, wastes which were really part of southern Spain, near Almeria.

Lawrence's grave lay at the far end of the new cemetery, cut out of a field, under a silver cypress still only half grown. I saw that there were bunches of yellow tulips and other flowers on the grave, one with a card from 'Tom and Helen'. Then I realized,

Lawrence's headstone in the graveyard of St Nicholas's Church, Moreton, Dorset.

with quite a shock, that by coincidence I had arrived on the anniversary of his death, May 19.

Again it was all so English: those rows of modest white stones. Next to Lawrence was the grave of an old lady called Ethel Shrimpton, who had died in 1968 aged 83. There were artificial red roses on her grave. No mention of Arabia on Lawrence's stone, nor yet of T.E. Shaw, the name which he had taken by deed-poll. The emphasis was all on Oxford, with 'Fellow of All Souls' under his name, and at the foot of the grave there was a replica of the open book from the University arms with the words *Dominus illuminatio mea*. I felt that the rest of the wording on the stone, obviously the choice of his mother, who had been on missionary work in China at the time of his death, would not necessarily have pleased him, 'The hour is coming and now is when the dead shall hear the voice of the Son of God and they that hear shall live.' The words 'Son of God' stood out more boldly than Lawrence's own name.

I went next to Moreton church by the river, and as I listened to the tremendous spring birdsong I remembered photographs of Winston and Clementine Churchill among the mourners on that same road under the trees, past bluebells, elders, brambles and nettles, past lines of solemn villagers: that was a cooler day perhaps, judging by the overcoats in the pictures. Sir Ronald Storrs had been the chief pall-bearer; other bearers included Lawrence's neighbour and help at Clouds Hill, Pat Knowles, and Eric Kennington, who afterwards sculpted the recumbent effigy of Lawrence, lying like a crusader in Arab clothes, in St Martin's Church, Wareham. The funeral had been private, dress informal. Lady Astor, Augustus John, Siegfried Sassoon, Mrs Thomas Hardy, General Wavell, Liddell Hart and some RAF and Tank

Eric Kennington's recumbent effigy of Lawrence in Arab costume in St Martin's Church, Wareham, Dorset (detail).

Mourners at Lawrence's funeral at Moreton, 21 May 1935, included *(left)* Sir Winston Churchill and *(right)* with his back to the camera, holding a hat, Augustus John.

Corps ex-comrades had been there. Although the church was in such a remote spot, it had been hit by a bomb during the last war. All the same, the mid-Victorian red and black tiles, the font and the pews still looked in a pristine state. The five apse windows behind the altar and the east window had been replaced with glass engraved by Lawrence Whistler. The simplicity of the view of the sky and parkland through the emblematic designs seemed appropriate to the later life of Lawrence, and to his longing for solitude and peace in retirement, a 'boundless prospect of leisure... about the only experience I have never had.'

Lawrence is supposed to have discovered Clouds Hill on a walk soon after his arrival at Bovington in 1923. It had then been lent rent-free by the Framptons to Pioneer-Sergeant Dick Knowles, father of Pat, on condition that he repaired it. Eventually Lawrence took over the lease, and in 1929 he bought it, with five acres, for £450. He wanted to escape from the animal spirits of barrack room life at Bovington Camp and also to have the chance of getting on quietly with the revisions to *The Seven Pillars of Wisdom*; as he put it, he hoped for a 'warm solitary place to hide in sometimes on winter evenings'. In point of fact he usually had some fellow 'slaves' with him, two in particular called Russell and 'Posh' Palmer. There was no water, let alone drainage or damp course in these first years, and the roof especially was in a derelict state. Later on Dick Knowles, who built himself a bungalow on the other side of the road, and then Pat helped him with repair work.

E.M. Forster remarked on the happy casualness of the place, and on the feeling that no one in particular owned it, but Corporal Alec Dixon, who had literary ambitions and had soon made friends with Lawrence, said after he had been invited there, 'I must confess that when they invited me to tea he looked very like Colonel Lawrence with several aides de camp'. Lionel Curtis, on whom Lawrence unloaded his horror of Bovington, also went to tea at Clouds Hill with his wife, expecting some rough bachelor hospitality. But, he wrote,'the party, confined to ourselves and two privates from the Tanks, was a work of art, so quietly conceived for our pleasure that we had not noticed the skill behind it till we came to look back on it'. And Dixon, who became a regular visitor, spending most weekends at Clouds Hill, described how everyone was impressed to spring clean the cottage before E.M. Forster arrived. Lawrence on that occasion even made sure that his wireless worked, so that Forster could 'hear Big Ben strike'.

Dixon's description of life at Clouds Hill between 1923-25 has often been quoted:

> T.E. was an expert at "mixed grills" where men were concerned. He presided over the company, settling arguments, patiently answering all manner of questions, feeding the gramophone, making tea, stoking the fire and, by some magic of his own, managing without effort to keep everyone in good humour. There were many picnic meals (stuffed olives, salted almonds and Heinz baked beans were regular features) washed down with T.E.'s own blend of China tea. Some of us used chairs, others the floor, while T.E. always ate standing by the side of the wide oak mantelshelf which had been fitted at a height convenient for him.

Only the two upstairs rooms, one largish with a sloping roof, the other small and dark, were habitable. The two downstairs were filled with lumber and firewood. Lawrence told his old friend Hogarth, Keeper of the Ashmolean, that the sale of his gold Meccan dagger had paid for the repair to the beams of the roof (which he left exposed), something however being left over for the furniture.

Clouds Hill.

In recent years there have been revelations by various writers concerning birchings at Clouds Hill, so the matter cannot be ignored even if some evidence is decidedly suspect. This has been mostly based on an account by Jock Bruce, who for a while acted as a kind of unofficial barrack-room bodyguard for Lawrence at Bovington, and who moreover claimed that he once prevented Lawrence from shooting himself in the cottage. It has also been suggested that the famous scene with the Turkish pasha at Deraa in *The Seven Pillars* was fantasy on Lawrence's part. So many of Lawrence's contemporaries who wrote appreciations of him after his death compared his forsaking of fame for the simple anonymous life of Aircraftman Ross or Private Shaw to that of a mediaeval *condottiere* retiring into a monastery, and Lawrence himself made an equivalent comparison. Maybe therefore it is best for the present to accept his biographer Montgomery Hyde's suggestion that the beatings were in the nature of a penance rather than a perversion.

The front door of Clouds Hill with Lawrence's inscription OU ΘPOVTIS from Herodotus in the lintel.

When, after leaving Moreton church, I reached Clouds Hill I could see no sign of any of the 'tame flowers' which Lawrence had felt were so out of place there, 'spoiling the picture'. Before his mother went to China, she had stayed in the cottage, putting in – as he told his publisher Jonathan Cape – 'dozens of daffodils and things, garden flowers'. However, he added, 'the rabbits seem to like them and I have offered Mrs Knowles the rest'. The rhododendrons were not yet in bloom, but were obviously going to be spectacular. There were a few shrubs of tall golden broom, which perhaps he had consented to have planted. The red tiles of the roof, whose condition had once worried him so much, were immaculate. The four dormer windows were painted grey, and the outside walls were cream. Through a downstairs window I could see the Goslett bath (Captain Goslett had been in Ordnance at Akaba) that had been paid for out of Lawrence's translation of the *Odyssey*, worked on while he was in India. As he had said, the bathroom did seem somewhat of a 'demi-cupboard'. Then, above the front door, I saw the inscription from Herodotus that he had freely translated as 'Why worry?'.

As I climbed the steep staircase I remembered P.N. Furbank telling me how Forster had watched Hardy's bald head emerging and how he had thought that this was a sight to be remembered. It had been Robert Graves who had arranged for Lawrence to call on Hardy ('You know the old thing, don't you?' Lawrence had asked) at Max Gate, Dorchester, and it had been Lawrence apparently who had introduced the Hardys to the Bernard Shaws – 'A gorgeous mixture!'. Lawrence referred to Shaw in one letter as the 'Great Spadebeard'. He had bought eight reproduction Jacobean candlesticks before Shaw's visit to Clouds Hill, and had been nervous lest Mrs Shaw might find the place 'unclean'. Shaw had come in 'sniffing the air and taking stock of everything like a sergeant-major'. A rumour developed that Lawrence was Bernard Shaw's illegitimate son because he had taken the name of Shaw. This pleased them both.

———————————

Forster went to Clouds Hill several times, the first being on March 23 1924, to help with revisions to *The Seven Pillars*. He stayed at Lawrence's expense at the Black Bear at Wool, which with The Lion at Winfrith (the model for the Quiet Woman in *The Return of the Native*) was another recommended inn for guests. 'I reached here at 8.0', he wrote to his mother, 'and found a little private soldier waiting for me. This was the romantic L. He was rather shy and so was I. He had to go at 9.0. Today I went out to his cottage by car. He shares it with two other private soldiers – also little. They spend their leisure there but have to sleep in camp. A charming place in a hollow of the "Egdon Heath" described by Hardy at the opening of *The Return of the Native*. It is all among rhododendrons which have gone wild. We worked for a couple of hours on his book, then had lunch on our knees – cold chicken and ham, stewed pears and cream, very nice and queer; a fine log fire. I like L. though he is of course odd and alarming. In the afternoon the man who is about to print his book came down from town, so I suggested to one of the other soliders we should go for a walk: a cockney youth, intelligent and musical. We got on well. L's identity has leaked out of course but as the cockney said "people aren't interested as soon as they are sure – it's doubt that excites them so". We returned to tea and a most beautiful gramophone. I walked back to Wool (about 4 miles) and got wet crossing "Egdon Heath" though not to the skin.'

The cottage from Clouds Hill with Egdon Heath beyond.

Forster came again in July. It must have been on that occasion that Lawrence invited the Hardys, for he had written to Mrs Hardy: 'E.M. Forster is coming to my cottage on Friday, to stay till Monday or Tuesday. Probably it is out of pity, to cheer me up. He would be shocked to know that I am pitying him, or rather his sojourn among the beetles and the fallen rhododendron-bloom'. Forster brought a copy of *A Passage to India* with him as a present. This time he actually slept at Clouds Hill and was kept awake by a nightjar in the roof.

The gramophone, with its enormous papier mâché horn and made by Ginn, 'one of the best obtainable and obviously cared for' according to Lawrence's dentist who

An old photograph of the upstairs room *(Bodleian Library)* and *(below)* as it is today.

was also a friend, is the first thing that strikes you in that 'brownish' room. At the time of Lawrence's death there were over 200 records at Clouds Hill, including 32 of works by Beethoven. Lawrence played Boccherini when he felt 'rebellious', Bach's Concerto in D. Minor when he was 'disgusted' with barrack-room horseplay at Bovington. He admired Clara Butt but could not abide Galli Curci. Lawrence hated jazz. Looking at the gramophone I remembered his fan-letter to the aged and dying Elgar after he had listened to the 2nd Symphony, 'This Symphony gets further under our skins than anything else in the record library at Clouds Hill'. 'You would laugh at my cottage', he had added. 'A one-man house I think.'

The rest of the furniture in the room consists of a sofa covered with undyed leather with cushions to match, two somewhat ecclesiastical chairs covered in the same leather, and an oak coffin-stool given to Lawrence – presumably used for writing on. There is also a wrought-iron, somewhat art-nouveau-like fender designed by Lawrence; and above the red brick fireplace there is a candle sconce, also wrought-iron. Judging from an old photograph, a deck-chair or two must have been stacked near the log box filled with Forster's 'rhody-wood'. Two pictures have now been hung in the room. One is by Henry Tuke of Lawrence as a cadet undoing his puttees before bathing on a beach near Falmouth; the other is a landscape of Egdon Heath by Gilbert Spencer, giving a useful sense of airiness to the place, in contrast to the trees pressing in from outside.

No doubt in the early days the tiny room opposite was mainly used for storing what Forster called tinned dainties and the like; Lawrence preferred to buy in bulk, a hundred one pound jars of jam at a time for instance. One can see the three glass domes that he used for keeping the flies off the bread, cheese and butter. Later he put an exceedingly narrow bunk into this room, with drawers beneath it for clothes. I put my hand on the mattress and thought it horribly hard. To lighten the room he inserted a ship's porthole, obtained from a scrapyard. The walls are lined with aluminium foil, supposedly to keep it warm in winter and cool in summer. Also on display is an Arab robe with a complicated history: it was bought by Sidney Cockerell when he was wrecked off Sinai with Wilfrid Blunt in the 1880s; given to Lawrence as a dressing-gown, then to Bernard Shaw, who also used it as a dressing-gown; then given back to Sidney Cockerell, who gave it to Alec Guinness who played Lawrence on the stage, in Terence Rattigan's play *Ross*. Finally it was presented by Alec Guinness to Clouds Hill.

Although Lawrence found the camp 'protracted torture' he cannot have been overworked, and occasionally he even joined in the barrack room rough and tumble. On the face of it, judging from *The Mint* (which I regret to say is one of the great unread books, in spite of the immense trouble he took in writing it), the drudgery and the tedium could hardly have been worse than at Uxbridge with the RAF. Yet he became utterly depressed by the lack of ambition or even hope at the camp, and above all by having to lie night after night listening to squalid 'streams of fresh matter from twenty lecherous mouths'. Eric Kennington was alarmed on arriving for the first time at Clouds Hill to see him looking 'scared and savage', as if 'possessed by devils'. Lawrence wrote to Wavell on 27 December 1923, 'This place is like Rowton House without cubicles, Xmas night was like sleeping – or lying rather – in a public lavatory with a choked drain... The old army, in my recollection, did at least carry its drink.' A letter to Edward Garnett at his publishers in June 1925 was so worrying with its hints of suicide that an appeal (from Bernard Shaw and John Buchan) was sent to the Prime Minister to have him transferred back to the RAF.

Nevertheless Lawrence was considered to have been the most popular man at Bovington, and was known as 'Broughie Shaw' because of his Brough-Superior racing motorcycle. Altogether in his lifetime he owned a succession of eight

Lawrence talking to George Brough, the manufacturer of his 1932 Brough Superior 10 h.p. SS-100 motorcycle.

motorcycles, though the last one was not delivered until after his death. He had a sidecar and 'seldom went out without a recruit as a passenger'. His madcap, fearless speed became legendary. George Brough, the maker, defended him as one of the finest riders he had ever known, never taking a risk. On the other hand a Dorset friend has said to me, 'I had an aunt living near Wareham who often used to say, "That young man is going to kill himself". She also complained about the motorbike's ghastly noise.'

He called his cycles Boanerges appropriately enough. He wrote about 'riding gloriously at speed along the sunset' and of the 'lustfulness of moving swiftly'. Boanerges was his 'wild beast' and as he told Dixon it gave him 'an opportunity to see Dorset in my spare time'. He would take his passengers to bathe in the the sea or out to a breakfast treat. Dixon went with him to look at Salisbury Cathedral Close and

Lawrence called all his motor-bikes by the biblical name 'Boanerges' after James and John, the 'sons of thunder'.

Stonehenge at sunset. Corfe Castle was another favourite outing, and he would drive off for miles to see some rhododendrons in flower or a patch of heather contrasting with the dark wall of a pine wood. 'When I cross Salisbury Plain at 80 or so', he said, 'I feel the earth moulding herself under me.' Dixon said, 'I sometimes felt that his Bedouin taste showed itself in his love for the barren wind-swept moorland of Dorset. He had a particular affection for Egdon Heath.'

With a certain amusement I read somewhere that the Bere Regis road was a spot where Lawrence had liked speeding. Whilst driving along there I had thought to myself, 'This is just where T.E. would have let rip'. Indeed, Hardy's Wessex is full of roads with open views that would have appealed to him. As I drove on towards Cornwall, I felt sure that he would have thought Black Down, between Dorchester and Bridport, ideal for his 'beast', with Posh Palmer riding pillion or bumping in the sidecar.

Exactly why Lawrence 'walked away' from fame and 'became a nobody' will always be a fascinating and complex mystery. He wanted, he would repeat, to forget and be forgotten. As Bernard Shaw wrote, 'He had to do the most diabolical things with his own hands, and see their atrocious result close up... A highly sensitive and imaginative man cannot do such things as if he were doing no more than putting on his boots.' An aeroplane crash, in which he broke some bones and the pilots were killed, may have been responsible for a kind of snapping of his nerve, just as the crazy speeding on his motorcycle, and for that matter the birchings at Clouds Hill, could have been in the nature of endurance tests – atonement for running away from responsibility. Apsley Cherry-Gerrard, who had been a member of Scott's last Antarctic expedition said, 'Lawrence never settled to himself that problem we should all solve as early as possible, FEAR. To the world he is one of the bravest men of a century: but to tell Lawrence he was brave made him feel physically sick.'

Bernard Shaw persuaded Lawrence to suppress his bitter introductory chapter to the original limited edition of *The Seven Pillars of Wisdom.* This and the morbidly introspective Chapter 100 provide clues to Lawrence's state of mind after what he considered to have been the betrayal of the Arabs at the peace conferences. 'To endure for another in simplicity', he wrote, 'gave a sense of greatness. There is nothing loftier than a cross from which to contemplate the world'. But after the march from Akaba he had already repented of his involvement in the Arab Revolt, 'with a bitterness sufficient to corrode my inactive hours'. Elsewhere he spoke of the 'immoral and unwarrantable risks I took with other people's lives and happiness in 1917-18'. On one level, as a private soldier he was obviously hoping to find that ideal of simple comradeship he had known with the Argeyl tribesmen in the desert; on another he was looking for a 'cold storage of character and Will'. At first, after the war, he had actually enjoyed his new public glamour as 'Lawrence of Arabia', the great hero, created by Lowell Thomas's illustrated lectures at the Albert Hall, and he secretly went to five of them. He had not attempted to refute the legends that had grown up. Then he became ashamed of his attitude, of 'the craving to be famous and the horror of being known'.

Other factors would have contributed to his depression; the death of his father, the loss of the first draft of *The Seven Pillars*, the strain of rewriting it and reliving the experience. He also dreaded the exposure of his illegitimacy, and the effect that such a revelation might have on his mother and brothers.

When Lawrence at last managed to be transferred back to the RAF and was posted to India, he let Clouds Hill to two army friends at 12 shillings a week. He went to say goodbye to the Hardys at Max Gate. Afterwards Mrs Hardy wrote, 'Hardy was much affected by this parting, as T.E. Lawrence was one of his most valued friends. He went into the little porch and stood at the front door to see the departure of Lawrence on his motor cycle. As the machine was difficult to start Hardy went indoors to fetch a shawl.' Lawrence hurried off, afraid that on the 'raw and miserable' afternoon the old man might catch a chill. Both must have had a presentiment that they would never see each other again – which was in fact to be the case.

His farewell to the Shaws was also painful, but 'we managed that good-bye occasion very well, I think', he wrote to Charlotte Shaw, who had become not only his confidante but had confided in him – after her death GBS was taken aback by the revelations in their correspondence.

'I am being hunted, and do not like it,' he wrote to Forster in February 1929, after his precipitate return from India, following drummed-up press rumours that he was involved in the rebellion in Afghanistan. 'When the cry dies down I'll come out of my hole and see people'. Meanwhile he offered to lend Forster Clouds Hill. He also said that some anonymous person or persons had bought him a large new 'apolaustic' Brough. Those anonymous persons were the Bernard Shaws.

He joined Commander Sydney Smith's flying-boat squadron at Cattewater, later renamed Mount Batten, near Plymouth, and helped to organize the Schneider Trophy Race. It was a happy time. From Cattewater he wrote to Jock Chambers about Clouds Hill, which he had been able to visit for one hour only. The cottage was as lovely as ever. 'Only chimney-pots are added as a monument to the new tenants' taste. Jock, the old tenants were some people. You & me, & Guy, of the RAF, and the brothers Salmond (Marshals of sorts): Hardy, Graves, Siegfried Sassoon, poets: Forster, Tomlinson, Garnett, prose-writers. Spencer & John, artists. It was a good place while it lasted.'

Soon he was planning more improvements at Clouds Hill. Dick Knowles had built himself a bungalow across the road and was at first in charge of the work; later his son Pat took over. A thatched garage was built, as was a reservoir which could be used as a swimming pool. An ingenious hydraulic water machine or ram was devised for bringing the water uphill. Bookshelves were also a priority. Lawrence wrote in 1930, 'My life is full of books and I get heaps of them, every week.' By then he reckoned that the total had grown to two thousand.

So the larger downstairs room became known as the Book Room, and it is the one to which most visitors nowadays gravitate first. The little room opposite, the bathroom, is kept locked. When I enquired if there ever had been a lavatory, or if it was just a question of going out into the rhododendrons, I received an embarrassed reply: a chemical lavatory had been put in when Mrs Lawrence had stayed there.

Actually the first thing that strikes one on entering the Book Room is the enormous couch, covered in the usual undyed leather and with its head under the widow that Dick Knowles enlarged. It looks like a bed, wide enough for three, but apparently was not considered as such, for Lawrence wrote to a bookseller, K.W. Marshall, who wanted to stay at Clouds Hill, 'A word of warning. Since last visit the cottage has changed, somewhat. The bed is thrown out. There are two sleeping bags, six loose blankets, and a shabby quilt. Many sheets. A large couch in the book-room downstairs... There are no cups or plates yet: but some on order. I cannot say how long it will take to make them. Six knives, six spoons, six forks. A small kettle: no pots or pans. Enough towels...' The sleeping bags were embroidered 'Meum' and 'Tuum' by Lawrence himself, and the Meum one still lies folded on the couch though Lawrence slept on the floor (as guests were supposed to do). The cups, of blackish glazed earthenware, were designed by Lawrence and are also on show. There being no kitchen, I asked about Lawrence's eating habits, though of course I knew about the tinned dainties and jam. I was told that he used to go across to Pat Knowles for a large breakfast, and would make tea and toast for himself in the evening. I was shown the kettle and a specially designed expandable toasting fork. The wooden candlesticks I assumed were some of those bought for Bernard Shaw's visit.

Ever one for economies in effort, Lawrence did away with socks and wore instead some sheepskin-lined slippers. In the Book Room there are various relics of Lawrence's pre-Clouds Hill days, including photographs that illustrated his *Crusader Castles* and some taken by him during the Arab Revolt: El Kur, Rumm, Ghadir Uswan, 'Near Resape discussing terms of surrender' and so on. There is also a bust by Eric Kennington. Four of the photographs of portraits of Lawrence are of paintings and drawings by Augustus John. Lawrence was always fascinated by likenesses of himself, hoping that they would reveal aspects of a personality that 'puzzled the owner as much as anyone else'. He was particularly pleased with the Kennington bust and considered it 'magnificent'.

The books on the shelves are replacements of those that were in Lawrence's possession when he died. In *T.E. Lawrence by His Friends,* edited by his brother, there is a complete list of the originals. The first entries in the list show something of the range of his taste: Adams, H., *The Degradation of the Democratic Dogma, The Education of Henry Adams*; Aeschylus, *Tragedies, Oresteia*; Aesop, *Fables*; Agar, W. and others, *One Hundred and One Ballades*; Aiken, C., *The Jig of Forslin*; and – ironically, in view of his notorious and vicious debunking biography of Lawrence – Aldington, R., *Death of a Hero*. There were very few women writers represented in the library. *My Early Life* had written inside 'To Lurens from Winston S. Churchill' and *The World Crisis* had 'Inscribed by Winston S. Churchill for Lurens to replace stolen property, February, 1934'.

Lawrence complained of books disappearing at Clouds Hill. In Shaw's *Saint Joan* was written, 'To Shaw from Shaw to replace many stolen copies until this, too, is stolen, 7th Feb 1934', and Lawrence wrote in it, 'G.B.S. gave me first a copy of the acting version of S. Joan. It was borrowed from me by an A.T.C. reader, who lent it to another, and he to a third. So it disappeared. Then G.B.S. sent me another Joan, like this, inscribed "To Pte. Shaw from Public Shaw". This was one of my chief joys at Clouds Hill: but in 1932 it also vanished. Hence this third copy with its pessimistic inscription. T.E.S.' Bernard Shaw had apparently found some inspiration for the

An old photograph of the book room.

character of Joan of Arc in Lawrence.

'The everlasting effort to write', the 'one craving... for the power of self-expression in some imaginative form', had obsessed Lawrence; consequently as Bernard Shaw said he had a 'perfectly ridiculous adoration of literature and authors'. Lawrence's chief literary hero was Doughty. According to Graves, when Lawrence asked Doughty his reasons for his Arabian journey, Doughty had replied, 'To redeem the English language from the slough into which it had fallen since the time of Spenser'. Graves said that this had made a big impression on Lawrence, and largely accounted for his 'furious keying-up of style in *The Seven Pillars*'. Although Shaw considered Lawrence to have been one of the greatest descriptive writers in the English language, Lawrence often felt that he had failed as a writer. He told Sir William Rothenstein, 'My style is a made-up thing, very thinly encrusted with what seemed to me the tit-bits and wheezes of established authors'. 'By measuring myself against such people as yourself and Augustus John,' he said to Graves (obviously flattered), 'I could not feel I was made of the same stuff. Artists excite and attract me: seduce me.' So he had tried something which was the opposite in style to *The Seven Pillars,* that 'iron, rectangular, abhorrent book', *The Mint,* one which no man 'would willingly read'. 'Powerful and capable as his mind was', Shaw summed up, 'I am not sure that it ever reached full maturity.' A little hard perhaps.

Doughty and Spenser were thus well represented at Clouds Hill, as were other favourite writers such as Fredric Manning, Swift, Norman Douglas, Pater, Cunning-ham Grahame, and of course Hardy, Forster and Lawrence's two biographers, Graves and Liddell Hart (but not Lowell Thomas). In his copy of *The Mirror of the Sea* was written 'Signed for T.E. Lawrence with the greatest regard by Joseph Conrad 1922'; Lawrence considered that this, with *Moby Dick*, was the first sea book of our times.

As February 1935, the month of his discharge from the RAF, approached, Lawrence began to look forward more and more to the quiet of Clouds Hill. He quoted Flecker; there would be a 'great Sunday that goes on and on'. He would be 46: 'Remaineth twenty-three years of expectancy'.

But he could not escape public interest in the mystique of 'Lawrence of Arabia', or speculation about his future. Alexander Korda wanted to film *Revolt in the Desert*, an abridged version of *The Seven Pillars*, which was still not on public sale. In 1935 I was aged eleven and remember being presented with Robert Graves's *Lawrence and the Arabs* as a school prize (I found its style tough going, even if the book was supposed to have been written for boys). Lawrence had become interested in William Morris, and now had an idea of building a small printing press with Pat Knowles. Maybe he would write a biography of Roger Casement. Always hard up, even though he had been generous financially to friends, he was worried about money, with only £2 a week to live on. Perhaps he would have to give up his motorbike. He was suffering from rheumatism.

When finally he reached Clouds Hill, he found himself besieged by reporters. He gave one of them a 'terrific sock', hurting his thumb in the process, and then slipped away secretly through the rhododendrons and made his way on a 'push-bike' to London. An American friend Ralph Isham drove to Clouds Hill on March 17. 'As we neared the cottage I noticed a group of, perhaps, four men, talking earnestly together. They seemed very curious at my arrival. I knocked, then shouted for T.E. but there was no response. On the few feet of lawn that had separated the cottage from the surrounding rhododendrons, I saw fragments of thick old tiles'. Apparently the *paparazzi*, not knowing that Lawrence had escaped, had hurled stones at the roof, damaging it, in the hope of driving him out. Lawrence wrote to John Buchan on April 1, telling him that he had been to the Newspaper Society, various photographic agencies and Esmond Harmsworth, representing the Newspaper Proprietors, 'with a plea to leave me alone'. 'They agree, more or less, so long as I do nothing that earns a new paragraph: and on that rather unholy compact I am back here again in precarious peace, and liking a life that had no fixed point, no duty and no time to keep'. But still he had to ask for help from the local police.

He sent out cards 'To tell you that in future I shall write very few letters', and to Kennington he said, '"You wonder what I am doing"? Well, so do I, in truth. Days seem to dawn, suns to shine, evenings to follow, and then I sleep. What I am going to do, puzzle and bewilder me. Have you ever been a leaf and fallen from your tree in autumn and been really puzzled about it? That's the feeling'.

On May 7 he wrote to E.M. Forster, 'Your arrival will be marked by the setting of a white stone into the new wall... any day after the 14th superb'. On the next day he wrote to Lady Astor, who had tried to inveigle him to Plymouth and then to a weekend at Cliveden, where the Prime Minister would be a fellow guest, 'You will never regret it', she had said. There was a clear suggestion that he might be offered a job in Home Defence. 'No' he replied. 'Wild mares will not at present take me away from Clouds Hill'. In his present mood, he added, he was not interested in any job at all. 'Am well, well-fed, full of company and innocent-minded'.

Soon a new kind of temptation appeared. Lawrence had admired Henry Williamson's writing, and Williamson hero-worshipped Lawrence. Williamson also hero-worshipped Hitler, whom he considered to be 'a very wise and steadfast and truth-perceiving father of his age: a man like T.E. Lawrence.' He foresaw a new age, preceded by mass-meetings of ex-servicemen at the Albert Hall with Lawrence on the platform. 'England was ready for peace – Lawrence was the natural leader of that age in England. I dreamed of an Anglo-German friendship, the beginning of the pacification of Europe. Hitler and Lawrence must meet. I wrote this to him'.

Even in 1934 Liddell Hart was to write, 'I told him [Lawrence] of the many people who were approaching me to seek him as "dictator". He said that the Fascists had been after him... no doubt there was a big call for a new lead'. Robert Graves made the comment that Lawrence was 'without a reverse gear' – 'He had finished with digging up the past, making a new military history, trying to be an "artist", being a plain man. Now came the temptation to dramatize himself politically'. Whatever Lawrence really felt about Williamson's letter (which has mysteriously disappeared), on May 13 he sent the fatal telegram inviting him to Clouds Hill. On the way back he swerved on his motorcycle to avoid two boys on the road. He was thrown over the handlebars and never recovered consciousness. He died on May 19. Immediately there were wild rumours of assassination, even of suicide.

Liddell Hart drove down to the funeral along the Salisbury-Blandford road, 'T.E.'s favourite speed-stretch'. He was among those who assembled first at the cottage, waiting for the hearse with its small, plain unmarked coffin. To Forster, 'the real framework, the place which his spirit will never cease to haunt, is Clouds Hill', and Lawrence's friends must have felt just that as they left the house for Moreton church.

Eric Kennington at work on the stone effigy of Lawrence for St Martin's Church, Wareham.

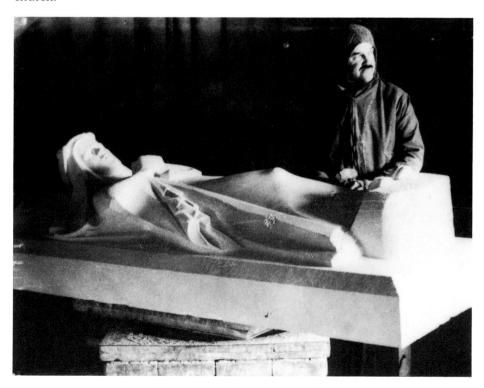

Leonard and Virginia Woolf at Monk's House

John Lehmann

How strange it is that small things often bring back the past more vividly than the big and central things. When I revisited Monk's House a few years ago, it was not the absence of Leonard and Virginia, which of course I had been prepared for, and for Virginia's absence long before Leonard died there, but the absence of two features which I had always associated with the house during my visits when one or both of them was a living presence there. The first was Virginia's books, so many of them rebound in fancy coloured papers prepared by herself, which filled the sitting-room shelves beside her chair and seemed so powerfully redolent of Virginia's writing life. They were gone, sold to some ardent collector on the other side of the Atlantic, and replaced only by a few miscellaneous Hogarth Press publications which did nothing to fill the yawning personality gap. The second thing I missed was Leonard's potted plants: elaborately blossomed double begonias, gloxinias, and heavily perfumed lilies, which he had nurtured in his carefully tended greenhouse in the garden and brought into the house when they were at the peak of their blossoming. He took great pride in them, and they filled the little room with their bright colours and (sometimes) scent.

The Woolfs had first spotted Monk's House when they were living at Asheham House nearby and considering moving to the Round House in Lewes, which Virginia actually bought on a sudden impulse. They would take walks round Rodmell, and Leonard, peering over the fence, was strongly attracted by the layout of the garden, with its division into little patches in which flower-gardens and vegetable-garden pressed close to one another. There were apples, pears, plums, cherries and figs. In July 1919 they bought it, for what today seems the ridiculous sum of £700, though one must remember that at that time it had no gas, electricity, or water. The grounds amounted to about three-quarters of an acre, and had beautiful views over the surrounding countryside.

The history of the house was obscure, but Leonard in the course of the years, set himself to explore it. The chief fact he discovered was that it had never been a house for monks: the name was only the picturesque description invented, perhaps by a house agent, many decades before. The deeds, he found, went back to 1707, and the various owners could be traced by name all through the eighteenth and nineteenth centuries. It was a low, rambling house, which gave one the impression of having grown by itself in a shambling way; no over-all plan to it, with short, worn staircases appearing in unexpected places. When they bought it, it had no mains sanitation. The additions the Woolfs made, bit by bit, as Virginia's novels began to make money, did not add any sense of order to the house, but a great deal to the amenities: a bathroom with running water; electricity; a sitting-room on the first floor which took over from the large garden floor room as the place for relaxing, reading and entertaining friends; and a bedroom for Virginia to one side on the ground floor, which, when it was added on in 1929, she imagined she might make into a work

Virginia Woolf (1882-1941) in the upstairs sitting room at Monk's House.

The view from Virginia's hut.

room, but never in fact did. Her writing was done in what she called her 'hut', (which appears originally to have been a tool-house), the studio summer-house at the end of the garden, near the stone wall that marked off the little church and its churchyard, and half shaded by trees. There she was insulated from all the distractions of the

160

Downstairs at Monk's House.

(Right) 'Leonard and Virginia'.

household, and could work in peace. I do not think anyone, except Leonard, was allowed in there while she was at work.

When they built the new rooms, Virginia managed to obtain some painted chairs from Vanessa Bell, and a low square table, for which Duncan Grant made a tiled top. She also ordered some pottery from France (Aubagne). In the garden, near the lawn, was a small pool filled with goldfish which Leonard regularly fed, and beside which they used to sit out on summer afternoons. Behind it grew two tall ancient elms, and the Woolfs decided that they would be buried there, one at the foot of each. The one under which Virginia was buried blew down in a great gale one night in 1942. The reproduction of Donatello's *David* which one now sees in the middle of the garden, was bought, after Virginia's death, one day when I was driving on an afternoon spin with Leonard, and spotted it in an antique shop we were passing.

In 1919 the Woolfs still had six more years in Hogarth House, Richmond, before they moved to Tavistock Square. In *Downhill All The Way* Leonard writes movingly of the inner peace these two houses gave them: 'In both one felt a quiet continuity of people living. Unconsciously one was absorbed into this procession of men, women and children who since 1600 or 1700 sat in the panelled rooms, clattered up and down stairs and had planted the great Blenheim apple-tree or the ancient fig-tree. One became part of history and of a civilization by continuing in the line of all their lives. And there was something curiously stable and peaceful in the civilization of these two houses. In 1919 when we bought Monk's House, Virginia was only just recovering from the mental breakdown which I have described in *Beginning Again*; in 1919 we still had six years of life in Hogarth House before we moved into London. Those six years were, I am sure, crucial for the stabilizing of her mind and health and for her work...'

One of the advantages of Monk's House was that it was in easy motoring – even

Leonard and Virginia Woolf, and 'Sally', by the fishpond at Monk's House.

walking – distance of the old converted farmhouse, Charleston, where Virginia's sister, Vanessa, Clive Bell, Duncan Grant, and the children, Julian, Quentin, and Angelica (later Mrs David Garnett) had established themselves, and there was a continual *va-et-vient* between the two households. It was also not far from Tilton farm where Maynard Keynes and his wife Lydia Lopokova lived. So they were pleasantly surrounded by friends and relations.

Both Leonard and Virginia were sociable people – too sociable I sometimes used to think for the continuity of Virginia's work – and liked to invite their friends for a week-end at Rodmell. Before they began to extend the house, they only had one spare bedroom, so it was a matter of one guest at a time: they included Lytton Strachey, T.S. Eliot and Morgan Forster. By the time I came to work at the Hogarth Press in 1931, there was hot water and a bathroom, and the upstairs sitting room had been built, which was the favourite place for us to sit after dinner. We always ate in the long scullery kitchen, Virginia dishing out stew which she had warmed up and cutting us hunks of delicious white bread in the baking of which she had become an expert. The sitting-room was filled not only with Leonard's begonias, gloxinias and lilies, and on the tables all the current weeklies and monthlies, but with Virginia's favourite books on the shelves beside the chair on which she usually sat, smoking a cigarette she had just rolled in her long holder. The conversation was apt to turn very soon to our mutual friends, their affairs and their *amours*. Virginia had an insatiable curiosity about their sexual adventures, and a gift for drawing one out to be indiscreet. Nothing, I believe, could shock her, though some revelations I made surprised her, particularly about the way of life of friends like myself in London. Leonard, puffing at his pipe which was always going out, would nod his head sagely while I uncovered the hidden life that seemed so often news to Virginia – though

T.S. Eliot and E.M. Forster at Monk's House.

news that she triumphed in having drawn out. My retaliation was to make them both talk about the early life of Bloomsbury, the personalities, the interconnecting liaisons. It was sometimes quite late before we broke up for bed.

When the war broke out, and I was back in the Hogarth Press after an interval of a few years, the week-end visits were renewed. As I had the responsibility of the Press on my shoulders when the bombing began – we had emigrated to Letchworth when Mecklenburgh Square was made uninhabitable – there were fewer opportunities to go down to Rodmell. Leonard usually came up once a week, or for a couple of nights every two weeks, to have a business conference with me in London. He was very amusing about the early trials of the evacuation period in the Lewes area.

> We have been working like coolies here the last 48 hours. Yesterday 18 pregnant women, accompanied each by 3, 4, or 5 already born children arrived · in omnibuses. Half an hour later 11 more pregnant women arrived ditto, but with rather fewer already born children. These had to be distributed in inhabited and uninhabited cottages. We spent hours carrying furniture about. On Saturday we expected 100 school children but they got lost on the way and never arrived.

When the war in the air started in earnest, that part of Sussex between Newhaven and Lewes was constantly in the front line, with raids and bomb-dropping by the Germans and dog-fights between their bombers and our fighters continually taking place high in the skies above. What I soon became aware of was that this warlike activity left Virginia remarkably cool and self-possessed. If there was to be an invasion, it would quite possibly begin in that part of the country; but as the summer wore on and the Nazi airforce had not gained the necessary superiority, far-sighted people – and Leonard was one of them – came to the conclusion that the invasion was

Angelica and Clive Bell, Virginia Woolf and Maynard Keynes outside the hut.

Monk's House today.

(Right) part of the garden at Monk's House with the reproduction of Donatello's *David* bought by Leonard Woolf on an excursion with Lohn Lehmann.

off; and he certainly communicated his reasoned optimism to Virginia. She was confident; she was in fact almost euphoric, and calmly carried on with her work on the biography of Roger Fry and her (still secret) work on the new novel, *Pointz Hall*, or as it finally came to be known, *Between the Acts*. Her *sang-froid* is clearly shown in a letter she wrote to me when I had to refuse an invitation to pay them a visit during this period: 'We could have offered you a great variety of air-raid alarms, distant bombs, reports by Mrs. Bleach who brought a stirrup pump (installed needless to say in my bedroom) of battles out at sea. Indeed it is rather lovely about 2 in the morning to see the lights stalking the Germans over the marshes. But this remains on tap, so you must propose yourself later.'

The story has been told too often for me to repeat it here of how, in the following March, fearful of recurring madness, Virginia walked out one morning and drowned herself in the river Ouse, and how Leonard, after a desperate and fruitless search, came back to Monk's House to find her suicide letters.

It is in *Between the Acts,* though transformed and at a distance, that I believe it is not too fanciful to detect Virginia's feeling for Monk's House and the immemorial Sussex landscape that surrounded them – had surrounded them since Asheham House.

In later years, after my partnership with Leonard in the Hogarth Press had come to an end, and the interim between Virginia's death and that break, more than once I went down at his invitation to stay at Monk's House. I remember one weekend in particular, at a time when the bombing of London had revived in 'tip-and-run' raids. We had had the idea of preparing an anthology of the best of the poetry that the Hogarth Press had published since its earliest days – and poetry had always been prominent on its list. Twenty-five years! So we had decided to call it *The Silver Anthology*, and to devote this week-end to selecting the poems. Afterwards I wrote in my diary:

> We decided to do the job at Rodmell, as Leonard had a complete collection of Hogarth Press publications down there, and work right through Saturday evening to Sunday afternoon. When I arrived, I found him at the back of the house, sawing wood in his old corduroys and what I had come to call his "French poacher's jacket". The house struck me as cold and damp, but it was filled with a great litter of books and papers and stores of the season's apples and jars of honey and jam that nevertheless created a warm atmosphere. We polished off our routine work between tea and dinner. As soon as we had eaten, we began our work on the anthology, with all the Hogarth books of poetry spread out around us.
>
> We had not got very far when sirens sounded, followed almost immediately by a noise of gunfire on all sides and a droning of aeroplanes that seemed scarcely to stop for several hours. One or two extremely violent bursts of firing shook the house. It flashed into my mind that Nazis could be carrying out an exceptional reprisal raid on London in answer to our raid on Berlin just before. Sure enough this proved to be so, for when I rang up the BBC at Bush House and asked to speak to my friends in the Austrian section, I was told they were all down in the shelters. The raid died down again before midnight: Leonard and I had found the situation too noisy for clear thoughts about poetry, and had returned to one of our favourite tussling arguments about the future of Germany and the organization of Europe after the war. In the middle of the night the clatter began again, with violent house-shaking gunfire and the continuous mosquito-persistent droning of aeroplanes. We learned next morning that there had been two attacks on London, not as heavy as we could have imagined, but an opportunity on our side for a gala warning display of the

The author with Leonard Woolf.

terrific new London barrage that had been developed since the 1940-41 blitz. A little hollow-eyed, but nevertheless cheerful we again spent several hours crouching over the fire in the sitting room, picking up the little volumes, arguing but mostly agreeing, and making notes of our choices. From time to time Leonard would say, "No, he's a hopeless poet", or "You know we really *did* print rather well" (not in every case my own view), or "That was one of Dottie's insane choices..." By lunchtime we had broken the back of the job, and I left on the afternoon train for London.

During another weekend Leonard discussed with me the vast tasks he felt he must undertake of sifting and preparing for publication Virginia's uncollected literary remains. As he described them, I was staggered by their extent and richness – and so they have indeed turned out.

Nothing in the appearance of the house, either outside or inside had changed. There was only the one great difference, that haunted me every moment of my visits, and during this one in particular: the absence of Virginia herself.

A Bloomsbury Circle in East Sussex

Quentin Bell

Visitors to Monk's House find themselves in a literary shrine which is also a very attractive property; very likely they know rather more about Virginia than about Leonard Woolf and they may well be unaware that they are entering a region which has been inhabited and has been in some sort recorded not only by the Woolfs but by their friends, some famous and some obscure, but nearly all of them interesting. This region has been called 'Little Bloomsbury by the Sea'. The phrase has in fact been attributed to the writer of these words, wrongly I hope, for although convenient it is inexact and in some ways unfortunate. It is inexact because the area in question lies to the north of the South Downs and has therefore been saved from that urban rash with which nearly all the Sussex Coast has been affected; it has not, as will be seen, quite escaped the effects of industrial enterprise, but by and large this is indeed an 'area of outstanding natural beauty'. Drive through the hills along the A27 from Brighton to Eastbourne; when you have passed Lewes the hills to your left will retire from view until on that side it is all timber and rich grazing land, but to your right the Downs continue; they have neither the magnitude nor the asperity of mountains, but in their gentle contours offer scenic effects which are both charming and dramatic; and here and there they draw aside in a very graceful manner to allow some lazy circuitous stream to slip away towards the Channel.

Even for the visitor who is content with purely visual delights and travels without any thought of historical enlightenment this is an enchanting stretch of country. But for the historically imaginative traveller who gains an additional pleasure from the sight of an old house because he knows who lived there, or who can find a special magic in landscapes which have been described by the brush or the pen of artists about whom he knows, there is much more, and indeed the tour may be extended by a visit to the Brighton Museum and the Towner Art Gallery in Eastbourne. Others may be content with the special and intimate charms provided by the 'Bloomsbury' settlements at Rodmell, Firle, Charleston and Upper Berwick.

But this brings me back to the other unfortunate element in my unfortunate phrase, if mine it be. For the word Bloomsbury darkens counsel. Today there are Bloomsbury enthusiasts (a recent phenomenon) and, ever since I can remember, Bloomsbury haters. The opposing parties resemble each other in that they both seem very unsure as to what the word 'Bloomsbury' means and very uncertain as to who was and who was not a 'member' of Bloomsbury. Their confusion is pardonable in that formal 'membership' never existed, and the more one knows about it the less easy it is to define the term. It seems necessary then to try and say what we are talking about. Of the people who can rightly and reasonably be called 'Bloomsbury' – men who were at Cambridge about the turn of the century, their wives and sisters and a few painters – only five or six were closely connected with this part of Sussex: Leonard and Virginia Woolf, Clive and Vanessa Bell, Maynard Keynes, Duncan Grant and perhaps Roger Fry and David Garnett, the former but lightly attached to Sussex, the latter to Bloomsbury.

Clive, Julian and Quentin Bell with Maynard Keynes at Asham, 1914.

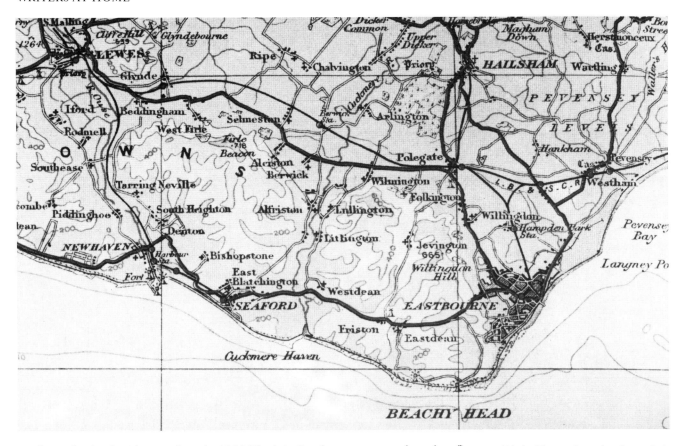

The 'colonisation' began thus: in 1910 Virginia Stephen was at work on her first novel, *The Voyage Out*. She was finding a new and difficult path in the art of fiction, she was easily upset by noise and by social disturbance, she wanted some very peaceful spot, not too far from London, in which to work. She came to Lewes, stayed there and explored, finding, as one may suppose, exactly what she wanted in the village of Firle. It is hard to think that Firle can ever have been a deafeningly noisy place; it must have become even quieter when the turnpike from Brighton to Eastbourne, which used to run along the foot of the Downs, was replaced by a new macadamised high road (itself now replaced) which runs a little erratically to the north of the village. Thereafter the turnpike slowly declined into a cart track until it came to Firle where it became the main street of the village, a street which shyly veers away from the out-buildings of Firle Place (very well worth a visit but none of my business) and descended in gentle curves down to the pub, the school and the new high road. It was a village street where you would hardly find anything louder than the hesitant perambulations of a pensive cat. It was on this street, at the centre of the village, that Virginia found a dwelling; it was almost the only ugly house in Firle. Today, time has mellowed its appearance and the visitors who now survey it (it is not open to the public) are not shocked by a raw red crudity which time has removed. They will be pleased to notice that one semi-detached is called Little Talland and will remember Talland House, St Ives, where Virginia spent the happiest part of her childhood. But around 1910 when the name was given, the place looked so uncouth amongst its discreet neighbours that Virginia called it the village eyesore.

Virginia's sojourn in Firle was not long. She arrived at the beginning of 1911. The following year she married Leonard Woolf, in whose company, exploring westwards along the foot of the Downs, she discovered Asham House. Asham (or Asheham) lies

'Little Bloomsbury by the sea'. A road map of 1932.

just off what is now the main road to Newhaven. At one time a traveller upon that road could have caught a glimpse of it far up the wooded valley which descends from Itford Hill toward the River Ouse. Even at a distance the beauty of the gothic facade, perhaps one should say 'gothick' for the house dates from early in the nineteenth century, would have been evident and perhaps if they had walked up towards the house they would have felt not only its charm but also something slightly uncanny which so many visitors have felt and which, for some, remains even to this day. Both Virginia and her sister Vanessa fell in love with the place. It was remote, it was hard to get help or to get provisions, it was dark and, lying between high woods, damp. It could certainly be very cold, as the Woolfs discovered when they held their house-warming party in February 1912; but they leased it, sharing it for a little time with the Bells, delighting in its distinction and its peculiar atmosphere.

Virginia Woolf's short story *A Haunted House* is a description of Asham; in her imagination she peopled the house with amiable spectres; it is a ghostly but not a frightening story. Other imaginations have been, and still are, excited by the sense of a supernatural but not a malevolent presence and I have known sceptics who would allow that if any house be haunted it is Asham.

Here Leonard and Virginia spent seven summers, in some ways the most eventful of their lives; it was here that they began their honeymoon; it was here that they saw the beginning of the war when seemingly endless columns of troops marched down past the house towards Newhaven; it was here that Virginia convalesced after her terrible breakdowns of 1913 and 1915, and here that the Webbs came to stay with them in 1918 full of the brave new world that was to come with the peace.

The lease expired in 1919 and they had to leave. They did not go far but found a house on the far side of the river. In this situation they had the misery of seeing Asham taken over by a cement-making company which cluttered the landscape with monstrous iron sheds, and tore open the hillside dumping the spoil in a great midden in front of the house; letting the woods run wild until the view was utterly ruined, filling the air with noxious fumes and covering the hills for miles around with gritty, dirty white dust. Asham House still stands; it is partitioned to provide two labourers' cottages and, the cement-makers having withdrawn, the excavated shell of Asham Hill now serves as a dumping ground for the refuse of Brighton. The road leading up to the house is adorned with a notice telling the traveller that he must not enter. Perhaps, everything considered, it had better be obeyed.

While the Woolfs were still living at Asham, Vanessa Bell applied to her sister for help in finding a house in the country. Her companions, Duncan Grant and David Garnett were conscientious objectors: if they were to escape imprisonment they had to work on the land. Vanessa also wanted to bring her children out of London so when Leonard discovered Charleston Farm House under the Beacon and on the western boundaries of Firle parish she was delighted. She visited the place, loved it and in the autumn of 1916 this curious party arrived to stay, which they did until the death of their last survivor in 1978.

It was cold (a morning wash might entail the breaking of ice), there was no hot water save that heated on the kitchen range, there was very little coal and so we children went gathering wood, and, of course, there was no telephone or electric light. The taxi from Berwick was an enormous luxury. A bicycle was the only vehicle to take you to Lewes; but for children and for painters it was perfect whichever way you looked – over the pond to Tilton, into the walled garden, across the fields to the Folly Tower or due south to the farm buildings. There were immensely paintable subjects as may be seen in galleries and private collections all over the country. Some combination of light and space made it seem proper to use any room as a studio, and indeed most were. At the same time this happy luminosity invited decoration. To

The Farm Pond, Charleston, by Roger Fry, 1918 *(Wakefield Art Gallery)*.

Asham House, by Roger Fry, *(Monk's House, The National Trust)*.

Charleston Farm, Firle, Sussex.

paint the walls of any house which they might, even for a short time, inhabit, seemed to Duncan Grant and Vanessa Bell the simplest and most necessary of tasks. They began at once and, from this first period of their residence date some of the most striking decorative schemes in the house. Despite the exigencies of war it was a fertile moment in their joint *oeuvre*. It was a difficult, anxious and in many ways an unhappy time but Charleston was a constant source of pleasure and seemed in many ways superior to Asham.

The Woolfs might dispute that. But when they had to leave Asham, they despaired of finding an alternative as good as the one that they had found for the Bells.

In the summer of 1919 Virginia and her sister had a sharp difference of opinion concerning *Kew Gardens*, this work having been decorated by Vanessa with designs which she found quite inadequately reproduced. Virginia was so ruffled by this that, when she got back to Lewes, she could only assuage her feelings by buying a house. She purchased the Round House. Once a mill, it stands high above Lewes and although by no means lacking in charm was not really at all what they wanted. Nor, on further reflection, did it seem a completely satisfactory answer to Vanessa's comments on the material form of *Kew Gardens*. A few days later, on their way to visit their new property, they saw a notice describing a house for sale: Monk's House, Rodmell; it diverted them from their purpose, they sold their Round House (I don't think they ever spent a night there) and at an auction held at the White Hart, Lewes, on the 1 July 1919 they bought the place for £700, not quite as cheap then as it seems now.

A few years later Asham again became available and they could have bought it for £1500. They were strongly tempted and I think often regretted having missed the chance, particularly in view of what happened later on; but by then they had established themselves too firmly in Rodmell to be able to contemplate another move. Monk's House is a pleasant place, two labourers' cottages knocked into one, with a very agreeable garden ending at the walls of the churchyard, and a splendid view of Caburn to the north across the water meadows. The Woolfs certainly made the best of it. Leonard enriched and continually improved the garden. As Virginia's books sold in increasing numbers and the Hogarth Press published Vita Sackville West's enormously popular novels further additions became posssible: electricity and hot water, W.C.'s and bathrooms, extensions to the north, improvements in the upper stories, outlying fields saved from speculative builders, ponds and greenhouses gave the house increasing importance and beauty and made its garden famous.

The Bells at Charleston, although not owners, also introduced comforts and extensions. The austerity of the first years was mitigated although it remained, even by European standards, a cold house. A new studio was built on the west side of the house. It was designed by Roger Fry, who had also invented the very efficient rectangular fireplaces on the ground floor. With his own hands and a borrowed chisel he altered and greatly improved the interior design of the dining-room.

In the 1920s Charleston was inhabited by Vanessa Bell and her children, the youngest of whom was born there in 1918. With her lived Duncan Grant, Clive Bell and, for many years, Maynard Keynes. For Keynes, Charleston was a second home; here he came to repair the effects of over-work at the Treasury and later at Versailles. It was here that he rapidly and angrily attacked the injustices of the Allies in the work that made his name, *The Economic Consequences of the Peace*. In 1925 Keynes married Lydia Lopokova, the comic genius of the Dhiagilev Ballet, and needed a home of his own. After some experiments in the neighbourhood he settled in Tilton, the roofs of which are just visible from the upper windows of Charleston.

Far more than the other colonists Maynard felt that he belonged to this part of Sussex, or at the very least that it belonged to him. He wanted to put down roots which had once flourished in the clay and the chalk of the Rape of Lewes, that demesne which Keynes or Cahannes, so he asserted, had been granted by the Conqueror, along with Horsted Keynes and other places. I do not know what evidence could be adduced in support of this claim, but to Maynard, although he had no children, it seemed not unreasonable to take a 99 year lease not only of Tilton House but of the farm and cottages. He himself became active as a farmer; he reared and preserved birds in Tilton wood and on the arable land to the south, employing a professional keeper and inviting a few 'guns' at the appropriate season of the year. And yet Maynard, who died in 1946, and his wife, who for many years survived him, have left very little tangible evidence of their tenancy. The great collection of pictures – it included two Cezannes, a sketch for Seurat's *Grande Jatte*, a Bracque, a Matisse, several Delacroix and much else – has gone to hang in the Fitzwilliam Museum. There were neither murals nor mosaics to leave behind and I think that the only visible trace of the great economist is Kennedy's 'Sun Trap' built to provide a sheltered retreat looking toward the Downs.

Lydia Keynes has indeed left a legend which I hope and believe survives in the district. The chatelaine of Tilton might sometimes be met stark naked amidst the raspberry canes of Tilton garden; her speech could be artlessly free, her manners endearingly unconventional. As the years went by she came more and more to resemble some aged moujik who had the strange fancy to go abroad wearing a flying helmet. Surely there must still be some bewildered Sussex farm labourers who can astonish their cronies in the bar of the Barley Mow or the Rose and Crown with stories of her whom they invariably called 'Madame'. Maynard could at least be placed in a category which the country understood: he was the gentleman farmer whose efforts and experiments served to amuse his neighbours, but there was far more of respect than amusement amongst those who had struck a bargain with him; in that line of business he was certainly no amateur. But 'Madame' was the really sensational character; she was the *stupor mundi* of our little world.

Maynard Keynes and Lydia Lopokova in 1925, and *(below)* a family snapshot of Tilton.

Maynard and Lydia Keynes by William Roberts, 1932 *(National Portrait Gallery)*.

It was about 1927 that Bloomsbury found that the motor car, hitherto an undreamed-of luxury, was within its reach. Now Tilton and Charleston were within fifteen minutes of Rodmell and although Mrs Woolf might sometimes be unwell and incommunicado, and Mrs Bell disinclined to waste the precious hours of daylight upon even her oldest friends (for a time Charleston gate bore a placard with the simple message OUT), Mrs Keynes, half amused and half afraid of what she called Bloomsbury, at times socially cautious and at times socially foolhardy, brought the most unlikely people to visit.

A number of people who were old friends of all three households got into the habit of visiting one house and then making the easy journey to the other two. Such were Lytton Strachey and later his niece Jane Bussy, Roger Fry, Desmond MacCarthy, E.M. Forster and Saxon Sydney Turner; while the Memoir Club met, once at Tilton and once at Charleston. There would also be some really large entertainments with fireworks and theatrical displays. Such were the elaborate entertainments provided by the Keyneses in, I think, 1927 when J.T. Shepherd (later Sir John Shepherd, Provost of King's) made an unforgettable appearance in drag, and the host and hostess danced a *pas de deux*, and a few years later the celebrated 'grouse party' at Charleston when T.S. Eliot explained the history of Mrs Porter and her daughter. In an essay such as this, long vanished junketings cannot be recalled, the echoes of laughter which was itself the echo of gossip and teasing, fun and youthful nonsense would sound pointless if reproduced. All that I want is to remind any reader who may visit these sites that although the inhabitants were workers – and for the most part hard workers – their summer holidays were also devoted to cruder delights, to bathing, sailing or walking and to the pleasures of conversation. At Monk's House conversation was the rule; the body was decently though certainly not richly provided with food and drink; but literature, politics and fantasy was there in abundance. Virginia Woolf's diaries are there to give us a taste of it. Charleston, with Clive Bell to look after the cellar and Duncan Grant to aid and abet the enterprises of the juvenile element in the household, was equally conversational but less austere. When the evening landscape had to be abandoned, and the canvases and easels driven home – for the painters went as far afield as Arlington, Cuckmere and Newhaven – the painters were able to join the writers over a drink before dinner. They then joined a conversation which had been in progress for some time. For the writers downed pens before lunch and started to talk for the rest of the day. Sometimes indeed Desmond MacCarthy would tell us at breakfast that he had a deadline, he would be working against time all that day and far into the night. On such occasions the talk would start immediately after breakfast and work would be forgotten. After dinner there might be music and sometimes someone would organise a play of some kind. Tilton could be even more frivolous and theatrical, particularly while Lydia was still young and mobile and there, if Maynard took charge of the conversation, the evening might be dazzling. Maynard, far more than the others, enjoyed and provided intellectual fireworks. But there were moments when Tilton was attacked by a bout of austerity, a spirit of teetotal frugality governed the housekeeping. Virginia was certainly exaggerating when she declared (I quote from memory) that a whole snipe had been set before six persons at Tilton and washed down with mugs of lemonade – but there was a grain of truth in what she said. On the other hand there were times when the Keyneses could make their hospitality flow 'with pomp of waters unwithstood': only it was not water, it was champagne.

Thus three dwellings were inhabited by old friends who, when they passed from urban to rural pursuits, liked still to be in some measure united. If it is permissible to see in these houses workshops in which our century was shaped, and I think it is, then, clearly, Tilton has the surest claim to fame, whatever we may think or try to think about Keynesian Economics there can surely be no doubt that the entire Western World during the past 40 years has to a very large extent been formed and framed by the doctrines and institutions which emanated from Lord Keynes's working couch at Tilton. But, as we have seen, the house itself has not very much for the sightseer; it is and is likely to remain a private house. Monk's House had much more in the way of permanent exhibits and, without attempting to assess the greatness of Virginia Woolf as a novelist, one can at least say that hers is a name with which to conjure, not so much in her own land as on the continent of Europe and, of course, in North America. Charleston is associated with no one figure of towering eminence and it is only within recent years that the contribution of the Bloomsbury painters has begun again to be noticed and reassessed. But, historically, Charleston is incomparably the most completely expressive monument to the culture to which both Maynard Keynes and Virginia Woolf belonged: for a monument must be a visible thing and Charleston is, eminently, a painters' house; a place where artists who, from the days when they helped to found and form the Omega Workshops, were never content to keep their art within the limits of a picture frame. At Charleston, for a space of 50 years, they painted and repainted the walls and the wallpapers, they expressed themselves on doors and cupboards, window frames and furniture; they dyed, printed, embroidered curtains, cushions, pelmets, chair-backs and even the covers of their radiators, they planted mosaics and sculpture in the garden. Their tiles and their tableware came from or were decorated in the home, and yet this is not quite true for they were also collectors, particularly of ceramics, their pottery coming from Spain, Italy, China and Africa. They put fairground figures sold by some Roman mountebank in the studio, heads from the Congo and the Orient and other objects too numerous to mention. Despite the catholicity of the artists' taste and their moments of wilful vulgarity which sometimes distressed Clive Bell, it is perhaps worth noting that a French seventeenth century landscape merged quite happily into that strange background; Duncan Grant, encouraged by Roger Fry, had bought it for a song in Paris and we thought that it might be of the school of Poussin. It was not until many years later that the Courtauld insisted that it really was from the hand of the master and as such it was purchased by the Poussin expert, Anthony Blunt. With passing years and declining fortunes there was much else that had to be sold, Picasso, Vlaminck, Juan Gris and other trifles which cost very little at the time of the First Post Impressionist Exhibition. There have also been other losses and yet the whole interior aspect of the house survives wonderfully. So much was

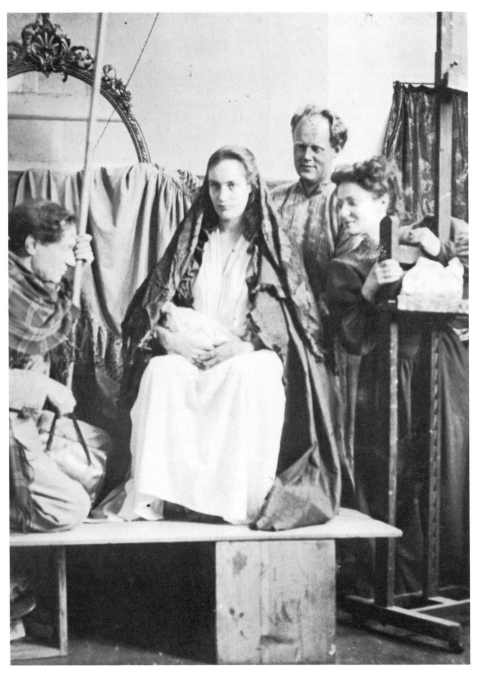

Duncan Grant, Chattie Salaman, Quentin and Angelica Bell posing for Vanessa Bell's mural of *The Nativity* in Berwick Church *(opposite)* finished in 1942 *(St. Michael and All Angels, Upper Berwick)*. Local people were asked to pose for the other figures, and the background landscape is of Mount Caburn, Lewes, seen from a barn at Tilton.

painted on the walls of that shabby much lived-in much worked-in house that it can survive very serious damage.

The task of preserving and tactfully reconstructing this house is not yet complete, but it is beginning to look as though it will be accomplished. When it is, a piece of cultural history immensely valuable in itself but valuable also because it completes our understanding of the cultural habitat of Monk's House and Tilton, will be preserved for posterity. The future traveller will be able to say with confidence – this was what it was like, now we can taste the aesthetic flavour of their lives. It is not often that the historian can see with such intimacy and with such a plethora of evidence the private achievements of such a group.

As though to complement the purely domestic decorations at Charleston we have in the church at Upper Berwick something entirely formal and public and, just as Charleston is quite unlike any other house that I have seen, so Berwick Church, which from the outside is like hundreds of other pleasant and pretty English country churches, becomes when you enter it quite extraordinary.

It was as the result of discussions between Professor Sir Charles Reilly of Liverpool and Dr Bell the Bishop of Chichester that Duncan Grant and Vanessa Bell were asked in 1941 to undertake the decoration of St Michael and All Angels in Upper Berwick. The village lies about five miles to the east of Charleston and so, even in wartime, was easy to visit. In the event much of the work could be done upon plaster boards in Charleston barn. It was settled that Duncan Grant should paint the west side of the

chancel arch, Vanessa Bell the walls on either side of the chancel, Quentin Bell the east side of the chancel arch and Angelica Bell the south aisle. Unfortunately she was never able to complete this work. But before the actual decoration could begin there had to be the most tremendous struggle, a conflict around which Anthony Trollope might easily have written three fat volumes. The Bishop was the hero in this encounter; he fought the artists' battles and fought his own, frequently against formidable odds; he persuaded committees to be reasonable; he encouraged church dignitaries to be open-minded; he wrote and talked and cajoled and charmed. But there was a lady in the parish who was equally redoubtable; she mobilised public opinon; she dominated parish meetings, she played upon protestant feelings (glass is 'low' but paint is 'high') and in the end the matter could only be settled by the Chancellor of the Diocese sitting in judgement in the church and listening to evidence from both sides. Thus the Consistory Court met on the 1 October 1941 and having heard the testimony of experts, of whom Sir Kenneth Clark was one, together with the voices of the people, gave judgement in the artists' favour and a faculty was granted.

The local opposition was sincere and personally, looking at the sketches which we produced on that occasion, I cannot but feel some sympathy with the protesters. No doubt one wants to worship in familiar surroundings and it was clear that the surroundings would be very unfamiliar indeed if this plan were put into effect. But new decorations, no matter how peculiar they may be, eventually grow old. Today, I gather, the opposition has evaporated, the decorations bring visitors but they are well-behaved. When a few months ago I repaired some murals which had been destroyed, it was the damp and not the outraged parishioners which had destroyed them. This was not always the case: 20 years ago someone did quite wilfully destroy the Vanessa Bell decorations on the pulpit (they were repainted by Duncan Grant) but whether it was some furious parishioner, or a Bloomsbury-hater or just some drunken lout one cannot tell. The artists themselves received nothing but kindness from the village even when, in their usual manner, they began to go beyond their original brief. Some of the added work was on a large scale, like the big crucifixion at the west end. There was also an altarpiece and an altar cloth, decorations on both sides of the screen and on both walls of the chancel, as well as the pulpit. Sir Charles Reilly wrote:

> I have seen it. I have been to Berwick. I went yesterday with Duncan Grant. It's wonderful. It's like stepping out of foggy England into Italy. I felt such a heavenly feeling as I sat there... .

The 'heavenly feeling' is not always experienced either in Berwick Church or in Charleston; but I think that Sir Charles was perceptive when he pointed to the un-English, the Italianate character of the work of these decorators in their colour, their hedonism, their indifference to some of the demands of 'good taste'. They, like so many northerners, looked to the south. At this point it would be tempting to embark upon a theory of the Bloomsbury aesthetic as manifested in its interior decoration. I shall refrain, for all that needs to be said here is this: whether you like or dislike the work of these artists, it now belongs to history and for that reason it is being preserved. Berwick and Monk's House are open to the public, Charleston we hope will be. If you have an historical imagination and an eye for the visual arts a considerable treat awaits you along the A27.

Acknowledgements and bibliography

The National Trust and the Publishers are grateful to the following for supplying photographs and for permission to reproduce them: The Ashmolean Museum, Oxford, 140; Mr & Mrs T.W. Beaumont 151; The Bodleian Library, Oxford, 149; BBC Hulton Picture Library 60, 83 (top), 112, 125, 148, 167; British Information Services Library, New York, 102; Bronte Society 15 (left); Camera Press 120, 139; Cornell University Library, Ithaca, New York, 56 (left); *Country Life* 11 (left), 18, 20 (right), 96, 97 (top & right), 114, 116; Cowper and Newton Museum, Olney, 32 (right); Crafts Council XIV; Dickens House Museum, Broadstairs, 21; Dorset County Museum, The Thomas Hardy Memorial Collection, Dorchester, 79, 84, 85; Harvard University, Houghton Library, 95 (left); John Hillelson Agency (photo Giselle Freund) 160; Lady Lorna Howard 110, 113; *Illustrated London News* 88; Anne James 172 (top); A.F. Kersting 37; Dr W.M. Keynes 175; Dr J.C. Lawrence 53, 58; Mrs David Lytton Cobbold 25; H. Montgomery Hyde 101; Derry Moore XVI; The National Gallery of Scotland XI; The National Trust 19, 27 (left), 28 (left), 31 (left), 38, 41, 42, 43, 50, 54, 63, 65, 68, 69, 71, 72, 73, 75, 92, 95 (left), 97 (left), 98, 99, 104, 115, 117 (below), 122, 129, 142, 143, 144, 145, 147, 149, 152, 155, 161, 164, 170, 173, 178, 179, I, IV, V, VII, VIII, IX, X, XII; (Trustees of Dove Cottage 34, 36, 45, 46, 56 (right), VI; Trustees of Dr Johnson's House 28 (right); Lamb House 95 (right)); National Portrait Gallery, London, 11 (right), 15 (right), 20 (left), 24, 27 (right), 31 (right), 32 (left), 48, 52, 103, 107, 117 (top), 176, III, XV; The Photosource 118, 121; Popperfoto 127, 133, 134, 138; Salford Museum and Art Gallery 23 (right); Shakespeare's Birthplace Trust 9; Wing Cdr. R.G. Sims 157; Somerset County Record Office, Taunton, 56 (top); J. Stevens Cox 76, 83 (below), 87, 89, 91; Tate Gallery, London, 168; Victoria & Albert Museum II; Clive Wainwright 23 (left), 24 (below); Wakefield Art Gallery & Museum 172 (below). Whilst every effort has been made to secure permission to reproduce photographs, it has in some cases proved impossible. We therefore apologise for any omissions in this respect.

Wordsworth — Mary Moorman
Poetical Works of William Wordsworth, ed. E. de Selincourt & H. Darbishire, Oxford University Press, 1940-1949 (5 vols).
The Prelude, complete edition 1979, ed. Jonathan Wordsworth & others, W.W. Norton & Co, New York and London; *see also* 1958 edition ed. E. de Selincourt & H. Darbishire, Oxford University Press.
The Letters of William and Dorothy Wordsworth, revised edition, ed. Chester Shaver, Mary Moorman and Alan G. Hill, Oxford University Press, from de Selincourt's original edition, 1967-1982 (7 vols, further volumes to follow).
Journals of Dorothy Wordsworth, re-edited by Mary Moorman, 1971, Oxford Paperbacks.

Coleridge — Ronald Blythe
Coleridge & Wordsworth in Somerset, Berta Lawrence, David & Charles, Newton Abbot, 1970.

Carlyle — Ian Campbell
Collected Letters, Duke University Press, vols. 1-12 (up to 1840) so far in print.
Reminiscences (London, 1972).
The Carlyle's Chelsea Home, Reginald Blunt, London, 1895.
Homes and Haunts of Thomas Carlyle, London, 1895.
I Too Am Here, ed. A. and M.M. Simpson, Cambridge, 1977.
Thomas Carlyle, Ian Campbell, London, 1974.
The Carlyles at Home, Thea Holme, Oxford, 1965, 1979.
Carlyle, 'Past Masters', A.L. LeQuesne, Oxford, 1982.

Hardy — Desmond Hawkins
The complete poems of Thomas Hardy, edited by James Gibson, Macmillan, 1976.
Under the Greenwood Tree, New Wessex Edition, Macmillan, 1974.
The Collected Letters of Thomas Hardy, edited by R.L. Purly & M. Millgate, Vol. 1, Oxford University Press, 1978.
The Life of Thomas Hardy, F.E. Hardy, Macmillan, 1962.
Young Thomas Hardy, Robert Gittings, Heinemann, 1975.
The Older Hardy, Robert Gittings, Heinemann, 1978.
Thomas Hardy, Michael Millgate, Oxford University Press, 1978.

James — Frank Tuohy
The Story of Lamb House, Rye, H. Montgomery Hyde, 1966.
Henry James at Home, 1969.

The Life of Henry James, Leon Edel, Penguin, 1977.
I wish to express my grateful acknowledgement of the assistance provided by these works, and also to Sir Brian Batsford, for allowing me to see Lamb House 'out of hours'.

Kipling — Jonathan Keates
Something of Myself, MacMillan, London, 1937.
Rudyard Kipling and his World, Kingsley Amis, Thames & Hudson, London, 1975.
Kipling: Interiors and Recollections, MacMillan, London, 1983.

Lawrence — Raleigh Trevelyan
The Letters of T.E. Lawrence, ed. David Garnett, Jonathan Cape, 1938.
Lawrence of Arabia and his World, Richard Perceval Graves, Thames and Hudson, London, 1976.
T.E. Lawrence to his Biographers, Robert Graves & B.H. Liddell Hart, Cassell, London, 1963.
The Secret Lives of Lawrence of Arabia, Phillip Knightley & Colin Simpson, Nelson, London, 1963.
T.E. Lawrence by his Friends, ed. A.W. Lawrence, Jonathan Cape, 1937.
T.E. Lawrence, Desmond Stewart, Hamish Hamilton, London, 1977.
P.N. Furbank kindly directed me to the letter by E.M. Forster dated March 23 1924; this is © 1984 The Provost and Scholars of King's College, Cambridge, and I am grateful to the Society of Authors, as literary representatives of the Estate of E.M. Forster, for permission to quote from it.

Shaw — Michael Holroyd
Michael Holroyd is currently working on the authorized biography of Shaw.
The Genius of Shaw, ed. Michael Holroyd, Holt, Reinhart & Winston, New York, 1979.

Virginia & Leonard Woolf — John Lehmann
Downhill All the Way: autobiography vol. I, and *The Journey not the Arrival Matters*: vol. II, Leonard Woolf, Hogarth Press, London, 1967–69.
Virginia Woolf, a Biography, Quentin Bell, Hogarth Press, London, 1972.
A Marriage of True Minds, George Spater & Ian Parsons, Jonathan Cape, London, 1977.

Bloomsbury — Quentin Bell
Vanessa Bell, Frances Spalding, Weidenfeld & Nicolson, 1983.
Omega and After, Isabelle Anscombe, Thames & Hudson, 1981.
Bloomsbury Portraits, Richard Shone, Phaidon, 1976.

Index

The page numbers in italics indicate illustrations

Ronald Blythe is the author of a number of books including the *Akenfield: portrait of an English Village*, which won the Heinemann award in 1969, and *The View in Winter, Reflections on Old Age*, 1979. He is a Fellow of the Royal Society of Literature, and lives in East Anglia.

Ian Campbell is Reader in English Literature at Edinburgh University. He is the author or editor of a number of books about the Carlyles, including *Thomas Carlyle*, 1974, and President of the Carlyle Society.

James Lees-Milne worked for the National Trust for thirty years from 1936 and was their Historic Buildings Adviser from 1956-66. Since then he has published, among other things, the three volumes of his autobiography – *Another Self*, 1970, *Ancestral Voices*, 1975, and *Prophecying Peace*, 1980.

Raleigh Trevelyan was born in 1923 and lived in Italy until 1946. Previous books include *The Fortress*, *Princes under the Volcano*, and *The Shadow of Vesuvius*. He has just published *Shades of the Alhambra* (1985).

Mary Moorman is the author of *William Wordsworth, A Biography* (3 vols. 1957-1970), the second volume of which won the James Tait Black Memorial Prize in 1965, as well as other volumes on William and Dorothy Wordsworth. She has been a Trustee of Dove Cottage and recently published a memoir of her father, the historian George Macaulay Trevelyan.

Michael Holroyd is well known for his acclaimed biographies of Lytton Strachey and Augustus John. A past Chairman of the Society of Authors, he edited *The Genius of Shaw* (Holt, Reinhart & Wilson, 1979). He is married to the writer Margaret Drabble.

John Lehmann was a partner and General Manager of The Hogarth Press from 1938-1946, and since then has been reponsible as author or editor for more than forty books, including three volumes of autobiography. In 1975 he published his recollections of Virginia and Leonard Woolf in *Virginia Woolf and Her World*.

Professor Quentin Bell is Emeritus Professor of the History and Theory of Art at Sussex University. He spent much of his childhood and adolescence at Charleston and the neighbouring haunts of his parents Clive Bell and Vanessa Stephen, and worked with his mother and Duncan Grant on the decoration of Berwick Church. Professor Bell has written much about the 'Bloomsbury circle', most notably in his *Bloomsbury* (1968) and his authorative *Virginia Woolf, A Biography* (1972) which won the James Tait Black Memorial and Duff Cooper Memorial Prizes.

Desmond Hawkins, OBE, worked for many years for the BBC, founding the Natural History Unit in 1957 and becoming Controller, South & West, in 1967. His work as a critic includes studies of John Donne and D.H. Lawrence as well as three books on Thomas Hardy, the latest of which *Hardy's Wessex* appeared in 1983.

Frank Tuohy has taught English at Universities in North and South America, Poland and currently Tokyo. As a novelist he has received great critical acclaim and recognition in the form of the Katherine Mansfield Memorial (1962), Geoffrey Faber Memorial (1964) and E.M. Forster Memorial (1972) Prizes. For his volume of short stories, *Live Bait*, he received the Heinemann Award in 1979.

Jonathan Keates was born in Paris and went to Bryanston School and Magdalene College, Oxford. He has been Assistant English Master at the City of London School since 1974. His *Allegro Postillions*, 1983, won the James Tait Black Memorial Prize and his most recent book is *Handel, the Man and his Music* (1985).